W9-BXO-760

The Skills of Document Use: From Text Comprehension to Web-Based Learning

The Skills of Document Use: From Text Comprehension to Web-Based Learning

Jean-François Rouet
Centre National de la Recherche Scientifique

2006

LAWRENCE ERLBAUM ASSOCIATES, PUBLISHERS
Mahwah, New Jersey   London

KH

Lawrence Erlbaum Associates, Inc., Publishers
10 Industrial Avenue
Mahwah, New Jersey 07430
www.erlbaum.com

Cover design by Tomai Maridou

Library of Congress Cataloging-in-Publication Data

Rouet, Jean-François
The skills of document use : from text comprehension to Web-based learning / Jean-François Rouet.
p. cm.
Includes bibliographical references and index.
ISBN 0-8058-4602-6 (cloth : alk. paper)
1. Computers and literacy. 2. Functional literacy. 3. Reading comprehension. 4. Web-based instruction. 5. Cognition. I. Title.
LC149.5.R68 2006
02.2'244'0285—dc22 2005052083
CIP

Books published by Lawrence Erlbaum Associates are printed on acid-free paper, and their bindings are chosen for strength and durability.

Printed in the United States of America
10 9 8 7 6 5 4 3 2 1

9/5/06

Contents

Foreword

As I write this foreword, I have open a copy of the manuscript by Jean-François Rouet as an electronic file, along with a separate copy of the concluding chapter, and another file of the tables and figures: three documents—in this case, parts of a single larger document—in addition to this under-construction foreword. What Rouet calls *complex documents*, which are "artifacts that include more than one piece of coherent, continuous text," are commonplace raw materials to the work of the modern scholar.

Of course, we should not think that the use of complex documents emerged only with the age of computers. Scholars through the ages have sat slouched over piles of open books, journals, letters, and other documents to create their understanding of some topic, problem, or event, so as to produce their story concerning this topic or to find text to support their arguments about the topic. The use of complex documents is far from new. But what seems to be relatively new are two things: the pervasiveness of complex document use and the discovery that this use is an object of study itself.

The pervasiveness extends well beyond the expert scholar to the middle-grade student. With her social studies book already open, my fifth-grade daughter opens a world atlas to consult a map, going back and forth between text and map while writing about the location of a city. (My second-grade daughter so far sticks to one-at-a-time reading, but this will soon change.) Furthermore, complex document use is not restricted to academic work by students and professors. The tourist on the street corner opens a copy of a guidebook along with a street map to figure out how to get to the Louvre. The frugal shopper may stand in the aisle of the supermarket comparing a coupon that states a special price for a package of a certain brand of spaghetti with the price posted on the box itself. These mundane examples illustrate the range of functional literacy that ordinary life demands. Clearly, how people come to skillfully navigate complex documents is a topic worthy of understanding.

That this topic has not been central in the cognitive psychology of text comprehension reflects a natural priority of scientific enquiry. The first problem for the field of text comprehension was to establish the study of texts as a scientific problem and to characterize the understanding of texts in cognitive terms. There has been some success in this effort, and the field can now support a more ambitious program in which the processes of text (singular) comprehension remain important but are supplemented by a wide range of additional considerations. Because there is neither a single purpose nor a single circumstance for complex document use, there can be no single paradigm for its study. There can be, however, a general framework to examine at least some of its features, and Rouet provides that in his use of functional literacy, with attention to the knowledge and text-experience of the readers along with the features of the text and of the reader's task in relations to the text.

It is a special pleasure for me to write this brief foreword. Jean-François Rouet spent a post-doc with me in the mid-1990s. It was a time when (with Anne Britt) I was working on how readers negotiated texts by different authors who provided overlapping but partly contradictory accounts of historical texts. This work on what I called *text-based reasoning* benefited greatly from collaborating with J.-F. Rouet around shared ideas and experiments. Although the ideas that Britt, Rouet, and I tossed around then left some traces, this book's treatment of complex documents includes a great deal of new research and a very rich context of functional literacy, technology, and education. It uniquely defines a new area of research, demonstrates its agenda, and provides some of the research answers to questions about the use of complex documents.

—Charles Perfetti
University of Pittsburgh
July 14, 2005

Preface

This book presents a reflection about people's ability to read, comprehend, and make use of complex documents. The chapters review psychological theories of text comprehension, and discuss the processes at work in document integration, document search, and the use of electronic information systems. My core purpose is to offer a new, comprehensive look at the concept of document literacy. Document literacy encompasses a set of basic skills needed to perform language activities, such as reading and writing, but also more complex, experience-based comprehension strategies. Those complex strategies are necessary for individuals to make use of print and electronic documents in a purposeful, context-sensitive fashion. They include the integration of information across multiple sources, and the selective browsing of document sets in order to locate information. Document literacy also includes the knowledge and use of digital information technologies, which have brought new ways to display, organize, and navigate complex document sets.

The idea of this book is rooted in my experience, first as a student of language psychology and information systems, and then as a research scientist interested in reading, comprehension, and the uses of written language in purposeful situations. As I was specializing in those areas, I was struck by an apparent gap between two conceptions of text comprehension. The first conception arises from the work of language theorists who have extensively studied text comprehension, but mostly in basic, well-controlled situations. They have examined how people (most often university students) read simple texts in order to perform simple tasks, based on the literal encoding of the materials. The second conception arises from the informal observation of everyday reading situations. Millions of readers (younger, older, educated or not) have to exert their reading comprehension skills on a daily basis in order to study, to work, or for other purposes. Considered from the latter perspective, text comprehension involves a wide range of materials, tasks, and strategies. First, people often have to cope with complex, lengthy, and heterogeneous documents. Second, they need to use selective, goal-based strategies in order to make their way through complex information, locating and extracting relevant pieces, and tying such pieces together across texts. Most of those aspects of reading comprehension fall out of the scope of traditional research. Consequently, most of the problems people face when performing those activities are not easily interpreted in light of the available theories.

A central goal of my research work has been to find out if a scientific approach to text comprehension could be extended to capture the complex processes involved in naturalistic text processing. I have tried to investigate this issue by looking at processes of text evaluation, multiple text integration, and document search. I have also reflected on the impact of new information technology on reading, text comprehension, and text-based activities. This book is an attempt to communicate some of my findings and conclusions regarding those issues.

Understanding the nature of document literacy, analyzing strategies of document use, or reflecting on the interactions of technology and cognition are not just topics of great interest for cognitive research. They are also issues of utmost importance for those who design information systems, those who write and publish documents, and those who teach students how to use them. In addition to extending current models of reading and comprehension processes, the purpose of this book is to inform practitioners about research developments and their potential applications. In reviewing the research literature, I have tried to avoid unnecessary technical details. In summarizing and drawing conclusions, I have tried to establish explicit connections with various areas of practice.

The layout of the book reflects my objectives. The first two chapters introduce some important aspects of text comprehension considered from a psychological standpoint. In chapter 1, I examine the language and memory processes involved in text comprehension. In chapter 2, I analyze the linguistic and visual devices that represent the organization of complex texts, and their role in comprehension. Those two perspectives—memory-based and text-based—are needed in order to understand what people do when they interact with complex documents.

Chapters 3 and 4 examine document-based activities that go beyond the mere comprehension of a text's content. Chapter 3 deals with the integration of information from multiple documents. Document integration is an important and yet underrepresented issue in current discourse processing research. Observing people's strategies when they read multiple documents highlights the role of evaluation and perspective taking in comprehension. Chapter 4 considers document search, an activity that is complementary to multiple document integration. Information search is what happens when people need to locate information of interest among a large repertory of documents. Efficient search requires sophisticated strategies that rely heavily on one's knowledge of document structures and text organizers. Chapters 3 and 4 show that the knowledge and skills at work in document integration and document search must be considered part of document literacy, while showing that they are acquired quite late in the curriculum, if they are at all.

In chapters 5 and 6, I focus on computerized information systems. I question the influence of new information systems on the way people read and comprehend text. In chapter 5, I examine the use of hypertext systems for general comprehension purposes or for more specific search tasks. Chapter 6 focuses on Web-based learning. I review recent research suggesting that the effectiveness of the Web as an instructional resource is a matter of "cognitive compatibility," that is, the system's ability to support the learner's strategies, and the learner's ability to consider critically the characteristics of document information in a versatile, expanding, and unregulated environment.

Chapter 7 offers some broader considerations about literacy skills and the spread of information technology in our society. Recent advances in information and communication technology have created wonderful opportunities, but also dreadful challenges for the teaching and mastery of functional literacy in the general public. The romantic view of computers as friendly devices that facilitate the sharing of knowledge must now be seriously questioned. Computer technologies only contribute to people's personal development to the extent that people master the skills and knowledge required to use them effectively. With over 800 million people lacking basic literacy skills, and an access rate to the Internet lower than 10% in poorer countries, this is a very serious challenge for tomorrow's global world. Electronic information systems mean more, not less, time, effort, and money devoted to education. I point out some of the issues that lie before us, as well as some directions for future research.

This book owes a lot to my experiences as a postdoctoral fellow at the University of Pittsburgh, USA, and at the Institut National de Recherche en Informatique et Automatique (INRIA) in Grenoble, France. I am grateful to the Lavoisier program and to the research institutions where I belonged for making these experiences possible. I acknowledge the great intellectual stimulation that I received from my colleagues, and especially André Bisseret, M. Anne Britt and Charles A. Perfetti. I also acknowledge my colleagues and students at the Laboratoire Langage et Cognition (LaCo), a research center funded by the Centre National de la Recherche Scientifique and the University of Poitiers, France, where I presently belong. Thanks to Alain Bert-Erboul and Nicolas Vibert for their useful comments on an earlier version of the manuscript. Very special thanks to Emily Wilkinson at Lawrence Erlbaum Associates, for her encouragements and patience. Finally, I extend my deepest appreciation to my spouse, Monica Macedo-Rouet, for her continued support, care, and love during the completion of this project.

Introduction

Ever since the earliest writing systems were created, information technologies have played a steadily increasing role in people's lives (Fig. I-1). Finding new ways to write, print, duplicate, and communicate documents has been the subject of a constant and intense quest in most human cultures. And the production of printed materials has kept increasing at an accelerated rate. It is estimated that during the 16th century, about 200,000 books were produced in the world. The production was perhaps 8 million during the 19th century, five million for the single first quarter of the 20th century, to reach probably over a million a year at the beginning of the 21st century. Computerized information systems have accelerated the advent of the "information society." Com-

FIG. I-1. Drawing of a clay tablet. This clay tablet was molded some 5,000 years ago in ancient Mesopotamia. It is interpreted as a tool used to teach a young scribe how to write. The tablet is divided in two areas by a horizontal line. On the lower part, the "teacher" has drawn three lines to be copied by the "student." On the upper part, the student (a novice?) has tried—rather clumsily—to copy the symbols (drawing by the author after a bronze replica).

puters allow individuals and organizations to produce documents faster and to store them at a reduced cost, virtually independent from the amount of information. In addition, electronic information systems have generated new types of documents and information sources (e.g., online databases, Web sites, and multimedia documents).

Parallel to the increased production of printed and electronic documents is the dissemination of reading and writing skills among humans. Access to basic literacy skills has undergone constant increase in the world throughout recent decades. According to UNESCO, the percentage of people over 15 years old with alphabetization skills has increased from 63% in 1970 to 79% in 1998 (UNESCO, 2000). Sadly, however, 880 million adults still could not read or write in 1998. Ninety-eight percent of them lived in the least developed countries, and three out of four were women. Thus, significant as it may be, the progress of reading literacy in modern times is far from being evenly distributed across political, cultural, and social territories. Meanwhile, in the wealthiest parts of the world, reading literacy skills play an ever-increasing part in people's social, professional, and personal lives. Mastering the use of written information is key to academic success, professional development, personal culture, and autonomous use of all kinds of devices. Operating a digital telephone set, requesting social security benefits, safely preserving frozen food, or looking for a job, to cite just a few widespread activities, all require the reading and use of multipage documents including text, pictures, and various types of symbolic information. Being literate was an important skill in yesterday's developed world. It is now becoming a vital one.

But exactly what is reading literacy? Despite the widespread use of the phrase and its utmost importance in modern societies, literacy is far from a simple and unambiguous construct. Heath (1991) emphasized that the modern definition of literacy is often reduced to a distinction between those who can read and write in a vernacular language (usually their native language) and those who cannot. In recent years, however, there has been a growing awareness of the need to broaden the definition (Kirsch, Jungeblut, Jenkins, & Kolstad, 2002). The United States National Adult Literacy Survey used the following definition: "using printed and written information to function in society, to achieve one's goals, and to develop one's knowledge and potential" (Kaestle, Campbell, Finn, Johnson, & Mickulecky, 2001, p. 2). The Organization for Economic Cooperation and Development's Programme for International Student Assessment (OECD-PISA) offers a similar definition:

> Reading literacy is understanding, using, and reflecting on written texts, in order to achieve one's goals, to develop one's knowledge and potential, and to participate in society. The assessment of reading literacy requires students to perform a range of tasks with different kinds of text. The tasks range from retrieving specific information to demonstrating a broad understanding and interpreting text and reflecting on its content and fea-

> tures. The texts that are used will include not just standard prose passages but also various types of documents such as lists, forms, graphs, and diagrams. (OECD PISA, 2004)

Thus, reading literacy covers a wide range of activities that rely on the use of written materials. Reading literacy obviously requires, but is not limited to, the ability to read and write words. The concept encompasses more complex mental processes that combine reading and text-based reasoning, decision making and problem solving. Literacy is among the most empowering skills that an individual can gain through education. And the teaching of literacy skills is one of the dearest objectives of most current educational systems. In the common language, being literate is often associated with a sense of empowerment. "The state of being literate removes the individual from dependence on only immediate senses and direct contacts" (Heath, 1991, p. 4). Heath further argued that literacy skills are closely intertwined with critical thinking skills—the ability to reason about written information, to question, to build up and communicate sound arguments, and to solve problems (see also Kuhn, 1991). Thus, there is much more to literacy than the mere ability to read and write words.

A common feature of most literacy activities is that they involve the use of complex documents. I use the expression *complex documents* to designate artifacts that include more than one piece of coherent, continuous text. This is certainly far from a precise definition, but it is nevertheless of some use. A textbook page, a scientific report, a technical manual, or a Web site are basic examples of complex documents (see, e.g., chapter 3, Fig. 3.1). The concept of complex documents calls for theories of reading, comprehension, and literacy acts that are far more diverse and complex than those proposed by language specialists so far. It is my contention that broadening our scientific approach to literacy acts and literacy skills is an issue of utmost importance at theoretical and practical levels.

At the theoretical level, we need comprehensive theories of the cognitive structures and processes that underlie our ability to deal with complex documents. So far, however, psychological research has mostly concentrated on a very restricted range of reading and comprehension activities. This was done on behalf of sound principles of scientific investigation, such as the rational ordering of research questions, the need for specific hypothetical constructs, refutable theories, and controlled empirical research settings. Concentrating on basic issues and basic processes has allowed reading psychologists to come up with extremely accurate and robust models of reading and, to some extent, of text comprehension. But it is fair to say that the application range of these models is rather narrow compared to the versatility of literacy acts. In the current state of knowledge, psychological theories have little to say on the cognitive processes that underlie activities such as scanning newspaper pages, making informed decisions based on medical or legal documents, or searching information of interest in printed or digital libraries, to cite just a few examples. The kinds of knowledge structures, mental operations, and skills involved in these activities remain to be found, as well as the reasons why document-based tasks sometimes prove very difficult to perform, even by people with normal reading skills.

To come up with an extended theory of text comprehension, one must reconsider the nature of the interactions that unfold as people use written materials. The range of variables of potential interest is much broader than those usually considered in the scientific literature. Especially critical is the notion that the task context that surrounds the reading act plays a critical part in the nature and organization of mental processes during reading. Thus, comprehension theories need to shift from the traditional "reading as text-reader interaction" to a broader "reading as context-text-reader interaction" (Fig. I-2; see also Snow, 2002). Very often, the actual encounter of a text and a reader is determined by a set of contextual parameters, like the presence of human or artificial mediators. Thus, "text comprehension" encompasses the intention of authors, teachers, experimenters, and the design of books, pharmaceutical leaflets, Web sites or online databases. It is also the context that tells a reader whether he or she should read quickly or slowly, extensively or selectively, and with or without calling on his or her prior knowledge, beliefs, and biases. Thus, a theory of comprehension should look at how people represent texts, but also at how they represent the context in which reading takes place.

From a practical standpoint, understanding the true nature of literacy is a problem for educators and information system designers. For example, in many countries secondary education professionals are puzzled and frustrated by the seemingly increasing proportion of students who fail to complete basic text comprehension assignments. Many higher education specialists are worried by the number of students who lack the basic skills required to complete course requirements (Nist & Simpson, 2000). Yet, there is no agreed-upon instructional approach for training literacy skills beyond primary education. Another example is the recurrent problem of designing usable documents for professional use. There are numerous cases of errors and accidents that can be attributed, at least in part, on poor or inappropriate design of technical documents (see, e.g., Reason, 1990). Despite the large number of published

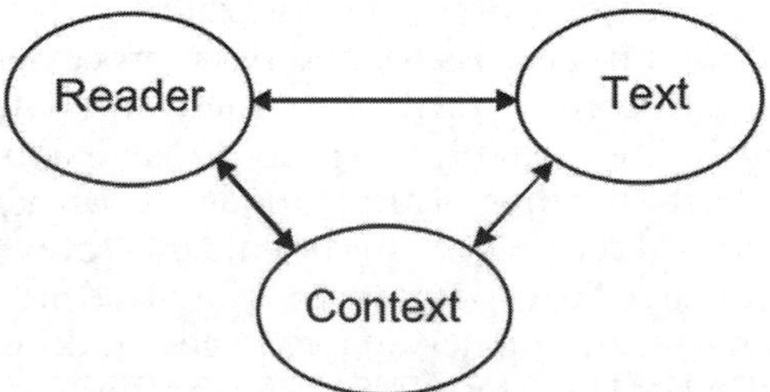

FIG. I-2. Comprehension as context–text–reader interaction.

works on the topic of information quality, little is known about the nature of literacy skills and comprehension strategies actually used by professionals. A third example has to do with designing usable Web-based information systems. Web sites are often of mediocre quality, and empirical studies suggest that their usability is limited. Web resource publishers are generally concerned with the users' needs, but they often lack reliable guidelines as to how they can concretely identify these needs and take them into account. A theory of how people interact with complex documents in various task settings would certainly be of some use in those areas.

Secondary education, professional document writing, and Web-based publishing are just a few examples of professional activities that could benefit from a more comprehensive theory of human information usage. As a general working hypothesis, I suggest that current problems in these areas lie in part in a lack of awareness of the diversity and complexity of the cognitive and language processes involved in literacy acts. Educational policymakers, instructional designers, and professional developers must be informed of the constraints and prerequisites that come with the use of complex information systems. Better educational and training programs, as well as more usable technologies and materials, might result from increased exchange of information between communities of research and practice.

The aim of this book is to present and define some of the skills and mental processes that underlie our ability to read, comprehend and make use of complex documents in real life situations, or what I call *functional literacy*. Because the issue is such a complex one, however, this volume focuses on a few key aspects that have been investigated in recent years by me and others. Thus, the book is mostly concerned with the individual use of complex documents, as opposed to the collaborative production and distribution of documents. Also, I have chosen to restrict the scope of this book to text-based information systems, as opposed to multimedia and virtual reality systems (see, e.g., Mayer, 2001; Rouet, Levonen, & Biardeau, 2001). Finally, I deal mostly with complex comprehension activities in adult readers, with only a few incursions into the acquisition of literacy skills by children and adolescents (see, e.g., Barr, Kamil, Mosenthal, & Pearson, 1991).

In many places, I refer to the concepts, theories, and research methods of cognitive psychology. Providing detailed background information about these is, however, beyond the scope of this book. For a general introduction to cognitive psychology, the reader may consult the popular works by Anderson (2000) or Sternberg (1999). Comprehensive overviews of research in psycholinguistics and comprehension theories are available in Gernsbacher (1994), Graesser, Gernsbacher, and Goldman (2003) or, for readers of French, Blanc and Brouillet (2003). And the book by Kintsch (1998) offers a firsthand presentation of a leading approach in comprehension theory.

The present book is organized in three sections of two chapters each. The first two chapters introduce some important aspects of text comprehension considered from a psychological standpoint. In chapter 1, I examine the language and memory processes involved in *text comprehension*. I briefly review the situation model and mental model theories, and I present current accounts of memory-based processes in comprehension. In chapter 2, I examine the issue of *text organizers*, that is, linguistic and visual devices that help readers figure out the structure and find their way in complex texts. Both the nature of online memory processes and the role of text organizers are needed to understand what people do when they interact with complex documents.

Chapters 3 and 4 deal with the psychological processes typical of complex documents comprehension. Chapter 3 deals with the *comprehension of multiple documents*. This is a complex, important, and underrepresented issue in current discourse processing research. Yet, in many everyday situations people have to confront more than just one piece of text or discourse. For example, students acquire knowledge from sets of instructional texts and documents; media consumers learn about events in the world through collections of news articles and radio and television messages; and taxpayers calculate their dues with the help of forms, guidelines, and sometimes telephone assistance. How do we manage to build coherent representations from such multiple and heterogeneous sources? To what extent do we truly integrate information from different texts in memory? Do we just merge any new information with what we already knew, or are there more subtle mechanisms involved? And does it help to study from primary sources, as opposed to single, integrative texts? These are some of the questions discussed in chapter 3. The answers highlight some of the limitations of the more classical text comprehension theories reviewed in chapters 1 and 2.

Chapter 4 considers *information search*, an activity that is somewhat symmetrical and often complementary to multiple document comprehension. Whereas in multiple document comprehension the reader has to connect various sources together, in document search the reader has to eliminate most of the information in order to locate only the one or the few pieces of information that are relevant to the task. Again, a closer look at information search processes highlights the limits of traditional text comprehension research. Theoretical constructs of information search shed some light on key aspects of functional literacy.

In chapters 5 and 6, I focus on the issue of *computerized information systems*. The core question addressed in those two chapters is: How do new information systems affect the way people read and comprehend text? Do these systems call on new, distinct psychological processes? And is it for better or for worse? In chapter 5, I examine the issue of using hypertext systems, for general comprehension purposes or for more specific search tasks. The distinction is important as these activities rely on quite different cognitive processes. Chapter 6 focuses on a question of great practical interest: Can students learn from Web-based information systems? Is learning improved, hindered, or simply unaffected? I review recent research suggesting that the answer is a matter of quality, and that quality depends to a large extent on "cognitive compatibility," that is, the system's ability to acknowledge and support the learners' cognitive states and processes.

Chapter 7 concludes this book with some broader considerations about literacy skills and the spread of information technology in our society. My main conclusion, in a nutshell, is that recent advances in information and communication technology have created wonderful opportunities, but also dreadful challenges, for the teaching and mastery of functional literacy in the general public. The romantic view of computers as friendly devices that facilitate the sharing of knowledge, which has prevailed among educators in past decades, must now be seriously questioned. Computer technologies only contribute to people's personal development to the extent that people are taught the skills and knowledge required to use them effectively. This will take more, not less, educational time, effort, and money. Making sure that no one is left beside the information highway is a new challenge for education systems. It is also a prerequisite to equal opportunity and social cohesion in the future. I point out some of the issues that lie before us, as well as some directions for future research.

1

The Psychology of Text Comprehension: Current Theories and Issues

OVERVIEW AND CONTENTS

What do we do when we read, comprehend, memorize, and utilize information from texts? This chapter offers an overview of current psychological theories. The chapter presents the propositional theory of text comprehension laid by Kintsch and his colleagues in the 1970s. Then, I review the role of knowledge in text comprehension as it was construed in theories of mental models and situation models. I emphasize the relationship between knowledge activation and the updating of mental text representations. Comprehension and updating rely on the online production of inferences and other, more complex memory-based processes. I review different approaches of those processes, including advances in the computerized simulation of online comprehension processes. Finally, I discuss some of the limitations of current research on text comprehension, especially when considering the case of complex or multiple documents.

Contents

INTRODUCTION

Reading and comprehending written discourse can be a rich subjective experience. As we read novels, newspaper stories, or popular science articles, to cite just a few examples, word meanings come to our mind, as well as related ideas, images, emotions, puzzles, and so forth. We often pause to reflect and elaborate about the text's content. We recall information read in previous portions of the text, or even in other texts. We sometimes anticipate or conjecture about what is coming next. We map incoming information onto the background of our personal experiences. We interpret, evaluate, and challenge the text against our personal beliefs and biases. We sometimes remember a text a long time after we have read it. In other cases, we seem to forget instantly what we have just read. Some texts leave us with rather detailed and vivid memories, others with just a few fragments. We may even remember a story without being able to tell where or when we read it.

Over the past decades, psychological research has attempted to integrate all these processes and experiences into comprehensive theoretical frameworks. As part of this effort, researchers have tried to explain how text information is turned into a mental representation of what the text is about. Researchers have also attempted to model the processes that occur in the reader's working and long-term memory as text comprehension proceeds. In this chapter, I review some current conceptions of the cognitive processes involved in text comprehension (for more comprehensive reviews, see Graesser, Gernsbacher, & Goldman, 2003; Kintsch, 1998; van Oostendorp & Goldman, 1999). My purpose here is to present a few key aspects of text comprehension theory that are essential to understand the more complex activities that are dealt with in the following chapters. I start with a summary of the propositional view of text meaning, a view that has dominated research on text comprehension during the past 30 years or so. Then I briefly introduce the well-known comprehension theory proposed by Kintsch, van Dijk, and their collaborators (Kintsch,

1974, 1998; van Dijk & Kintsch, 1983). I examine the theoretical construct of situation models, and I review current conceptions of the memory processes that underlie their construction. Finally, I point out some limitations of current theories of comprehension, and I discuss some key issues left open for further investigation.

1.1. CONSTRUCTING MENTAL REPRESENTATIONS FROM TEXT

As they undertook the task of describing the psychological processes involved in comprehension, researchers faced the problem of representing explicitly the semantic content of the text. Semantic representations are needed both for theoretical and methodological reasons. On a theoretical level, if we are to understand what a person *does* comprehend from a given text, we need to know what *can* be comprehended from the text. On a methodological level, comprehension is often assessed through tasks that require the reader to recall and use information from the text (e.g., recall, summary, question answering). An explicit representation of the text's content is needed as a template against which the reader's production can be confronted and evaluated.

1.1.1. The Propositional Approach to Text Comprehension

Various researchers have proposed methods to represent the semantic content of texts (see Meyer & Rice, 1984, for an overview). Kintsch (1974) proposed a detailed procedure, called *propositional analysis,* to parse the semantic content of short texts into constituent units. According to propositional analysis, any text can be decomposed into a list of basic semantic units, or *propositions*. Each proposition is made of a predicate (generally a verb or an adjective) and one or several arguments (generally a name or a referential expression). The number and type of arguments that come with each predicate are determined by the predicate *frame,* or structure. The verb "carry," for instance, involves an agent and an object, such as in "the hemoglobin carries oxygen." Moreover, a proposition can serve as an argument for another proposition. Thus, the meaning of the whole text takes the form of a propositional hierarchy. Propositional analysis has been presented in detail and discussed in many publications (see, e.g., Meyer, 1985; Perfetti & Britt, 1995; Perrig & Kintsch, 1985; Schmalhofer & Glavanov, 1986; Turner & Greene, 1977), and I only give a simple illustration borrowed from Kintsch (1998, pp. 61–64).

Table 1.1 presents a sentence and the list of propositions that results from its analysis. Each proposition is made up of a predicate (e.g., first, possess, four) and one or several arguments (chamber, heart). Furthermore, some propositions (e.g., P3) can serve as arguments in other propositions, as in possess (heart, four[chamber]).

The list of propositions that can be directly drawn from a text is called its *microstructure*. In addition, propositions can be organized into more global structures called *macropropositions*. Macropropositions can be ei-

TABLE 1.1

A Sentence Parsed Into Constituent Propositions

Sentence	*Propositions*
The first of the heart's four chambers, the right atrium, receives purplish blood, short of oxygen and laden with carbon dioxide.	1. FIRST (CHAMBER)
	2. POSSESS (HEART, 3)
	3. FOUR (CHAMBER)
	4. RIGHT (ATRIUM)
	5. IS (1, 4)
	6. PURPLE (BLOOD)
	7. RECEIVES (1, 6)
	8. SHORT OF (6, OXYGEN)
	9. LADEN (6, CARBON DIOXIDE)

Note. Adapted from Kintsch (1998).

ther explicit in the text or inferred by the reader. In the latter case, three rules called *macrorules* permit the construction of macropropositions from the text. The *selection rule* consists in the deletion of propositions that are not directly needed to interpret other propositions. The *generalization rule* consists in replacing a series of propositions by an overarching one. The *construction rule* consists in adding a proposition that results from, or is entailed in, a set of propositions. An example of the selection rule, as presented by Kintsch (1998) consists in replacing the series of propositions in Table 1.1 by the expression "the right atrium receives blood short of oxygen and laden with carbon dioxide" (p. 66). The set of propositions that is obtained by applying macrorules on the whole microstructure is called a *macrostructure*. Put together, the microstructure and the macrostructure form the *textbase*, that is, a hierarchical representation of the text's literal meaning.

Propositions and propositional analysis are basically a technique to represent the information contained in a text. However, Kintsch and his colleagues also demonstrated that they match the basic mental processes that occur during comprehension. For instance, Kintsch, Kozminsky, Streby, McKoon, and Keenan (1975) showed that the recall probability of micropropositions varied as a function of their hierarchical position in the text structure. Propositions high in the hierarchy are more likely to be recalled than other propositions.

Kintsch and van Dijk (1978) proposed a detailed account of how propositions are encoded during the reading of a text. Comprehension, they argued, unfolds as a series of processing cycles. During each cycle, a small portion of the text is read and parsed into a list of semantic propositions. Even though the specific parsing mechanisms that underlie the extraction of propositions are not specified (see Kintsch, 1998), the theory assumes that the reader builds up a "surface representation" (p. 54), that is, a mental representation of the linguistic code. The surface representation provides the basic materials for the extraction of propositions. The number of propositions that can be extracted during a cycle depends on the capacity of the short-term buffer, a parameter called "i" in the theory (Kintsch & van Dijk, 1978). In practice, it is assumed that one or two sentences can be parsed within each single processing cycle.

Once propositions have been extracted, they are organized into a propositional structure. Propositions that share arguments are connected together. Macropropositions are constructed by applying macrorules. And a subset of propositions is held active in the short-term buffer until the next cycle. The size and composition of this subset depend on another parameter of the short term buffer (parameter "s"), and on the reader's strategy. Kintsch and van Dijk (1978) described a basic strategy, called *leading edge strategy,* that consists in maintaining the propositions high in the hierarchy as well as the most recent ones. The carryover of propositions over processing cycles is important because it allows the reader to connect information from one cycle to another, that is, to establish textual coherence. If the propositions in a cycle cannot be matched to propositions from earlier cycles, then the reader must perform a search in long-term memory in order to retrieve or to construct connecting propositions.

The same process applies in iterations until the entire text has been read. The result is a mental representation of the textbase that takes the form of a hierarchical list of propositions. Forming a good textbase allows readers to perform a variety of tasks, such as checking new statements against those they have read, answering simple questions about the text, or recalling the text.

1.1.2. Textbases and Situation Models

Knowing the text at the level of the textbase, however, does not necessarily ensure that the reader understands it at a deeper level. Deep comprehension requires the reader to integrate text information with his or her prior world knowledge. Integration is achieved through the activation of knowledge from long-term memory, either on the basis of associative links or through deliberate reasoning. The importance of knowledge activation in comprehension was demonstrated in early studies such as those by Bransford and his colleagues (e.g., Bransford, Barclay, & Franks, 1972). It was further emphasized in the mental model theory by Johnson-Laird (1983), and in the situation model theory by van Dijk and Kintsch (1983).

Mental models and situation models are two theoretical constructs proposed to describe what a reader has in mind after reading a passage of text. The two theories share a number of characteristics. The contents of a mental model or a situation model cannot be entirely predicted on the basis of a linguistic analysis of the text. Instead, they are constrained by characteristics of the reader such as prior knowledge and reading purposes. Moreover, mental/situation models may include information other than semantic propositions. For instance, they may incorporate traces from prior perceptual experiences, emotions, or nonlinguistic symbols. In addition, mental/situation models are not bound by the reading episode. They are "updatable" (Glenberg, Meyer, & Lindem, 1987), which means that they can be modified dynamically as new information is encountered. Finally, mental and situation models can influence the way new information is processed by creating perspective or context effects.

The properties of text-based mental or situation models have been extensively studied in the past 20 years (see van Oostendorp & Goldman, 1999). Mani and Johnson-Laird (1982) showed that readers form spatial mental models for "determinate" descriptions of objects, that is, descriptions that match one and only one spatial arrangement. An example of a determinate description is "The table is to the left of the bed. The chair is to the right of the bed." Once a mental model has been formed, readers can easily discriminate descriptions compatible with their mental model from foil descriptions that do not fit the same spatial arrangement. However, they can no longer distinguish the actual text they have read from another text different in the surface form but consistent with the mental model (Bransford, Barclay, & Franks, 1972).

Thus, comprehending a text is a process in which the reader attempts to mentally represent the situation described in the text. The ongoing process of forming a mental model of the situation involves a great deal of activation from long-term memory (Kintsch, 1988). It also requires the reader to maintain concepts active in working memory while acquiring new information (Ericsson & Kintsch, 1995). Glenberg, Meyer, and Lindem (1987) demonstrated that the structure of the situation model influences the process of foregrounding, or the activation of discourse objects in working memory. They manipulated short narrative texts so that a main character, introduced early in the story, was either spatially associated or dissociated with an object. For instance, in the sentence "After a few warm-up exercises, John put on his sweatshirt and went jogging," the character "John" and the sweatshirt are spatially associated. In the sentence "After a few warm up exercises, John took off his sweatshirt and went jogging," the character and the sweatshirt are spatially dissociated. Sentences creating such associations or dissociations were followed by filler sentences in which the character, but not the object, was mentioned.

Whereas the propositional theory would posit that arguments from recent propositions are foregrounded (i.e., maintained active for integration with incoming information), the mental model theory predicts that objects associated to the foregrounded character will remain in the foreground. In three experiments, Glenberg et al. verified this and other predictions using recognition time as a dependent measure. In experiment 1, 20 undergraduate psychology students read short passages describing a character and an object that were, depending on the conditions associated or dissociated, like in the example already given. On certain trials, reading was interrupted after zero, one, or two filler sentences (i.e., a *delay* variable), and the object name (e.g., "sweatshirt") was presented. The subject's task was to decide if the object name had been presented earlier in the text. The main result was an interaction between delay and response time. When the target word was presented immediately after the sentence that mentioned it, the response time was short and there was no difference between the associated and the dissociated conditions. After one and two filler sentences, however, response time increased and was significantly higher in the dissociated than in the associated condition. Glenberg et al. also demonstrated (experiment 3) that the reading time for sentences containing an anaphoric reference to the critical object was much higher in the dissociated than in the associated condition, but only after a one-sentence delay.

Other experiments found that spatial aspects of the situation are encoded during the comprehension of narratives (e.g., Morrow, Greenspan, & Bower, 1987; Perrig & Kintsch, 1985). These experiments showed that the structure of a mental model (i.e., characters, places, objects, actions, features, and their relationships) determines the foregrounding of mental model elements as the reader proceeds through the text.

1.1.3. The Dynamics of Situation Model Construction

It is useful to distinguish the processes that take place during the formation of a mental or situation model from those that may take place once the model has been formed. McNamara, Miller, and Bransford (1991) defined the "working mental model" as a memory structure that describes the state of the situation as the reader is processing a particular passage. The "passage mental model," on the other hand, is the representation that integrates all the relevant information from a passage. This distinction is important because, in texts that describe causal and temporal chains of events, the status of characters, objects, and situations may evolve continuously. For instance, a character may be "walking on the beach" at some point in the story and "sitting in a bar" later on in the text. Thus, it is important for the reader not only to build, but also to update his or her mental representation if new information is encountered.

Research on the structure and functioning of situation models has shown that they can be structured according to several dimensions. Zwaan and his colleagues' Event-Indexing Model (Magliano, Zwaan, & Graesser, 1999; Zwaan, 1999; Zwaan, Magliano, & Graesser, 1995) rests on the assumption that comprehension consists in identifying and connecting the events that constitute narrative texts. Events can be connected according to five distinct dimensions: time (when did the event occur), space (where did the event occur), protagonist (who is the main agent in the event), causation (what enabled or caused the event), and motivation (what was the purpose of the event). The event-indexing model further postulates that each dimension is dichotomous: Either there is a relation or there is not. However, Zwaan admitted that this is a simplification based on methodological rather than theoretical reasons. The event-indexing model entails two more assumptions. The *processing load* hypothesis states that the integration of incoming information into the situation model under construction is facilitated by situational overlap, that is, when the event described in the new sentence involves the same place, time, causal chain, protagonist, and goal structure. The *memory organization* hypothesis states that events are connected in long-term memory to the extent that they are connected on a number of dimensions.

The processing load hypothesis received support in a series of experiments by Zwaan, Magliano, and Graesser (1995). They focused on three main dimensions of situation models: *time* (or chronological unfolding of events), *space* (or the position and moves of characters), and *causality* (e.g., dependencies in the occurrence of several events). They hypothesized that discontinuities on either of these dimensions would cause the reader to slow down in order to connect adjacent sentences. In the first experiment, they asked university students with a good level of exposure to print to read two excerpts from published literary works. They analyzed each text in order to identify discontinuities on each of the three dimensions. For example, if a sentence describes an event that occurs in a place different from the previous sentence, this would be a discontinuity on the spatial dimension. They hypothesized that discontinuities would increase reading times for sentences, as the reader has to update his or her mental model. Using multiple regression techniques, they found that discontinuities on the three dimensions significantly influenced reading times, independent of other structural characteristics of the sentences, such as number of syllables or serial position in the text. In the second experiment, they used different texts and a broader sample of readers. They found significant effects of time and causal discontinuities, but not of spatial discontinuities. They concluded that under "normal" reading circumstances, readers accurately monitor the *time* and *causal* dimensions, but not so much the *spatial* dimension.

The memory organization hypothesis received support in experiments using clustering techniques (Zwaan, 1999). After reading a text, the participants had to group verbs denoting story events. Each dimension of the situation model was positively related to the clustering score. In other words, events close in time or space were found more similar than events that were separated on either of those dimensions. Thus, when reading a passage for comprehension, the reader forms a mental representation that combines incoming information from the text and prior knowledge activated from memory. The result is a multidimensional structure, or situation model, in which concepts are organized according to the structure of the situation, rather than the structure of the text.

1.1.4. Updating Situation Models

The situation models constructed from texts are updatable; that is, they can be completed and reorganized as a function of new incoming information. The updating process has received less empirical support, compared to other aspects of the situation model theory. It seems, however, that the updating of previously constructed situation models faces a number of obstacles. For instance, Wilkes and Leatherbarrow (1988) asked students to read texts describing a fire in a storehouse. The story mentioned a possible cause for the fire (inflammable materials had been stored in a room next to the storehouse). The explanation was later dismissed by new information (i.e., that "the room was empty"). When asked about the possible cause of the fire, however, students still frequently answered using the initial explanation. Similar evidence was found in works by Johnson and Seifert (1999) and van Oostendorp and his colleagues (van Oostendorp, 1996; van Oostendorp & Bonebakker, 1999).

The reader's ability to modify a situation model in order to incorporate new information seems to depend on the amount of transformation needed in order to update the model. More specifically, Johnson and Seifert (1999) proposed a distinction between surface and deep updating. *Surface updating* occurs when the subject identifies the correcting information and notes that it contradicts prior information, without reorganizing his or her whole representation of the situation. Surface updating faces three types of obstacles. First, the reader may not notice or understand the correcting information. Second, he or she may not notice that the correcting information contradicts prior information. Third, the reader may be unwilling to reconsider his or her initial representation of the situation. Studies of the social/cognitive processes of persuasion have shown that people often use strategies in order to avoid questioning their prior beliefs or knowledge. For instance, they may deliberately ignore conflicting information, they may find ad hoc explanations in order to dismiss it, or they may question its source or its validity.

Deeper updating occurs when readers transform those aspects of their representation that have been challenged by new, incoming information. Deep updating also poses a number of specific problems. The main problem is that the reader needs to reconsider not only the old information that is contradicted by new information, but also all the inferences that he or she may have drawn from this old information. Johnson and Seifert (1999) cite previous research showing that in many cases, the subjects managed to notice and to accept the new information. Their inability to update their situation model does not seem linked to "surface" problems. Moreover, the influence of old information was reduced when the participants were given concrete information that allowed them to reconstruct a whole new explanation (as opposed to information that only contradicted old information).

Several studies have attempted to identity the conditions that facilitate the updating of situation models. For instance, Johnson and Seifert (1999) had students read a "fire in the storehouse" story with an initial explanation followed by correcting information. One group of students was asked to generate several alternate explanations for the fire. Then the subjects answered a series of questions about the events. The analysis of students' answers showed that old information (storage of inflammable materials in the adjacent room) still influenced students' answers. Thus, asking subjects to generate alternate explanations had little effect on updating. Van Oostendorp (1996) studied the effects of reading objectives, delay, and the "strength" of the initial model on adult students' ability to update their mental model. The students read two texts about the "Restore Hope" military operation in Somalia. The first text mentioned that the operation was under United States command, whereas the second text mentioned that it was under United Nations command. The second text was presented either immediately after the first one, or after a 1-day interval. Half the participants were asked to read the text "attentively," whereas the other half were asked to read normally. After the first text, the subjects received a series of questions aimed at measuring the "strength" of their situation model, that is, the extent to which they had understood the events. After reading the second text, participants performed an inference verification task. About 30% of the answers were erroneous, and the participants made more errors on inferences concerning central events in the story. Neither the directions nor the delay had any influence on the judgment performance. According to van Oostendorp, the centrality effect could be due to the participants' superficial processing of new information, because of their feeling of already knowing this information. Verbal protocols collected as the participants read the second text tended to support this interpretation. In order to further confirm it, van Oostendorp and Bonebakker (1999) had students read "storehouse fire" types of stories, in which the old information was either weakly contradicted, strongly contradicted, or contradicted with an alternative explanation. After reading the stories, the participants answered inferential questions about the causes of the fire. Only the latter condition increased the proportion of answers based on the new scenario.

These experiments suggest that readers tend to "stick" to the explanations build initially as part of situation model construction. In fact, the degree and scope of updating seems to depend on both passive memory process and explanation-based comprehension mechanisms (Guéraud, Harmon, & Peracchi, 2005; Zwaan & Madden, 2004). It should be noted, however, that most experiments on updating were conducted using materials that do not provide any explicit reason for the discrepancy between the old and the new fact, feature, or explanation. In van Oostendorp and Bonebakker's (1999) study, for instance, both the old and the new explanation were attributed to "the police," with no explanation of why the initial police report was erroneous. This may prevent the participants from trusting either version more than the other. In fact, a further study by van Oostendorp (2002, experiment 1) found a rather different pattern of results. University students read a 16-sentence expository text that contained a clear cut contradiction concerning the duration of a process (i.e., a process takes "some days" vs. "a few minutes"). The participants were 93 first-year university students. Students overwhelmingly selected the new (latest) information when answering comprehension questions, regardless of whether they had been warned that some information in the text could be subsequently modified.

In three subsequent experiments, however, van Oostendorp (2002) found that students' preference for old or new information varied as a function of the degree of textual elaboration of either information. For instance, the old information stating that "the process takes some days" could be reinforced by a sentence mentioning that "(a device) plots a graphic every 10 hours." This would encourage students to stick to this version. Van Oostendorp concluded that updating one's situation model upon encountering conflicting information is a strategic behavior that depends on the salience of old versus new information, the nature of the contradiction (e.g., logical inconsistencies vs. changes in states), explicitness of correction, and credibility of old versus new information. Concerning the latter point, García-Arista, Campanario, and Otero (1996) found that students were more likely to detect inconsistencies when they read information presented as a *science report* than when it was presented as a *newspaper article*. These findings suggest that the *source*, in addition to the *content* of information, plays an important part in readers' ability and willingness to accept new information. I return to this aspect of text comprehension in chapter 3.

1.2. MEMORY PROCESSES IN TEXT COMPREHENSION

Text comprehension rests to a large extent on readers' ability to maintain information active in memory and to generate timely inferences while processing text information. An inference may be roughly defined as any idea that is generated from the reader's long-term memory, in reaction to incoming textual information. For example, upon reading "Sam fell from the ladder. The ambulance arrived quickly," one may infer that Sam is a human being, that Sam got injured, that someone called an ambulance, that the ambulance came to pick up Sam, and so forth. Inference generation has always represented a tough challenge to comprehension theorists. To what extent are readers able to generate inferences as they read texts? When, and how, precisely, are inferences generated during reading? Among all the potentially relevant inferences, which are those that will or will not be actually generated, and why?

1.2.1. Categorizing Inferential Processes

To address these complex issues, it is first necessary to establish the distinctions among several categories of inferences. Kintsch (1998) suggested that inferences can be categorized along two dimensions. First, some inferences are due to simple retrieval mechanisms, whereas others come from active memory processes that generate new information. Second, some inferences are generated automatically, whereas others depend on controlled mechanisms. This results in four main categories of inferences.

Automatic retrieval inferences occur based on strong associative links between information in working memory and prior knowledge. For example, the phrase "John nailed down a board" automatically activates the concept of a "hammer." According to Kintsch, this is made possible by an intermediate retrieval structure that links information in working memory to long-term knowledge structure, or "long-term working memory" (Ericsson & Kintsch, 1995).

Controlled retrieval inferences are generated when automatic activation fails to deliver information needed to build up a coherent representation. This is the case, for instance, when the reader attempts to connect two simple pieces of information, such as "Danny wanted a new bike. He worked as a waiter." The inference that Danny worked as a waiter in order to get the money needed to buy the new bike cannot be generated on the basis of associative links. Search must be directed by some control mechanism, that is, the search for causal links that is typical of narrative comprehension.

Automatic generative inferences result from structural properties of the situation model already constructed as part of comprehension. An example of automatic generation of inference is the deduction "The knife is to the right of the plate" when the passage "The spoon is to the right of the plate. The knife is to the right of the spoon." In this case, the reader uses his or hereading r prior knowledge of spatial relations to further specify his or her mental model of the situation.

Controlled generative inferences make up a widely open and heterogeneous category. They denote virtually all the deliberate thinking processes that may occur in connection to one's reading of a passage. Controlled generative inferences rely heavily of the individuals' prior knowledge, on their ability to manipulate information in working memory, and, most important, on their willingness to do so. Controlled generative inferences are not specific to text comprehension, but they are an integral part of deep comprehension. Kintsch argues that controlled generative inferences may be based on the application of explicit rules or on the properties of situation models, depending on the knowledge domain or type of representation considered.

1.2.2. What Inferences Do Readers Actually Generate During Text Comprehension?

The notion that some inferences may be generated automatically does not imply that they are generated in any circumstances. The problem, then, is to find out what inferences are *actually* generated as a particular reader reads a particular text in a particular context (McNamara, Miller, & Bransford, 1991; see also Fig. I-1 in the introduction). This issue has raised some controversy among comprehension theorists (see, e.g., Garnham, 1992), and it is not fully resolved yet (see, e.g., Shears & Chiarello, 2004). At the heart of the controversy is the question of whether readers normally generate global inferences about the meaning of a story, or only the inferences that are necessary to connect pieces of discourse locally. Some comprehension theorists have claimed that only the inferences strictly needed to maintain local coherence were systematically generated (McKoon & Ratcliff, 1992). This view is known as the "minimalist" theory of comprehension. Other studies, however, have shown that under some circumstances readers can manage both local and global coherence when comprehending narratives (Albrecht & O'Brien, 1993), or even expository text, provided that they possess the requisite knowledge (Noordman & Vonk, 1992).

The alternative to a minimalist view of comprehension is known as the "constructionist" theory of comprehension (see, e.g., Garnham, 1992; Graesser, Singer, & Trabasso, 1994, Graesser & Wiemer-Hastings, 1999). The constructionist theory states that when reading stories, readers generate inferences in order to achieve a global, integrated representation of the events. More specifically, the theory rests on two main assumptions, namely the "coherence assumption" and the "explanation assumption." Because these assumptions are central to the issues discussed in the following chapters, I review them in more detail.

The *coherence assumption* is that readers routinely attempt to link the events that make up a story at both local and global levels, according to coherence relationships. At the *local level*, linking is achieved when two consecutive statements share common values on the various relevant dimensions of the situation (Zwaan, 1999). For example, the reader monitors whether the agents (or protagonists) are identical, whether the timeline is continuous, or whether the event or action described in the statement is consistent with the agents' plans and goals. Any break in local coherence on any of the dimensions results in a processing difficulty, as it prevents the reader from applying the local coherence strategy. At the *global level*, coherence exists when actions and events can be grouped into meaningful chunks, and chunks can be organized into a global scenario or scheme. Achieving global coherence sometimes requires the reader to connect information in a statement with information read much earlier in the text. The constructionist view of comprehension suggests that readers will do so provided that the story is well written, and they have the motivation to do so (i.e., readers "search after meaning"; Graesser, Singer, & Trabasso, 1994).

The *explanation assumption* is that the reader normally attempts to know why actions and events take place, or why the author of a text mentions a piece of information or uses a particular rhetoric or writing style. Explanation-based inferences are more likely to be generated than, for instance, inferences about the spatial context or the means used to perform actions. Empirical research has provided evidence that readers do generate knowledge-based inferences while comprehending texts, and that words representing causal antecedents or superordinate goals are more active in memory than words representing consequences or subordinate goals.

One interesting aspect of the constructionist approach is that it acknowledges the role of pragmatic agents (e.g., the author, the narrator, the reader) in constructing explanations from texts. The theory assumes that "the reader does not build these agents unless there are non canonical features in the text that signal such agents" (Graesser & Wiemer-Hastings, 1999, p. 85). "Noncanonical features," in the context of story comprehension, include the narrator using the first person instead of the more common third person. In other discourse genres or discourse comprehension situations, however, discourse features that make the author more salient may be more canonical, and thus the consideration of pragmatic agents may become a more central component of skilled comprehension. Again, this emphasizes the role of source information in discourse comprehension, a point discussed further in chapter 3.

Recent research has emphasized the role of memory-based mechanisms in the production of inferences, which helped reduce the gap between "minimalist" and "constructionist" approaches (Guéraud & O'Brien, 2005). For instance, Gerrig and McKoon (1998) argued that inferences are not generated from memory in an all-or-none fashion. Rather, prior knowledge is made available as a consequence of memory-based processes. Each new piece of information in a text is thus interpreted in terms of the knowledge that "resonates" when this piece of information is encountered. Such knowledge includes our general world knowledge and knowledge specific to some discourse types, for example, narratives. In Gerrig and McKoon's perspective, resonance makes knowledge-based information available or "ready" for integration with the incoming text information. But whether or not the information will be used depends on a number of other factors, including contextual ones.

The "readiness" theory presented by Gerrig and McKoon (1998) rests on a number of experiments in which they investigated the factors that influence whether information previously read can be easily (i.e., quickly) made accessible again in memory. They demonstrated that rather weak discourse cues were able to increase the accessibility of characters in a story, even though these characters had been put in the background. In the first experiment, 15 undergraduate psychology students read simple stories where two characters talked about a third one (outsider), then parted, then reunited. On some trials, a keyword designating the outsider was presented either just before or just after the reunion sentence. The participants had to decide as quickly as possible if the word had appeared in the story. The mention of the reunion was enough to make information about the target character available again, as evidenced by faster response times when the keyword was presented after the sentence (experiment 1). A single sentence shifting the topic again was enough to decrease the availability of that target, suggesting that the fluctuation of readiness is a rather fast and flexible process. In their second experiment, Gerrig and McKoon (1998) showed that even though the "outsider" is fading away from short-term memory, it still interacts with the further content of the text. Words presented in a single story showed a significant priming effect, even though they were neither close in the text nor causally related. According to the authors, the fact that two characters reunite makes available information that was previously associated to either of them, or to the context in which they were initially introduced. This is a considerable extension of the situation model theory, inasmuch as it considers the discourse context as a dimension of situation models.

The role of "passive" resonance mechanisms in concept activation has been heralded by Myers, O'Brien, and their collaborators. Myers and O'Brien (1998) introduced a model of memory-based processes involved in reading comprehension, the *Resonance model*. They emphasized that memory activation processes are essential in building an integrated memory representation, that is, a representation in which text information is interconnected with information presented earlier, and with the reader's prior knowledge. Myers and O'Brien (1998) stated the basic assumptions of their model as follows:

> The model is based on the assumption that concepts and propositions derived from the sentence currently being processed (the focal sentence), or residing in working memory as a result of reading earlier portions of text, serve as signals to the memory representation. The intensity of these signals may depend on the degree of attention given to the text elements they reflect, but the process initiated by the signals is not under the control of the reader, it proceeds autonomously. (…) we assume that this process is one in which concepts and propositions in the discourse representation and in the reader's knowledge base resonate as a function of the degree of match to the input. This match depends on the overlap of semantic and contextual features among concepts and on the argument overlap of propositions. Memory elements that are connected by the initial signal in turn signal to other memory elements. During this resonance process, activation builds, and when the process stabilizes, the most active elements enter working memory. (p. 132)

Myers and O'Brien further define the resonance process as continuous (i.e., there is a constant flux of activation and deactivation in working memory) and dumb (i.e., information is activated regardless of whether it will be ultimately used by the reader). They also suggest that a second, higher order process intervenes to evaluate the content of working memory. Contrary to the basic resonance process, the evaluation process is active and dependent on the readers' goals (see also

Kintsch's "controlled inferences" previously mentioned or van den Broek et al.'s "standard of coherence" following). Myers and O'Brien define the evaluation process as one that takes care of failures in the comprehension process. Examples of such failures are when the reader cannot identify a referent for a pronoun (e.g., "... Yesterday, President Chirac landed in Berlin and greeted *her.*"), when a break occurs in the coherence chain (e.g., no cause is found for an action), or when two pieces of information contradict each other. The evaluation process results in slower reading times as the reader engages in additional memory search, reasoning, or problem solving.

Myers and O'Brien (1998) listed empirical arguments supporting the assumptions of the Resonance model. First, the reactivation of antecedent information upon reading anaphora is faster when the anaphora and the antecedents share many conceptual features *(featural overlap, e.g., "Ms. Simpson ... The lady")*. Thus, antecedent activation is faster when the anaphor is explicit (a noun phrase) than when it is implicit (a pronoun). Reactivation of an antecedent is also faster when the anaphor is a direct repetition than when it is a synonym (Dell, McKoon, & Ratcliff, 1983), and when the antecedent has been more elaborated in earlier text portions (e.g., repeated, or described in detail), before it became deactivated.

The Resonance model further predicts that activation will decrease as there are more potential antecedents (or *"distractors"*). Experimental studies actually showed that reactivation slows down when the antecedent has been introduced in several contexts (e.g., episodes), creating a fan effect that reduces the activation. Increased *distance* between an antecedent and the anaphor will also reduce its accessibility, either because activation decreases over time, or because distance decreases the amount of conceptual overlap between the antecedent (and its context) and the anaphor (and its context). Finally, concepts explicit in a text also resonate with concepts present in the reader's *prior knowledge base*, provided that there are strong enough links between the two. This may result in confusions between concepts explicitly read in the text and concepts not present in the text but strongly associated to them.

Myers and O'Brien (1998) further argued that the reactivation of concepts is not a mechanism specifically aimed a resolving local coherence breaks such as pronoun ambiguity. Concepts present in long term or episodic memory may become reactivated regardless of local coherence issues. Evidence comes from studies by O'Brien and Albrecht (1992), who demonstrated that spatial inconsistencies were noted even though the local sentence context was coherent. Contextual effects may not be due to the reader's active "search after meaning" (Graesser, Singer, & Trabasso, 1994), but to a passive and undirected spread of activation or resonance mechanism. Another, related approach is Gernsbacher's Structure Building Framework (Gernsbacher, 1990, 1995). The Structure Building Framework states that readers comprehend texts by laying conceptual foundations (or substructures), *map-*

ping incoming information onto these foundations, and *shifting* to a new substructure when the new information is less related to the discourse context. These processes are fueled by memory processes of *enhancement* and *suppression*. Enhancement consists of an increase in a concept's activation due to strong positive associations with other activated concepts; suppression consists of a decrease in a concept activation due to a lack of association or relevance. Among other findings, Gernsbacher and colleagues demonstrated that mechanisms of enhancement and suppressions could account for the activation and deactivation of character information during the comprehension of simple narratives (Gernsbacher, Robertson, Palladino, & Werner, 2004).

Recent developments in comprehension research put a strong emphasis on memory processes, and in particular on the relationship between the knowledge stored in a person's long-term memory and the processing of information in working memory. Even though the researchers' purpose is to uncover the general "laws" that govern the comprehension of discourse, there appear to be huge quantitative and qualitative variations in connection to individual differences (see, e.g., Fincher-Kiefer & D'Agostino, 2004; Hannon & Danneman, 2004). Readers' tasks or purposes also play an important though somewhat overlooked role in the course and nature of the mental processes that underlie comprehension activities. I return to this issue in section 1.5 and in the conclusion of this chapter.

1.2.3. Simulating Memory-Based Comprehension Processes

As the hypotheses regarding the nature of memory processes involved in comprehension became more explicit, several researchers attempted to design computer programs that simulate text comprehension. These programs are useful because they allow researchers to test further hypotheses about comprehension processes. Kintsch's (1998) construction–integration model, Goldman and her colleagues' 3-CAP model (Goldman, Varma, & Coté, 1996), or Myers and O'Brien's (1998) resonance model are examples of theories that have been successfully implemented in the form of computer programs.

Among the recent attempts in this direction is the "Landscape Model" by van den Broek and his colleagues (van den Broek, Risden, Fletcher, & Thurlow, 1996; van den Broek, Virtue, Everson, Tzeng, & Sung, 2002; van den Broek, Young, Tzeng, & Linderholm, 1999). The Landscape Model rests on the assumption that a commonly used comprehension strategy consists in maintaining referential clarity (i.e., knowing what the text is about) and causal explanation (i.e., identifying causal links among events). In order to apply this strategy, the reader must hold in mind a subset of the concepts encountered during reading (see also Kintsch & van Dijk, 1978). Van den Broek et al. hypothesized that concept activation is a gradual phenomenon, and is partly predictable based on the status of the concepts in the text and in the mental model. More specifically, concepts may receive activation (a) if they are explicitly mentioned in the text, (b) if they were active in the previous processing cycle (in the sense of Kintsch & van Dijk, 1978), and (c) if they were active sometime during the processing of earlier text portions. The latter concepts are reactivated only when they are needed in the current processing cycle.

Based on these and other processing assumptions, van den Broek et al. (1996) proposed a set of simple activation and deactivation rules that simulate the functioning of working memory during text comprehension. They set the activation range as an arbitrary continuous scale of 0 to 5. Then, they postulated that:

- concepts explicit in the passage being processed receive an activation value of 5.
- concepts needed to establish referential clarity receive a value of 4.
- concepts that participate in sufficient causal explanations receive a 4.
- concepts that participate in necessary conditions receive 3.
- associations and elaborations receive an activation value of 2.

The Landscape Model further assumes that unless concepts are repeated or reactivated, their activation value decreases progressively. As a first approximation of the decay function, the activation value is divided by two at each cycle, and cancelled after the third cycle.

Van den Broek and his colleagues applied those rules to a simple narrative text that corresponded to 13 processing cycles. Concepts were equated to content words in the texts (i.e., nouns, adjectives, verbs). The activation value of each concept was computed at each processing cycle, and the result was represented as a tridimensional diagram, the "Landscape" of concept activation (Fig. 1.1).

In Fig. 1.1, concepts are represented on one axis of the diagram; reading cycles are represented on another axis, and activation values are represented on the third axis. The diagram shows which concepts are active at each reading cycle. To find out whether the activation levels predicted by the model were accurate, Van den Broek et al. (1996) asked a group of students to read each sentence of the text and to rate the relatedness of the sentence with each concept presented in a list. They found a high correlation between the activation level predicted by the model and the participants' ratings. Van den Broek et al. also used the Landscape simulation to predict the probability and order of recall of concepts. Recall probability was predicted by adding up the activation values received by each concept across processing cycles. This value represented the centrality of a concept of "node strength." The degree of relatedness of concepts was calculated by computing the cross-product of activation values of each pair of concepts. Thus, if two concepts are active during the same cycles, they will become highly related. In a text recall experi-

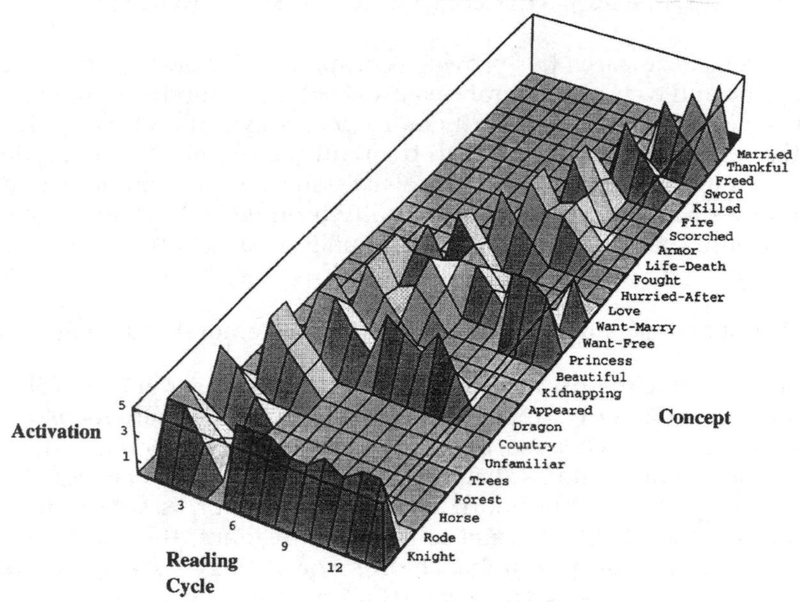

FIG. 1.1. Activation level of concepts from the "knight" story as a function of reading cycle (reprinted from van den Broek, Risden, Fletcher, & Thurlow, 1996).

ment, van den Broek et al. (1996) showed that the combination of node strength and relatedness predicted 64% of variance in recall probability.

Van den Broek et al. (1999) presented a revised version of the Landscape Model with a number of important modifications. They represented working memory as a limited pool of activation. Activation spreads across concepts according to a cohort function. The degree of activation of related concepts varies as a function of the activation value of the source concept, the strength of the association, and a propagation parameter that varies between 0 and 1. Furthermore, they assumed that the activation received by a concept across cycles decreases according to a learning curve. Finally, the connections across concepts are unidirectional: "prince" may activate "dragon" even though "dragon" does not activate "prince."

The more recent version of the Landscape Model was implemented in a computer program that allows researchers to test various hypotheses about comprehension processes (van den Broek et al., 2002). In a pilot study (Potelle & Rouet, 2001), we found that the Landscape Model software could be used to study the effects of headings and other content representations (e.g., concept maps) on concept activation during reading (see chapter 5). More generally, computer simulation tools seem a very promising means to formulate and test hypotheses about the fine-grain processes of text comprehension.

1.3. MANAGING THE COMPREHENSION PROCESS

Psychological research has provided comprehensive descriptions of the linguistic and cognitive operations involved in comprehending text, as well as detailed analyses of the memory processes that underlie such operations. Assuming a reader with the required cognitive and language skills, an important and yet unresolved issue is to determine whether, and how, memory processes are actually brought to bear during comprehension, that is, how the reader actually manages the comprehension process.

1.3.1. Context-Dependent Fluctuations of the Comprehension Process

Under normal circumstances, text comprehension is a purposeful, deliberate activity. The components of a text that are actually focused on, highlighted, comprehended, and remembered depend as much on what the reader wants to do as they depend on structural properties of the cognitive system. Furthermore, text comprehension is subject to frequent obstacles, incidents, and failure. For instance, the text may include unknown or unfamiliar words, or it may lack connecting information between two passages (Hacker, 1998). Conversely, the text may contain information that is unnecessary or irrelevant to the readers' goals (Gilabert, Martinez, & Vidal-Abarca, 2005; McNamara, Kintsch, Songer, & Kintsch, 1996). The reader must be able to deal with such problems by adjusting his or her reading rate, by initiating memory-based explanatory processes, or by selecting and applying more complex repair strategies. In short, the reader must be able not only to execute the basic process that lead to situation model construction; he or she must also be able to manage the memory processes so as to acquire information consistent with his or her goals, and to fix any potential incident that may occur en route.

Reading purpose (that is, the reason or goal that motivates a reader's engagement in text processing) has a strong qualitative and quantitative influence on the comprehension processes. The qualitative influence was demonstrated in studies where people were asked to take a particular perspective prior to reading a text. For instance, the perspective assigned to the reader—for example, reading the description of a house from the perspective of a burglar or a homebuyer—influences the information that is encoded and/or recalled (Anderson & Pichert, 1978; Baillet & Keenan, 1986; Bloom, 1988). Cues and questions inserted in texts focus the reader's attention on target information (Rouet & Vidal-Abarca, 2002) at the expense of other, nontarget information. Thus, the relative salience or centrality of information in the situation model is a function of both the structural importance of information in text and the functional, context-dependent importance of information given a particular purpose.

Readers' awareness of the situation demands may also modulate the amount of effort devoted to comprehending (Britton, Glynn, Muth, & Penland, 1985; Goldman & Durán, 1988; Lehman & Schraw, 2002). Postreading test expectations (e.g., reading for leisure or for work, reading in a science vs. a literature class) affect students' monitoring of text coherence and their production of inferences. For instance, in a study by Narvaez, van den Broek, and Ruiz (1999), "reading for entertainment" increased reading time, whereas "reading for study" increased recall, inference evaluation, and think-aloud comments. The perception of typical demands associated with content area reading also seem to affect students' monitoring of text information (Lorch, Lorch, & Klusewitz, 1993). García-Arista et al. (1996) asked tenth-grade students to read a series of short scientific texts, some of which contained contradictions. The students were assigned to one of two study settings: a language class where the texts were presented as newspaper articles, or a science class where the texts were presented as taken from a science textbook. They received explicit instruction to report any problem or inconsistency with the texts. The students reported more contradictions in the science/textbook than in the language/newspaper study setting (see also p. 89). García-Arista et al. concluded that high school students are sensitive to study contexts when they set up standards and comprehension strategies for themselves. Students tend to raise their expectation for coherence and internal consistence when reading texts with a high perceived epistemic authority—such as the textbook (see also Wineburg, 1991). However, because the source (textbooks/newspaper) and setting (language/science class) manipulations were confounded, it is unclear which of the two dimensions was the most influential.

In a similar vein, Lehman and Schraw (2002) hypothesized that reading a text with a specific purpose may compensate the effect of a decayed textual coherence. In the first experiment, they asked undergraduate students to read a historical narrative on "The quest for the Northwest passage" that was either coherent or less coherent. In addition, half of the participants were given basic, "low relevance" instructions (i.e., to read and remember as much as possible). The other half received an additional, more specific statement (i.e., to pay "particular attention to the explorers who made important discoveries and what these explorers discovered"). The high relevance instruction raised the quality of students' essays, whereas the coherence manipulation had no consequence. Neither relevance nor coherence affected students' performance on a multiple-choice test performance. In the second experiment, a combination of high coherence and high relevance gave significantly better essays than the other three conditions. The authors concluded that college students are flexible enough to compensate for reduced textual coherence through the active assignment of relevance.

1.3.2. Comprehension Strategies

Such evidence suggests that mature readers normally exert a high degree of control over their text comprehension processes. That is, normal comprehension involves metacognitive in addition to cognitive processes (Hacker, 1998; Nist & Simpson, 2000; Pressley, Van Etten, Yokoi, Freebern, & Van Meter, 1998; Winne & Hadwin; 1998). In the context of reading comprehension, metacognition involves both knowledge about texts and reading contexts, and a set of processes that allow the reader to prepare (or plan), control (or evaluate), and regulate the more basic perceptual, attentional, and cognitive processes involved in the construction of text representations (Hacker, 1998).

Mature readers generally do know quite a lot about the characteristics and constraints of a wide range of reading situations. Lorch, Lorch, and Klusewitz (1993) reported that college students are aware of the specific demands of tasks as different as leisurely browsing a magazine or studying in order to prepare for an exam. Wagner and Sternberg (1987, experiment 1) asked college students to read a series of text passages followed by comprehension questions. Based on the latency and accuracy of answers, the authors distinguished easier (gist, main idea) and more difficult types of trials (detail, analysis). They found that the most successful students tended to spend more time on the most difficult trials. In their second experiment, Wagner and Sternberg (1987) provided students with difficulty ratings and importance signals for each trial. Better able students made use of text difficulty ratings to plan their passage reading order. They also focused on sentences marked as important, but there was no relationship between this strategy and comprehension performance. The authors concluded that planning plays an important role in comprehension activities, and that some types of adjunct information may facilitate planning in more able students.

Researchers often use the phrase "comprehension strategy" to characterize the reader's activity at both the cognitive and metacognitive level (Garner, 1987; Nist & Simpson, 2000; Paris, Wasik, & Turner, 1991). Comprehension strategies involve thoughts, decisions, and actions that may take place at any point before, during, or after reading a passage of text. Furthermore, strategic behavior can be either local or global. Local strategies are directly attached to a particular piece of information/processing episode. They involve reading adjunct information (e.g., headings), pausing, rereading, backtracking, and so forth. Walczyk, Marsaglia, Bryan, and Naquin (2001) pointed out that poor readers may also need such strategies in order to compensate for their less efficient comprehension processes. Using a think-aloud procedure, they found evidence that college students with poor verbal skills used more compensations while reading a difficult text.

Global strategies characterize the comprehension activity as a whole. They involve choosing an appropriate time and place, and preparing additional equipment to assist comprehension (e.g., a dictionary); adjusting reading speed and depth of processing to time constraint and comprehension purposes; reflecting, asking questions, taking notes, summarizing the main points of a text; and generating external representations (e.g., diagrams, concept maps) of the semantic structure of the text (Nist & Simpson, 2000).

Studies of expert text comprehension suggests considerable interindividual variation in people's spontaneous use of both local and global comprehension strategies. For example, Lonka, Lindblom-Ylänne, & Maury (1994) found that students applying for medical school differed in their use of notetaking and other generative activities while studying a lengthy, difficult text. Furthermore, the use of comprehension strategies seems related to people's beliefs about knowledge and learning (Kardash & Noel, 2000; Lindblom-Ylänne & Lonka, 1999; Schommer, 1990). Thus, the actual unfolding of perceptual and cognitive processes during reading appears tightly related to readers' purposes, but also to their ability to manage the comprehension processes through higher level metacognitive strategies, which, in turn, appear partly dependent on people's conceptions of their own cognitive functioning.

1.4. CURRENT ISSUES IN TEXT COMPREHENSION RESEARCH

I have just summarized some of the main outcomes of research studies on text comprehension conducted in the past three decades, as well as a few of their recent developments. I want now to point out some important aspects of text comprehension that I think have been somewhat overlooked in mainstream research. More specifically, I want to introduce three issues that pose yet-unsolved problems to comprehension theories. The first issue concerns the relationship between *texts and situations;* the second issue has to do with coherence and *integration of information across texts;* the third issue concerns *readers' strategies and reading objectives*.

How do texts represent situations? Most studies of text comprehension rest on the basic assumption that texts are linguistic representations of situations, whether real or fictitious. Comprehension is defined as the construction of a mental representation of the situation described in the text. Thus, any given text is assumed to be a reliable and exhaustive basis for constructing such a representation. This assumption does fit the status of text in the fictitious narrative genre, which has been the focus of the vast majority of studies. In the fictitious narrative genre, a text is always a complete and reliable account of a situation, inasmuch as the situation has no existence outside the realm of the author–text–reader interplay. The text-as-situation assumption is challenged, however, as soon as one considers a broader definition of text. Such a definition is offered by the United States National Adult Literacy Survey. The survey distinguished three dimensions of literacy: prose literacy, document literacy, and quantitative literacy. Their definition of prose is as follows:

> Prose refers to any written text such as editorials, news stories, poems and fiction, and can be broken down into two types: expository prose and narrative prose. Expository prose consists of printed information that defines, describes, or informs, such as newspaper stories or written instructions. Narrative prose tells a story. Prose varies in its length, density, and structure (e.g., use of section headings or topic sentences for paragraphs). (National Center for Education Statistics, 2004)

Such a definition questions the text-as-situation assumption. Take, for instance, the case of newspaper articles. Typical articles describe the state of the world at a given moment. Experienced newspaper readers do not expect news articles to be complete and accurate representations, at least not in absolute terms. Instead, accuracy is modulated by characteristics that pertain to the source, for instance, the publication date of the newspaper. Other characteristics of information sources also play an important role in text comprehension and interpretation. As an illustration of this point, Table 1.2 presents two excerpts adapted from actual newspaper articles.

Excerpt 1, in Table 1.2, based on an actual newspaper report (L'Humanité, 23/08/1987), describes a controversial protest. Most comprehension theories reviewed in this chapter would claim that comprehending this passage amounts to forming a coherent representation of the situation. However, this simple text really describes more than just one situation. It includes at least three different depictions of the same event: One is offered by "the protesters" and claims that several

TABLE 1.2

Two Excerpts From Two Newspaper Accounts of the Protest in Noumea

Newspaper account #1	*Newspaper account #2*
"The protesters claim that about thirty people were wounded by the police, including one seriously injured, with a list of names for evidence. The government spokesperson, who was not present during the beating, declared that no one was wounded. A city physician has sewn up a few scalps and eyebrow arches. He has also cured many serious hematoma."	"I was there, and even through the tears provoked by the tear bombs, I saw no baby in the protesters' arms, no woman being beaten, not even a single wounded protester. When one points out to the organizers that nobody was taken to the hospital after the protest, they reply that the wounded were helped 'by private physicians.'"

Note. #1 adapted from L'Humanité, August 23, 1987. #2 adapted from Le Figaro, August 23, 1987.

people were wounded; another one is given by the "government spokesperson" and states that no one was wounded. Finally, the third depiction is indirectly provided by the physician, whose testimony is used by the author of the paper to support the view that there were indeed some casualties. Thus, a complete representation of the situation, as presented in this passage, should include not only a representation of the protest (i.e., a situation model), but also a representation of the characters mentioned in the text and what each of them has to say about the situation (i.e., a rhetorical model; see Graesser, Bowers, Olde, & Pomeroy, 1999; Perfetti, Rouet, & Britt, 1999).

Furthermore, the expert newspaper reader will probably want to know a bit more about the author of this passage before deciding, for instance, whether people were actually wounded during this protest. If one learns, for instance, that the article was published in a newspaper that opposes the ruling political party, one may infer that the author was trying to demonstrate that the government had used brutality to suppress the protesters. The reader will thus be able to estimate the distance between what was said and what might have actually occurred. This type of knowledge-based inference requires background knowledge of sources and rhetorical principles, in addition to knowledge of the events described in the text (Britt & Gabrys, 2000; Perfetti et al. 1999). More generally, it points to the need to acknowledge a pragmatic level of representation in discourse understanding (Graesser, Millis, & Zwaan, 1997).

The distance between individual texts and the situations they refer to is even greater in complex documents such as textbooks, magazine reports, or portfolios. There, the situation is represented as a collection of texts (i.e., individual articles, chapters, and supporting documents). The texts may be said to collectively represent the situation, but this is not true of each of them taken separately. Furthermore, complex documents do not just include information aimed at representing a situation. They also include a variety of text organizers, whose function is to describe the document and to help the reader perform various comprehension activities. Thus, complex texts provide both a representation of the situation and discourse cues and tools that assist the reader in his or her task. In order to achieve comprehension, the reader must bring to bear not only his or her prior knowledge of the situation, but also some knowledge of the many discourse cues, signals, and conventions that provide "shape" to printed discourse.

The distance between texts and situations, the connections that are made between contents and source information, and the interpretation that comes from the reader's knowledge of sources, rhetorical principles, and text organizers are hardly taken into account in current theories of comprehension. This is, in part, because comprehension research has focused on the comprehension of simple stories in which these issues are less critical. These aspects of text comprehension are nevertheless essential in many naturalistic reading situations, such as reading the press, studying historical texts, or even reading scientific information (think, for instance, about the growing body of self-proclaimed scientific, legal, or medical information pages published on the World Wide Web). They are the focus of chapters 2 and 3.

How is integration achieved across texts? So far, comprehension research has focused on the comprehension of single texts, with a strong preference for simple narrative texts. In real life, however, readers are often confronted by a variety of information sources that they have to integrate in order to achieve their purposes (e.g., learning about a complex subject matter, making an informed decision, solving a practical problem, and so forth). Integration across texts is often made difficult by the fact that the texts at hand present inconsistent or conflicting representations of the situations. Consider for instance the newspaper account #2, in Table 1.2.

This passage presents another account of the protest referred to in account #1 discussed earlier. Contrary to the previous account, this passage is strongly hedged toward the "no wounded" side. Suppose that, while sitting at a library, you find yourself reading these two accounts one after the other, in two different newspapers. How would comprehension proceed in this case and what would be the result? Current theories have little to say about multiple text integration. From a content analysis point of view, the two accounts are contradictory, and the reader is expected—at best—to notice the contradiction. Or else, theories of mental model updating would predict that the version provided by the first account has more chances to stick to memory, whereas the conflicting information given in the second one is likely to be ignored or dismissed.

Intuition suggests that this is not what the experienced reader would do. Here again, source information might play a critical part in the comprehension process. For instance, if the reader learns that the second article is from a major pro-government newspaper, then he or she might infer that the author is trying to downplay the violence of the protest. The result is a rhetorical structure where two authors—the journalists—argue for different evaluations of government policies through biased accounts of a protest, and through the citation and evaluation of various forms of evidence. How rhetorical relationships within and across sources are represented and what form the resulting memory representation takes remains to be explained. This is the purpose of chapter 3.

What is text information used for? Another issue that remains wide open is that of reading tasks, purposes, and objectives, and the role they play in expert comprehension. In most studies of text comprehension, readers are assigned recall or general comprehension purposes. This approach is valid to the extent that the texts are short, rather simple, and, literally, useless. On the other hand, those studies that have addressed the role of the reading context have found that it does indeed strongly influence readers' strategies. Thus, text comprehension appears to be strongly influenced by the situation. But how "purpose" is represented in the reader's mind, exactly when and how it affects the processing of text information, has not been examined very closely by comprehension theorists. Furthermore, reading purpose has mostly been examined through global manipulations of perspective-taking or postreading task expectations. These manipulations are hardly representative of the large variations of reading purposes reported in surveys of reading in study contexts (Lorch, Lorch, & Klusewitz, 1993) or at the workplace (Kirsch et al., 2002).

A broader view of comprehension should acknowledge the variety of comprehension tasks and strategies. This means that some basic assumptions of text comprehension research have to be challenged. For instance, text comprehension theories assume that "reading" involves the reader going through the whole text once from top to bottom. In real life situations, however, reading is frequently selective and opportunistic. People browse magazines for fun—they skim most pages and suddenly pause on a particular heading or passage that caught their attention. Or, people search a reference book for a particular detail on a topic of interest; they review course materials in order to prepare for an exam; they browse tourist guides for places to see and things to do. In these and other common situations, reading is neither exhaustive nor necessarily top to bottom. Instead, people use various strategies to search, locate, and make use of content information that is of interest to them. How does text search interact with the construction of long-term text representations? Again, this is a largely unknown side of comprehension behaviors, one that needs much more attention than has been devoted so far by researchers. Chapter 4 goes back to this point.

In summary, naturalistic text processing situations frequently involve dimensions that are hardly taken into account in current psychological theories of comprehension. Figure 1.2 synthesizes some critical variables characteristic of complex document comprehension. The first set of variables pertain to the *context* in which reading takes place. These include time and space constraints that surround the reading episode; the purpose of the task and its consequences (positive or negative) for the reader; the reading objectives and perspective taken on the materials. Sensitivity to contextual variables is critical in complex document comprehension. Readers' perception of temporal and other constraints determine their allocation of time and attention over the materials; readers' purposes and their perception of possible consequences modulate the amount of effort invested in the task; and reading objectives or perspectives provide criteria for assessing priority or importance of content information.

Resource variables characterize the amount and type of information available to the reader. Resources include single texts, document sets, and computerized databases. In addition, complex document processing often requires the use of organization and search devices (e.g., catalogs, content tables, or keyword search tools). Again, these variables are criti-

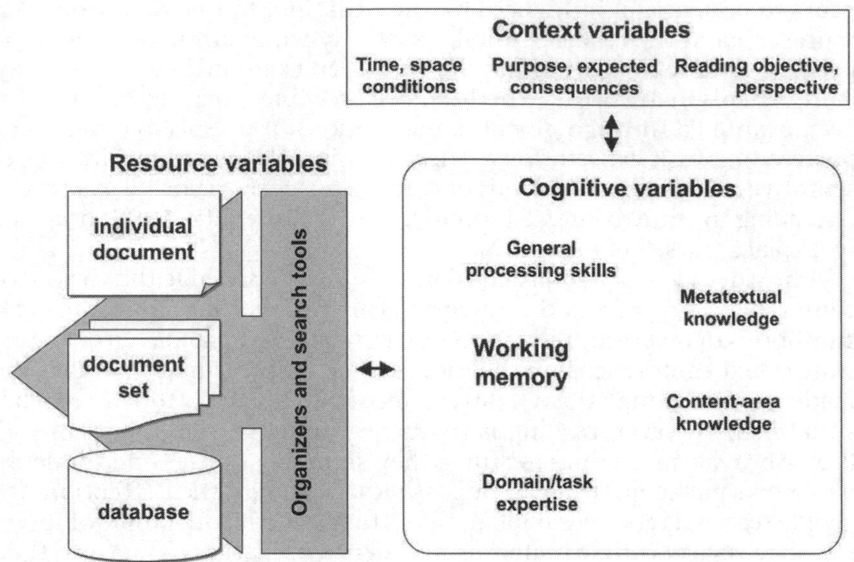

FIG. 1.2. An overview of critical dimensions in complex document comprehension.

cal in document comprehension because they determine readers' selection, processing, assessment, and evaluation of information. Single, short texts afford exhaustive, top-to-bottom reading and comprehension activities, whereas using a library or the World Wide Web obviously calls for additional evaluation and selection mechanisms.

Finally, *cognitive* variables characterize the level of skill, knowledge, and processing capacity available to the reader. Cognitive resources relevant to complex document comprehension may not differ from those involved in any language-processing activity. Some resources, however, play a more prominent role. For instance, metatextual knowledge (knowledge about texts, documents, and search tools) is more important in naturalistic document processing than in paragraph memorization tasks. And the level of familiarity or procedural expertise in the task is likely to affect the way lower level memory processes are initiated and regulated (see also Winne & Hadwin, 1998).

CONCLUSIONS

According to current psychological theories, comprehension is achieved when the reader constructs a mental representation of the situation described in the text. Such a construction is achieved through the use of text-based and knowledge-based mechanisms. Text-based mechanisms involve decoding words, parsing sentences into semantic micropropositions, connecting propositions across reading cycles, and subsuming micropropositions into global chunks like macropropositions. Knowledge-based mechanisms involve holding information active in working memory, activating relevant knowledge through either passive memory-based mechanisms (e.g., activation propagation, resonance), or through controlled, selective memory search mechanisms (e.g., global coherence inferences and deductive reasoning). Successful application of these processes results in the formation of a situation model, that is, an integrated knowledge structure that may be stored in long-term memory and later retrieved for further use and, possibly, updating.

The situation model view of text comprehension is widely accepted and it has, indeed, received considerable support from experimental research. I have claimed, however, that this view is valid only to the extent that researchers work under a restrictive set of assumptions regarding the very nature of texts and text processing situations. The first of these assumptions holds that texts are accurate representations of situations. The second assumption is that integration of information across passages or texts is achieved by linking information in an incremental way, using relevant dimensions of the situations (e.g., spatial, causal). The third assumption is that readers read texts entirely, at a constant depth of processing, using a general representation-building strategy.

These assumptions cannot be sustained in more realistic, complex reading situations. For instance, on some occasions the text may not be an accurate representation of reality (but readers will still want to read it!). On other occasions, readers need to use not just one, but two or more texts. These texts are not necessarily coherent; they may even contain blatant contradictions. But readers will still need to "integrate" them in some ways. Finally, in many situations, the reader is simply not interested in constructing a representation of the text as a whole. Instead, the reader may want to locate a particular detail, or to use information selectively in order to solve a complex problem. These uses also require comprehension mechanisms, although not necessarily the same as described in traditional comprehension research.

In the following chapters, my purpose is to address relevant issues in the comprehension of complex texts. I do not claim, however, that I can offer a coherent theory of comprehension that would account uniformly for all these situations. Instead, the research conducted so far only highlights a few aspects of this large and new area of investigation. But these highlights may be useful in explaining some of the problems associated with functional literacy, its learning, and its use in modern information-based societies.

2

The Role of Text Organizers in Expert Comprehension

OVERVIEW AND CONTENTS

This chapter deals with the role of text organizers (e.g., paragraphing, headings, and tables of contents) in the comprehension of complex texts. Complex texts include several layers of information. In addition to content information, they generally include a variety of text organizers, signals, marks, and other cues aimed at guiding the selection and comprehension of relevant contents. A comprehensive theory of text comprehension must account for the role of text organizers, that is, it should explain how these devices intervene in the construction of a mental representation from the text. In this chapter, I present a typology of visual and verbal organizers found in texts and complex documents. I review empirical studies showing their role in expert comprehension. The phrase *expert comprehension* is important here, as the use of text organizers assumes that the reader is aware of their functions. I discuss the role of individual differences in the use of text organizers, and the acquisition of knowledge about text organizers.

Contents

INTRODUCTION

Comprehending complex documents requires the reader to possess knowledge about the content and shape of the documents. The influence of content, or topic knowledge, is rather intuitive and straightforward. In order to understand a text about a baseball game, 19th-century Ireland, or the Panama Canal, for example, one has to possess at least some knowledge about the places, objects, events, purposes, and other aspects of the situations described in the text. The role of domain knowledge has been the object of numerous studies in text comprehension research. The oft-cited studies by Voss and his colleagues (Spilich, Vesonder, Chiesi, & Voss, 1979; Voss, Vesonder, & Spilich, 1980) showed that individuals with more initial knowledge of the baseball game have a better memory for verbal accounts of a particular game. Haenggi and Perfetti (1994) found that college-level reading comprehension is influenced independently by basic reading processes and domain knowledge. Studies using online measurements have shown that domain experts apply more efficient text comprehension strategies (Afflerbach, 1990) because they can activate more elaborate representations of the situation or problem (Means & Voss, 1985; Voss, Greene, Post, & Penner, 1983). Domain experts also apply more flexible rules when evaluating the importance of statements in a scientific text (Dee-Lucas & Larkin, 1986, 1988). In most cases, content area knowledge facilitates comprehension. In some cases, however, it may interfere with incoming information. This is the case, for instance, when readers try to apply irrelevant schema to unfamiliar stories (Deschênes, 1988).

Skilled comprehension, however, also depends on the reader's knowledge of the shape of discourse, that is, the visual and verbal devices that are used to structure the text. For example, it would be difficult for a reader to locate a specific date or name in a textbook without a minimal awareness of the table of contents, the index, chapter structure, and so on. It is not my ambition to cover all the visual and verbal devices used to structure any type of printed information (for a general introduction to the linguistic and cognitive issues involved in the design and arrangement of text, see Waller, 1991). I only discuss here those devices that are used to structure "continuous" texts, with a special emphasis on the texts that serve the purpose of description, exposition, and instruction (for a discussion of continuous vs. noncontinuous texts, see the OECD Program for International Student Assessment's Web site, OECD-PISA, n.d.).

Printed continuous texts come with a variety of "organizers" that guide readers' identification of the chunks, boundaries, topics, connections, and rhetorical schemata that underlie any coherent discourse. These organizers are universally present and a necessary condition to a text's readability. This book, for instance, would be of little use without its paragraphing, headings, chapters, page numbers, and so forth. Yet, the influence on text organizers has been somewhat overlooked in text comprehension research. This is, in part, because research has focused on simple, short texts in which text organizers are perhaps less essential. The purpose of this chapter is to review and illustrate the critical role of text organizers in the comprehension of complex, naturalistic prose passages. I start with a review of rhetorical organization in expository texts, then I examine the role of text organizers in expert comprehension. Finally, I discuss individual differences and the acquisition of metatextual knowledge in inexperienced readers.

2.1. SEMANTIC STRUCTURE AND RHETORICAL ORGANIZATION IN EXPOSITORY TEXTS

In order to understand why text organizers are so important, it is necessary to bear in mind that most texts are organized according to standard rhetorical schemata. Rhetorical schemata are consistent communicative patterns that authors use to represent situations in discourse. Rhetorical schemata reflect both regularities in the situations being conveyed by language, and also communication conventions. They are partly dependent on cultural standards, but many of them appear to be rather uniform across cultures. Different text genres—for example, narratives, argumentative essays, and expository texts—involve specific rhetorical schemata (see OECD-PISA's Web site for a typology). The role of story grammars in narrative comprehension has been extensively discussed in the literature (e.g., Brewer, 1985; Graesser, Golding, & Long, 1991). Most researchers acknowledge that stories form a discourse genre that describes events organized into general knowledge structures shared by the writer and the reader. Graesser et al. (1991) suggest that narratives normally include a number of typical components, such as characters, temporal and spatial relationships, character goals and communication acts, plots, complications, and resolutions. When reading a story, experienced readers expect to find these components and actively try to organize incoming information into their standard schema for stories.

The status of rhetorical schemata and grammars in expository text comprehension is less clear. The expository genre appears to be more diverse and heterogeneous than other forms of discourse. This has to do, perhaps, with the overarching goal of expository communication, which is to provide readers with information that was *not* previously known to them. Expository discourse relies on a complex communicative equation that involves: (a) the writer's expertise or knowledge of the domain; (b) his or her ability to communicate some of this expertise through discourse; (c) the reader's prior knowledge of the domain; and (d) his or her ability to update or expand his or her prior knowledge based on text information. Thus, the notion that discourse is governed by rhetorical rules, schemata, or grammars that are familiar and shared by the writer and the reader is less obvious in the case of expository texts than it is in narrative texts.

Nevertheless, several researchers have elicited structures or sequences that seem to be typical of expository text. One of the most elaborate typologies of the rhetorics involved in expository texts was proposed by Meyer and her colleagues (Meyer, 1975, 1985; Meyer & Poon, 2001; Meyer & Rice, 1982, 1984). Early versions of the typology included relationships of collection, description, covariance, comparison, and response. More recently, Meyer and Poon (2001) proposed that collection does not represent a rhetorical structure per se, but instead may be found within the other structures. Furthermore, they added "sequence" (i.e., temporal series) as a specific rhetorical structure. This resulted in a typology with five main categories, as summarized in Table 2.1.

Other researchers have proposed similar typologies in order to account for the rhetorical relationships found in texts. Stark (1988) proposed a taxonomy of relevance relations that, she argued, are typical of

TABLE 2.1

Basic Expository Structures

Structure	*Definition*	*Example*
1. Description	Gives attributes, specifics, or setting information about a topic.	newspaper story describing who, where, when, and how
2. Sequence	Ideas organized according to chronological relations.	cooking recipes; historical narrative
3. Causation	Ideas organized according to enabling, goal-related, or causal relations.	procedural directions; explanation of natural processes or events
4. Problem/solution	Ideas presenting a problem or question followed by a solution or response.	problems linked to energy production and how to solve them
5. Comparison	Ideas organized according to comparison, contrast, alternative relationships.	parallel description of two different countries, plants, species
6. Listing (collection)	Enumerates ideas that have a common point.	physical traits of a person or object NB. May be found within other types.

Note. Adapted from Meyer & Poon (2001).

local coherence relationships in expository text. She described six possible relations that can unite two discourse statements. Contrary to Meyer's typology, she took into account the order in which information appears in the text. Stark categories are reviewed in Table 2.2.

Although partly overlapping with the typology proposed by Meyer and her colleagues, Stark's list points out three specific aspects of the rhetorical relationships in expository texts. First, her typology takes into account the order in which statements appear in a text (see, e.g., subordinate vs. superordinate). Second, she considers relationships that are typical of argument (disagreement, evaluation). Third, Stark pointed out that rhetorical relationships may connect pieces of discourse at various levels, that is, clauses, sentence, or whole passages. Based on the content analysis of three expository essays, she found that over 80% of sentence pairs within paragraphs were related by one of her six local connectedness relationships.

A third example of a typology is presented by Weaver and Kintsch (1991). They categorized the rhetorical schemata that underlie expository texts based on three main classes of relations: general–particular, object-to-object, and object–part relations. General–particular relations involved *identification* (i.e., where/when is it), *definition* (i.e., what is it in terms of semantic relations), *classification* (i.e., what is in the cate-

TABLE 2.2

Six Local Connectedness Relationships. DS1 and DS2 represent two contiguous discourse segments (e.g., sentences)

Relation	*Definition*	*Type of connection*	*Relation with Meyer and Poon*
Contrastive	DS2 disagrees with DS1	adversative, concessive, comparative, disjunctive, alternative	5. Comparison
Coordinate	DS1 and DS2 are at the same level of generality	paraphrase, expansion, enumeration or temporal ordering	2. Sequence 6. Listing
Subordinate	DS2 more concrete than DS1	elaboration, detail, example	1. Description
Superordinate	DS2 more abstract than DS1	Summary, generalization	1. Description
Causal	DS2 reason or cause for DS1	causal, enabling, motivation, cause, justification	3. Causation
Evaluative	DS2 evaluation of DS1	emphasis, reinforcement, hedge, denial	—

Note. Adapted from Stark (1988).

gory), and *illustration* (i.e., what is an instance of it). Object-to-object relations were *comparison* and *contrast* relations (i.e., X is similar to or different from Y). Object–part relations defined the rhetorical process of analysis, which includes structural analysis (i.e., which parts are included, and what are their relationships), functional analysis (i.e., how it works), and causal analysis (i.e., what causes it and what are the consequences of it). Weaver and Kintsch's (1991) typology emphasizes the different strategies or perspectives available when analyzing a complex, functional referent.

The point in these typologies is that there is more to expository text than low-level propositional relationships. Texts are organized according to global, or macrostructural, relations, and these relations are marked using specific linguistic devices (see also van Dijk, 1980). Therefore, when reading a complex text, a reader has to deal with more than propositional information extracted from the surface linguistic form of a text. He or she also has to deal with a large number of cues, signals, and linguistic devices that do not convey meaning by themselves, but that facilitate the identification of rhetorical relationships between ideas. Expert comprehension relies heavily on theses cues, especially when reading and making use of complex documents.

2.2. HOW SKILLED READERS MAKE USE OF TEXT ORGANIZERS

Theories of skilled comprehension assume that readers normally attempt to identify the rhetorical structure underlying a series of statements (van Dijk & Kintsch, 1983). Meyer and Rice (1982) assumed that skilled readers use a "structure strategy" when learning from prose. The structure strategy is defined as:

> A search for organizational plans which can subsume all or large chunks of [text] information and tie it into a summarized coherent whole. Readers employing the structure strategy are hypothesized to approach text looking for patterns that will tie all the propositions together and the author's primary thesis which will provide the content to be bound by these schemata. (p. 162)

Meyer and Rice (1982) emphasized that the structure strategy is not a default strategy but a skilled, expert comprehension strategy. Meyer, Brandt, and Bluth (1980) found that half the readers in the ninth grade employed a more basic "list strategy" that consists of accumulating information in the form of lists or packages, with no attempt to organize it into meaningful structures. The list strategy was more prevalent in students with poor reading skills.

Complex documents come with a variety of cues and adjunct information that help competent readers identify the document's top-level organization, locate important information, and establish meaningful connections between discourse segments. I use the phrase *text organizers* to designate these cues. There are many types of text organizers that can be found either *within* a text (e.g., expressions such as "for example," "consequently"), *surrounding* a text (e.g., spacing, titles, headings, introductions), or *coming along* with a text (e.g., table of contents, page numbers). In addition to their position respective to the text, organizers may be categorized according to the type of symbols that they are made of. *Visual organizers*, on the one hand, use ordering, spacing, and material organization of written documents in order to convey or to emphasize the underlying semantic organization. *Verbal organizers*, on the other hand, use language to describe or cue the structural organization of texts.

These two types of organizers play a role at various levels within complex documents. For instance, spaces between words and typography may be considered local visual organizers, whereas the physical layout of a textbook page (i.e., where documents appear on the page), may be considered a global visual organizer. Similarly, connectives (e.g., "and," "since," "but") serve local coherence functions, whereas introductions, tables of contents, and index signal the text organization at a global level.

Research on expert comprehension has found both types of organizers to facilitate or improve the comprehension and recall of expository texts. In the following sections, I review some of the studies conducted on each type of organizer.

2.2.1. Visual Organizers

Printed text comes with a variety of visual features. Among the most obvious features are the size and the quality of the printed artifact. Novels, magazines, and newspapers are printed using very different page formats and paper quality. The choice of a particular page size and paper quality are informed by considerations of usage—the expected place, time, purpose, and lifetime of the printed artifact. Closer to the textual contents are the choice of font, page layout, and the presence of graphic cues (e.g., lines, diagrams). Again, text read from newspapers, novels, or scholarly articles are visually different from each other. The "pure," rectangular shape of a page from a classic novel contrasts with the visual chaos one may experience if taking a glance at a foreign newspaper (any newspaper reader will, however, quickly identify editorial standards among the jumble of symbols, columns, lines, and typographic signs.) It is an issue of importance to find out how these visual features influence text comprehension and text usage. A full discussion of these issues would take an entire volume or more. One problem, for instance, is that not all the visual characteristics of text are relevant to comprehension (for an extended discussion see Waller, 1991). I concentrate here on a restricted range of visual features whose relevance for text comprehension has been clearly established by psychological research.

The order of information in expository texts has a great influence on readers' comprehension processes. *Initial mentions* determine what readers consider main ideas or themes of the text. In a classical experiment, Kieras (1980) manipulated initial mentions (experiment 1) and paragraph order (experiment 2) of short texts excerpted from a scientific magazine. In experiment 1, 40 students read 16 one-paragraph texts with a thematic sentence either presented first or embedded in the paragraph. They were asked to type in or to write a main idea sentence after each passage. The participants' answers were scored for their similarity to the theme sentence or to the alternate sentence. Answers were rated as more similar to the theme sentence when the theme sentence was paragraph-initial than when it was not. In the embedded condition, however, participant-generated main idea statements were still closer to the original theme sentence than to the alternate first sentence.

In experiment 2, Kieras constructed two-topic texts such as the one presented in Table 2.3.The topics were chosen so that one could appear as an elaboration or an example of the other (thus complying with a rhetorical schemata typical of expository text). For instance, in passage (a) of Table 2.3, biochrystals may appear as an elaboration of the sea urchin skeleton description, whereas in passage (b) sea urchins may appear as an example of an animal with a biochrystal skeleton. Kieras manipulated the order of presentation of the topics, and found that students tended to consider the topic dealt with in the first part of the passage as the main topic. Kieras (1980) interpreted his findings as a consequence of readers' attempts to form a macrostructure of the passage, that is, a hierarchical representation of content information. Thus, using early information to initiate the hierarchy in a top-down fashion appears to be the reader's default comprehension strategy. The seman-

TABLE 2.3

Two Sections of a Two-Topic Text Used by Kieras (1980)

a. The sea urchin section of the passage	*b. The biocrystals section of the passage*
The development of the sea urchin begins when millions of microscopic eggs are ejected into the sea through pores in the spiny shell of the adult. The tiny embryonic sea urchin, which swims about freely and feeds on plankton, is so transparent that its internal structure is clearly visible. The skeleton of the sea urchin develops from two spicules which are made of biocrystals that eventually fuse to form a spherical shell.	Structures such as bone, tooth, and shell are made up of biocrystals which are two-dimensional arrays of calcium, silicon and phosphate and carbonate. These biocrystals are chemically undistinguishable from crystals found in the inanimate world.

Note. Adapted from Kieras (1980).

tic content of the passage remains nevertheless the main determinant of macrostructure formation, as illustrated by the fact that readers still consider a theme sentence as the main idea even if it is buried in the middle of the passage.

It is not the case, however, that "anything goes" with respect to ordering information within expository texts. Kintsch and Yarbrough (1982) reasoned that some arrangements of information form more coherent macrostructures than others. For instance, in a text describing the evolution of locomotion from apes to human, the chronological sequence appears to be the best "rhetorical shape." Kintsch and Yarbrough found that students' ability to answer conceptual questions was affected by reading the text in a scrambled order, even though the researchers attempted to minimize the impact of scrambled paragraphs on local coherence relationships. They concluded that the surface rhetorical structure plays a part in readers' construction of a macrostructure. Elshout-Mohr and van Daalen-Kapteijns (2001), using verbal protocols, also found that adult readers rely on typical rhetorical schemata when trying to make sense of a textbook passage about an unfamiliar topic. The best result, in terms of content comprehension, is obtained when the surface structure (e.g., the order of paragraphs) matches the organizing scheme in the semantic macrostructure (e.g., temporal ordering).

Another obvious visual organizer present in any text is paragraph marking. Paragraph marks are used in virtually any text genre and any language. Stark (1988) examined the functions of paragraphs in written discourse. She considered the issues of informativeness and effectiveness of paragraphs marks. As regards *informativeness*, the issue was to find out if paragraph cues convey information at all. On one end, they could be uninformative, simply repeating visually information that is already conveyed semantically. On the other end, they could be totally informative, conveying specific information that is independent from the text's content. An intermediate position considers that paragraphs reflect multiple writing conventions, that is, that a paragraph mark signals one among the many types of connections or disconnections that exist between sentences in a passage of text.

Stark (1988) also discussed paragraph *effectiveness*, that is, whether paragraphs actually affect the reader's comprehension. First, paragraphs may facilitate comprehension in a nonsemantic way, regardless of the content of the text or the position of the paragraph mark. For instance, they may guide eye movements in the text, and encourage the reader to pause and integrate information into global chunks. But paragraph marks can also facilitate comprehension by signaling semantic boundaries within a text. They may facilitate the structuring of information into main ideas, or, conversely, they may help the reader *not* integrate sentences that convey ideas about distinct topics or discourse parts. Finally, Stark considered the possibility that paragraphs may affect the meaning of the text. For instance, paragraph marks would modify the hierarchy of ideas constructed by the reader.

Stark conducted two experiments using three published expository essays of 487, 1253, and 1578 words. She defined expository essays as texts that "mention and bring together disparate aspects of the world, forming an argument" (p. 281). She pointed out that in expository essays, paragraphing is not strongly constrained by the structure of the discourse objects (unlike, e.g., in conventional description or in narration).

In experiment 1, 21 undergraduates read the texts presented without any paragraph mark. They were asked to place a slash between sentences that they felt would divide paragraphs. There was significant though incomplete agreement among the participants as to the placing of paragraph marks. Furthermore, the participants agreed to some extent, but not completely, with the author's actual paragraphing (Fig. 2.1).

On measures of agreement and accuracy, there was a significant variation across texts; some texts generated a higher agreement and accuracy than others. When asked to justify the placement of a paragraph mark, the students uniformly mentioned topic changes, or the introduction of a new topic, but they did not elaborate further on what constitutes a topic. Stark pointed out that subjects' choices were not predictable by simple parameters such as the number of sentences per paragraph or changes in sentences' surface subjects. The presence of a theme-marking device was significantly associated with paragraph markings. Thematic structure, expressed by both local coherence relations and global thematic relevance, also explained in part the place-

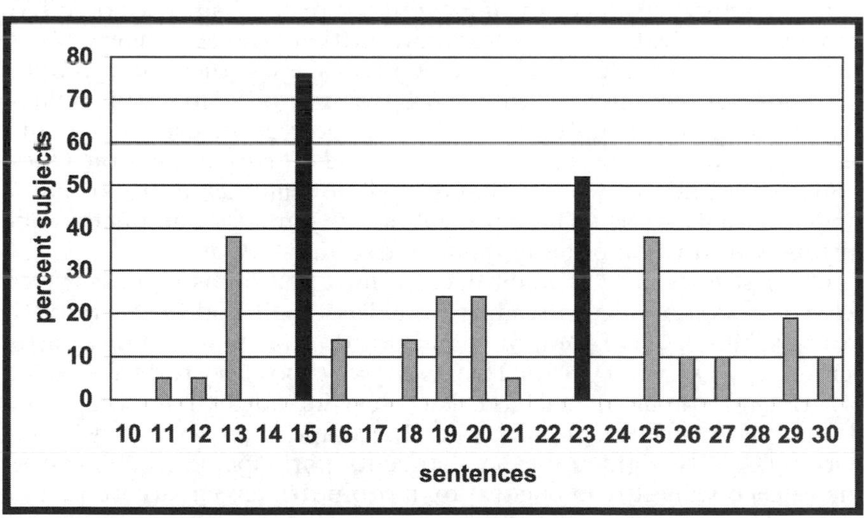

FIG. 2.1. Frequency of participants-generated paragraph marking for each sentence in a passage presented with no paragraph marks. Black bars indicate sentences that were paragraph-initial in the author's original text (based on the data for the Orwell text presented in Stark, 1988).

ment of paragraph marks. Finally, surface marks like overreference (e.g., using a full noun as opposed to a pronoun to identify a referent already mentioned in the text) coincided with paragraph marks. Stark concluded that paragraph marks cannot be entirely predicted by the text's literal content, and that they may be used to emphasize various types of discourse meanings and functions.

In the second experiment of her study, Stark (1988) attempted to capture the effects of different paragraphing strategies on readers' comprehension of the same three texts. The texts were presented either with their original paragraphing, with a random paragraphing that respected the original average length of paragraphs, or with no paragraphing. Twenty-one undergraduate students read the three texts, one in each version, measured their total reading time, and rated the texts for coherence, ease of reading, and goodness. Finally, they underlined the most important ideas in the text. Surprisingly, paragraph manipulations had no detectable effect on reading time or any of the ratings. They did, however, affect the underlining of important information. Paragraph-initial sentences were underlined more often than noninitial sentences, but only in the original paragraphing. In other words, merely adding a paragraph mark did not make any sentence appear more important in the readers' minds.

Two methodological aspects of Stark's experiments should be noted. First, Stark only performed a global reading time measure. It could well be that paragraphing affected differentially the reading time of initial, final, and other sentences. Second, Stark did not include an actual measure of comprehension or memory for text. Instead, she used perceived coherence and text quality as estimates. Other studies, however, have found that even adult readers cannot always assess their own comprehension level accurately (Glenberg & Epstein, 1985). Finally, it could be that some undergraduate students did not perceive or use the semantic signals contained in paragraphs as they read for comprehension. Questionnaire studies have found that a small but significant proportion of undergraduate students do not mention the semantic conjunction and disjunction function of paragraphs (see section 2.3 later).

Other studies have brought detailed information as regards the effects of paragraphing on reading time. Passerault and Chesnet (1991) examined the effect of paragraph marking on students' reading time for sentences in expository texts. They used two expository texts, one about camels and one about bacteria. Each text included three paragraphs dealing with various subtopics (e.g., the shape, location, and action of bacteria). Forty-eight university students participated in the experiment. Each subject read one text on a computer screen, according to a segmented presentation. The text was presented either in one block or in three paragraphs. Passerault and Chesnet hypothesized that paragraph marking could serve several functions in reading. First, the reader might delay integration of information across segments until he or she reaches the end of the paragraph. This would result in shorter reading times for nonfinal segments in a paragraph, compared to a control condition with no paragraph marking. Second, the reader might slow down on the final sentence of the paragraph (i.e., sentence position N-1 in Fig. 2.2) in order to integrate the ideas just read in the paragraph. Third, paragraphing might speed up the processing of segments immediately following the paragraph mark, as the reader no longer has to integrate information from the preceding text segments.

Passerault and Chesnet actually found limited evidence for each of the three predictions. The most notable finding was an increase in reading time of the final segment of the paragraphs, which was significant in three out of four instances of paragraphing included in the materials (see Fig. 2.2). Delayed integration and compensation effects were also found, but they were neither consistent across texts nor across paragraphs within texts. The results nevertheless supported a function of paragraphs as integration markers. An additional finding reported by Passerault and Chesnet was that the participants tended to reproduce the paragraph marking in their summaries of the texts. This latter finding may be interpreted in two ways: paragraph marking may influence the organization of the semantic representation of the passage in long-term memory, or people may retain a surface, maybe visual representation of the paragraphs that they retrieve when composing the summary. As pointed out by Goldman, Saul, and Coté (1995), however, Passerault and Chesnet's (1991) findings must be interpreted with caution, considering the peculiar presentation mode of the materials used in

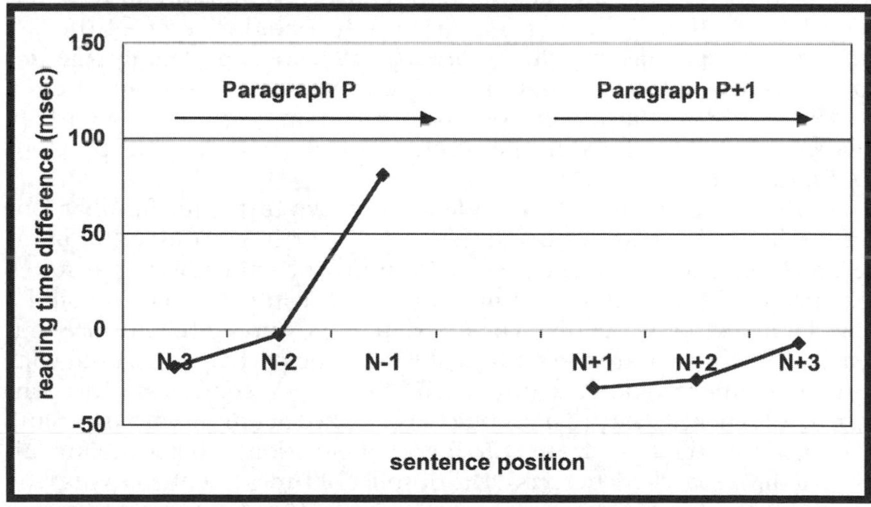

FIG. 2.2. Average reading time difference for sentences in a text as a function of serial order and paragraph marking. The zero value represents reading time in the no-paragraph condition (based on the data presented in Passerault & Chesnet, 1991).

their experiment. Furthermore, the lack of effect of paragraphing on paragraph-initial sentences may also be related to the particular semantic content of these sentences.

The effects of paragraphing may vary according to readers' prior knowledge of the topic. Goldman, Saul and Coté (1995) examined the effects of paragraph marks in interaction with reader and task characteristics. They pointed out that, in expository English, the topic of a paragraph is usually the first sentence. Thus, initial information sets up readers' expectations about the main points in a text. They suggested that main point identification follows a two-step process. In the first step, candidate main ideas are examined based on surface cues, for example, headings or paragraphing. In the second step, the reader processes the text content at a deeper semantic level and attempts to integrate information based on semantic connections. The latter phase is facilitated if the reader has prior content area knowledge because he or she can use prior knowledge as an integration scheme. Consequently, the effect of surface cues on the identification of main ideas should be weaker for familiar than for unfamiliar texts.

Goldman et al. tested these predictions in two experiments. They used four experimental passages, 250 to 345 words long, on topics of "distance," "nationalism," "cultural systems," and "multinational corporations." A pilot norming study established that the first two topics were more familiar to undergraduate psychology students. Each text was divided in six paragraphs. The first two paragraphs were introductory, while the remaining four each presented one subtopic (e.g., factors that contribute to the development of nationalism). Paragraphing was manipulated so that in the normal paragraph condition, each of the last four paragraphs began with a *thematic sentence* (e.g., "Language has been a factor influencing national consciousness in many countries."). In the conflicting paragraph condition, each paragraph started with an *elaboration sentence* from the subtopic dealt with in the previous paragraph (see Table 2.4).

In the first experiment, 32 students read two texts (one familiar, one unfamiliar) either in a "normal paragraph" or in a "conflicting paragraph" condition, with the assigned purpose of remembering as much as they could. Passages were presented on a computer screen using a special masking procedure. The entire text was presented at once, but each sentence appeared in a masked form. The participants could click on any sentence in order to unmask its content. As soon as another sentence was clicked, the previous one was masked again (Goldman & Saul, 1990; see also chapter 4, Fig. 4.5, for an illustration). This procedure allowed the researchers to record the number of times a sentence was read and the total reading time per sentence, without adding too much constraint on readers' behavior.

Online data showed that elaboration sentences were accessed more often when they were paragraph-initial, that is, in the conflicting paragraph condition. Moreover, the processing time of both thematic and

TABLE 2.4

Example of a Normal and a Conflicting Paragraph in the Study by Goldman, Saul, and Coté (1995)

Normal paragraph	*Conflicting paragraph*
(...)	
In nations where the rulers and the ruled have been of different faiths, religion has played an important role. This was especially clear in the case of Christians under Turkish rule in eastern Europe, and Muslims under British rule in northwest Africa. As these people began to express objection to foreign rule, religion was the essence of their feeling of being different.	(...) *In nations where the rulers and the ruled have been of different faiths, religion has played an important role.* This was especially clear in the case of Christians under Turkish rule in eastern Europe, and Muslims under British rule in northwest Africa.
Language has been a factor influencing national consciousness in many countries. The people who used to be called "Balkans" broke up into Greeks, Serbs, Romanians, and Bulgarians according to their languages. (...)	As these people began to express objection to foreign rule, religion was the essence of their feeling of being different. *Language has been a factor influencing national consciousness in many countries.* The people who used to be called "Balkans" broke up into Greeks, Serbs, Romanians, and Bulgarians according to their languages. (...)

elaboration sentences increased in the conflicting paragraph condition, but only for the less familiar texts. Finally, main point sentences were recalled more often than elaboration sentences, regardless of the paragraphing condition. Thus, placing elaboration sentences in paragraph-initial position did not increase their recall probability. Paragraphing, however, interacted with passage familiarity: In the normal paragraph condition, more-familiar passages were better recalled than less-familiar ones. In the conflicting paragraph condition, there was no difference between the two types of passages. The researchers interpreted the latter result as a consequence of the increased processing time of less-familiar passage sentences in the conflicting paragraph condition. In other words, reading an unfamiliar passage with a weird paragraph structure would force readers to "work harder" in order to learn the contents. This corroborates other studies' findings that slight decreases in text coherence may sometimes improve readers' comprehension and recall (e.g., Mannes & Kintsch, 1987; McNamara et al., 1996).

In experiment 2, 32 students read the same texts in the same conditions, but with the purpose of writing a summary. Again, conflicting paragraph organization led to an increase in sentence access, especially for the less familiar texts. But the conflicting organization did not significantly affect inclusion of main ideas in the summaries.

Several interesting conclusions emerge from Goldman et al.'s (1995) study. First, paragraph information is not processed independently from the semantic content of the passage. A conflicting paragraph organization seems to make it more difficult for the reader to sort out main ideas from elaborations, as evidenced in more frequent access (i.e., rereading) and longer processing time. It seems, however, that readers rely more on the semantic structure of the passage when integrating information into a global representation. Paragraph structure seems to have little influence on recall or summary measures, except that conflicting paragraphing boosted recall of less familiar materials, reflecting readers' effort to capture the actual thematic organization of the less-familiar texts.

Second, Goldman et al.'s (1995) study supports a two-phase process of main idea identification. In the first phase, readers identify "candidates" to main idea status, based on surface cues in the text. In the second phase, a hierarchical structure is actually constructed based on the semantic information extracted from the text or activated from long-term memory. The latter process may compensate, in part, for misinterpretations based on poor surface organization. Goldman and Saul's (1990) strategy competition model interprets main idea construction as an incremental process in which the reader gradually accumulates evidence for the thematic organization of the passage.

In conclusion, the order of information and visual breaks between paragraphs facilitate the identification of the text's main ideas as long as they are consistent with the text's rhetorical structure. Even though the use of visual signals does not correspond to formal rules, both writers and experienced readers seem to implicitly agree on the meanings conveyed by such signals. When consistent with the rhetorical organization of ideas in the text, appropriate visual organizers have a positive impact on text comprehension and memory.

2.2.2. Verbal Organizers

Most expository texts, especially lengthy and complex ones, use a variety of verbal organizers in order to represent and emphasize content organization. Verbal organizers generally convey two aspects of a text's content: its thematic structure (i.e., the main ideas conveyed by the text), and the semantic relations between ideas. Verbal organizers may help the reader integrate the upcoming information through the activation of relevant conceptual knowledge (Gaddy, van den Broek, & Sung, 2001) and the identification of the thematic structure of a text, facilitating the interconnection of information units (Lorch & Lorch, 1996).

Effects of Verbal Organizers on Text Comprehension and Recall. Numerous studies have found facilitative effects of verbal organizers on text comprehension (for reviews see, e.g., Mayer, 1984; Lorch, 1989).

Early demonstrations were performed by Bransford and Johnson (1972), using texts that were deliberately made ambiguous and difficult to understand. In such extreme cases, the presence of headings and other contextual aids was a prerequisite for readers' retention of textual information. Kozminsky (1977) also examined the influence of thematic titles on students' memory for texts. The participants had to read and to recall three texts presented either with a main thematic title, a secondary thematic title, or a mixed (main and secondary) thematic title. The recall of semantic propositions was higher with main thematic titles than secondary thematic titles. Kozminsky's interpretation was based on Kintsch's (1974) propositional analysis framework. During reading, macroprocesses extract the thematic information from the title and use it to organize the upcoming set of propositions. If a proposition extracted from a text does not correspond to the thematic title, the construction of the textbase is hindered.

More recent studies have replicated and extended these initial findings. A study by Loman and Mayer (1983) showed that signaling improved deep comprehension of an expository text. Studies by Lorch and his colleagues also provided ample evidence that verbal signals improve readers' comprehension and recall of the topic structure of a text. Lorch, Lorch, and Inman (1993) examined the effect of signaling topic structure on students' recall of an expository text. They hypothesized that expert readers identify the topic structure as they go through the text. Afterwards, the memory representation of the topic structure can be used as a cue to retrieve contents. Verbal signals can emphasize the topic structure without altering content. Lorch et al. discussed the conditions needed for such signals to be effective. First, readers must actually employ the structure strategy so that topic structure is effective at the time of retrieval. Second, the text must be fairly complex in order for the topic structure not to be evident in the absence of signals. Finally, signals may affect the recall of some but not all the information in a text. For instance, they may facilitate the retrieval of top-level ideas, but not the recall of subordinate information.

Lorch et al. conducted two experiments in order to check these assumptions. In the first experiment, 203 undergraduate psychology students read a text based on published scientific magazine articles on energy problems and solutions. The researchers manipulated the topic structure, signaling, and length of the texts. The version with a complex structure discussed 24 topics organized into three hierarchical levels. The simple structure version discussed 12 topics organized into two hierarchical levels. Each topic was discussed in more detail in the simple than in the complex version, in order to equate the two versions for length. Signaling was manipulated by adding four types of signals to the unsignaled versions: blank line between topics, overviews at the beginning of each major section, summaries, and headings that signaled each major section and subsection (Table 2.5). Finally, length was manipulated by adding or removing detail information. The short,

TABLE 2.5
Example of Text Organizers (Left) Added to the Unsignaled Text (Right) in the Study by Lorch, Lorch, and Inman (1993)

Text organizers	*Text contents (unsignaled)*
ENERGY PROBLEMS AND SOLUTIONS	ENERGY
	We are faced with severe problems created by our dependence on oil, coal, natural gas and nuclear power.
In this article we will discuss some of the major problems associated with our current methods of energy production, then we will discuss several strategies for solving these problems.	
I. Energy problems	
In the first half of this article, we will discuss some of the problems created by our current patterns of energy use, including: (1) the dwindling resources of fossil and nuclear fuels; (2) the environmental damage associated with fossil and nuclear fuels; and (3) health problems associated with fossil and nuclear fuels. We will discuss each of these major topics in turn.	
A. Dwindling fuel resources	
1. Hazardous production methods	
	Coal, oil and gas are not as accessible as they once were. The most accessible veins of coal have long since been exhausted and miners must dig ever deeper into the ground to recover coal reserves. The deeper and more extensive tunneling operations mean greater danger for the miners.(...)

unsignaled version was 2,400 words long, whereas the long, signaled version was 3,600 words long. The participants were instructed to read the text carefully. Immediately after, they were asked to recall as many of the topics as they could.

Participants recalled more topics in the signaled than in the unsignaled condition. They also recalled a larger proportion of the topics in the simple compared to the complex topic structure condition. The signaling effect was larger for the short and simple version. In this condition, the percentage of topics recalled varied from 47,7% in the unsignaled to

80,1% in the signaled condition. Finally, signaling increased the correlation between the order of topics in the text and in the students' essays.

Lorch, Lorch, and Inman's (1993) experiment 2 replicated those findings using a free recall task. The free recall task allowed the researchers to find out if signaling improved conditional recall, that is, the amount of information retrieved for each topic recalled. Experiment 2 also examined whether the signaling effect depends on the amount of elaboration of the topic. Eighty-two psychology undergraduates read a 2,000-word text discussing 12 topics about energy problems and solutions. Two versions were designed. In one version, six topics were discussed in a short section (4–17 propositions), while the six others were presented in more detail (17–33 propositions). In the other version, the status of the topics was reversed so as to control for content. In addition, the texts were either signaled or unsignaled as in experiment 1.

The participants read the text at their own pace and then recalled it as completely as possible. A topic was considered recalled if it was explicitly mentioned, or if at least a piece of subordinate information was correctly recalled. In the no-signal condition, recall was better for long than for short topics. Signaling increased the recall of short topics and did not affect the recall probability of long topics. As a result, recall of the signaled text was not sensitive to the length manipulation. Recall was also more consistent with the text organization in the signaled than in the unsignaled condition. Conditional recall, however, was poorer in the signaled than in the unsignaled condition.

According to Lorch, Lorch, and Inman (1993), the results support the view that signals help readers identify the top-level structure in a text. Subsequently, readers are able to use the top-level representation as a cue to recall the text's topics. This was especially clear for texts that only briefly discussed each signaled topic. For longer topic sections, the effect of signaling was not significant. Three features of their study need to be pointed out. First, the manipulation of signaling involved four different types of signals, making it difficult to know exactly what creates the observed effects of "signaling." Second, the effect of signals may take place at encoding or at retrieval. Signals may help readers encode more information, but they may also help readers retrieve more information from long-term memory at the time of writing a recall. Thus, it is not clear whether readers of signaled versus unsignaled versions encode the same amount of information from the text. Third, immediate recall of a text only partially reflects the reader's deep comprehension of a text. Immediate recall may rely on a type of literal, quasivisual memory for text, instead of a deep semantic representation. Thus, it remains to be found whether signals actually promote deeper processing of the text, as opposed to, for example, making visually salient the sections and subsections.

Other studies tried to unravel the respective effects of various types of signals. Spyridakis and Standal (1987) attempted to isolate the individual effect of headings, previews, and logical connectives, as well as their combined influence. Four expository texts dealing with technical materials were used in their study. Passage length varied from 362 words for the shortest text in the unsignaled condition, to 766 words for the longest passage in the signaled condition. The texts comprised between six and eight paragraphs. The texts always included a title, even in the unsignaled condition. Three types of signals were added to the nonsignaled version:

- *Headings* were inserted in order to signal the overall thematic structure. An example of heading for the text entitled "Nitrates" was "The risks." Three to four headings were inserted, depending on the text.
- *Previews* were expressions or sentence expansions that connected main ideas to subordinate ideas, and subordinate ideas among them. Previews were inserted at various places within paragraphs. An example of a preview is the sentence "Two questions are still unanswered," to introduce the risks associated with nitrates.
- *Logical connectives* were used to link various pieces of information within each paragraph. Examples are "for example," "therefore," "also," "additionally."

A total of eight versions were constructed for each text, resulting from the presence or absence of headings, previews, and logical connectives. The results were based on the analysis of 371 participants, all enrolled in preengineering courses. Each student read one passage in one of the eight versions. The participants were instructed to read the passages at their own rate. Immediately after reading the passage, participants answered a multiple choice questionnaire that included five questions about detail information and five questions about main ideas, either explicit or inferential.

The pattern of results showed a general trend toward beneficial effects of signals, but the pattern varied from one passage to another. Headings significantly improved comprehension only in the biomedical research text (See Fig. 2.3). Previews had a significant main effect on the "algae" and "biomedical research" text, whereas logical connectives were significant only in the "algae" text. A content analysis suggested that signals were most efficient for less familiar and less readable passages (i.e., passages on algae and on biomedical research).

The inconsistency of effects may be due to a lack of power, as each version of each text was read by only eight students. Interestingly, however, Spyridakis and Standal (1987) did not address the issue of signal quality. The effects of a heading, for instance, may depend on whether it uses familiar or unfamiliar words. On some occasions, the wording of headings in the Spyridakis and Standal experiment used technical terms. For instance, the passage entitled "Algae control in raw water supplies" included the following headings: "algaecide uses," "algaecide

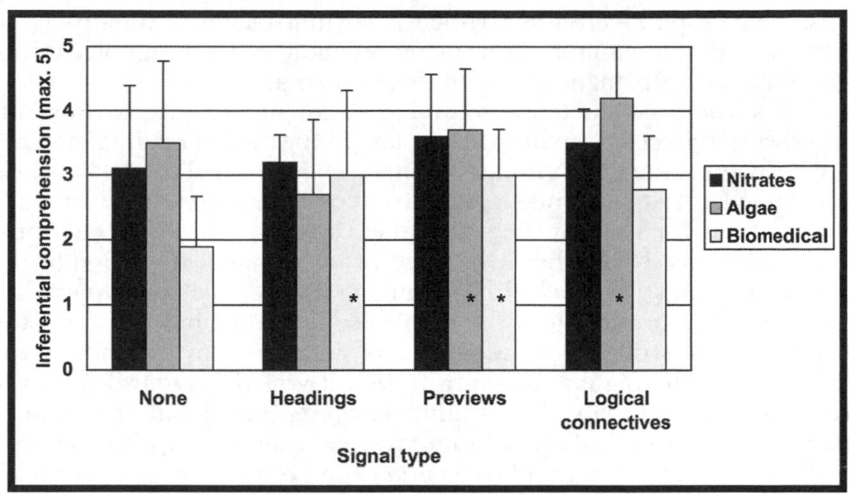

FIG. 2.3. Effects of three types of signals on the comprehension of three expository texts (based on the data presented in the study by Spyridakis and Standal (1987).

dosage," "species susceptibility," and "other factors affecting algaecides." Three of these four headings include the word "algaecide," which may be little familiar or even unknown to first-year students. Another uncontrolled factor is the propositional level of the information that was in the heading. The effect may depend on the quality of the match between the content of a heading and the propositional structure of the text (Kozminsky, 1977).

The issue of whether signals influence encoding or retrieval processes was addressed in a study by Lorch, Lorch, Ritchey, McGovern, and Coleman (2001). The study attempted to provide direct evidence that signaling the topic structure actually helps readers encode the topic structure of a text. They used a summarization task in order to elicit main idea selection and to minimize the impact of memory retrieval processes. In experiment 1, 73 undergraduate psychology students read a text about energy usage. The text addressed 10 topics about energy problems, followed by 10 topics about solutions. Three signaling conditions were designed. In the no-signal condition the paragraphs were just presented one after the other. In the full-signal condition, all 20 topics were signaled with headings; in the half-signal condition, every other topic was signaled. Two versions were created so as to control for which content was signaled.

Signals had a main effect on the total number of topics included in the summaries. Topic recall was better in the full-signal condition (66% included) than in the half (49%) and in the no-signal condition (42%). One key finding was that in the half-signal condition, signaled topics were more frequently included than in the full-signal condition, whereas unsignaled topics were less frequently included than in the no-signal condition. Partial signaling thus increased the salience of signaled information to the detriment of unsignaled information.

The authors conducted a second experiment in order to find out whether the effect of signaling takes place at the time of reading or at the time of composing the summary. They provided each of the 104 participating undergraduate students with two copies of the text: one for reading, and one for writing the summary. Depending on the conditions, participants received either a signaled or an unsignaled version at the time of reading. Then, within each group, half of the participants received either an unsignaled or a signaled copy at the time of writing the summary. The students included more topics if the copy available at the time of *summarizing* was signaled than if it was not, regardless of the version received initially. This finding suggests that signaling information is especially critical at the time of retrieving and using information.

The third experiment replicated and extended the previous two with 6th and 8th grade and college students. Two texts were used, one on dinosaurs and one on energy. The texts were either unsignaled, half signaled, or fully signaled. Signaling increased the inclusion of topics in students' summaries at the three grade levels. Older students, however, included more topics in their summaries than younger students did. Again, signaling increased the inclusion of topics signaled within a text. Unsignaled topics in the half-signal conditions were less frequently included than in the no-signal condition.

The general conclusion that emerges from this study is that signaling the topic structure of the text encourages readers at all levels of proficiency to shift to a structure identification strategy when reading and memorizing text.

Online Effects of Verbal Organizers. It has been demonstrated that titles can decrease the amount of time needed to read and understand a text (Lorch, Lorch, Gretter, & Horn, 1987; Smith & Swinney, 1992). The increase in reading time for difficult or untitled passages may be due to (a) more regressive eye fixations, (b) longer pauses at sentence boundaries, or (c) longer fixations on content words. Wiley and Rayner (2000) attempted to find out which of these processing components are affected by the presence of titles. In the first experiment, 32 students read four difficult passages adapted from previous studies. Each participant read two passages with a title and two passages without a title. Eye movements were recorded, and the participants were asked to free recall the last passage. The participants made more regressions and longer "wrap up" pauses at the end of sentences when reading texts with no titles. In addition, the presence of titles decreased gaze duration on individual content words (in contrast, the presence of titles did not have any effect on gaze duration of functional words, e.g., "sometimes"). Finally, recall was higher when the text was presented with a title than when it was not.

In two subsequent experiments, Wiley and Rayner found that facilitation at the individual word level reflected faster lexical access, rather than integration processes. In experiment 2, gaze duration on a sample of ambiguous words was shorter when preceded by a title. Thus, the title provided a strong contextual cue that helped select the appropriate meaning of words. For instance, a title mentioning the word "baseball" helped readers select the appropriate meaning of the word "pitcher." Titles had no effect, however, when a subordinate, infrequent meaning of an ambiguous word was to be selected. In experiment 3, there was no difference in gaze duration between ambiguous and control words when a title was present, except for low frequency meanings of ambiguous words, which took longer to identify. Wiley and Rayner's (2000) findings suggest that titles facilitate comprehension from the microstructural level of word identification, at least for texts that are difficult and ambiguous. Hyönä and Lorch (2004) found that headings inserted in expository texts specifically decreased reading time of topic sentences, suggesting that headings also facilitate the identification of a text top level's structure (i.e., at the level of macrostructure building). Thus, headings may both facilitate lower and higher order processes in comprehension.

Other linguistic devices used in expository texts, like introductions and conclusions, also facilitate content processing and memorization. Murray and McGlone (1997) found that an introductory paragraph that mentioned the topics dealt with in a multiparagraph text facilitated the processing of topic statements at the beginning of each subsequent paragraph. The introduction also improved memory for topics. The researchers suggested that prior exposure to topics created a background in memory that "resonated" as content information is processed, thus promoting the construction of an integrated representation (Myers & O'Brien, 1998; see also Chapter 1).

Recent research studies have attempted to provide fine grain interpretations of the effect of signals on text comprehension. Gaddy et al. (2001) discussed the effects of three types of textual cues in light of their "Landscape Model" of comprehension (see chapter 1, section 1.2.3). They introduced three categories of textual cues:

- Linguistic cues, for example, function indicators ("it is important to note that ..."), or pronouns (placed either after or before the referents),
- Typographic cues, such as boldface or underlining,
- Text-structure cues, such as titles and headings.

Gaddy et al. simulated the patterns of memory activations that result from the inclusion of signals in text. They argued that signals help the reader focus his or her attention on particular aspects of the text, creating a salience effect for some concepts. Thus, the centrality of these target concepts is reinforced by the presence of signals. The increased saliency of concepts prompted by textual cues affects the organization of the whole representation of the text, through "passive" propagation mechanisms as well as more active, strategic focalization mechanisms (see also van den Broek, Virtue, Everson, Tzeng, & Sung, 2002).

2.2.3. Organization Devices in Complex Documents

The studies reviewed here have been concerned mostly with the organization of rather short expository texts, that is, texts that include a few paragraphs or a few pages at most. Complex documents like manuals, textbooks, and Web sites come with higher level organizers. For instance, textbook chapters may come with outlines and tables of contents that signal the global rhetorical structure of the chapter. What are the effects of these complex organizers on text comprehension?

Mannes (1994) investigated the integration of information across an outline and a main text. She suggested that when reading expository texts, readers normally use a reinstatement-and-integration strategy, which consists in reactivating prior knowledge on encountering new information based on previously learned concepts. Mannes used a 2,131-word text on the use of bacteria in industry adapted from a published text. In addition, she wrote two outlines. One was compatible with the main text's expository structure; the other one emphasized a different expository structure, the classification of bacteria. The same and different outlines were 1,188 and 1,205 words long, respectively. Forty-five psychology undergraduates participated in the first experiment. In the learning phase, 15 participants read the "same" outline, 15 read the "different" outline, and 15 read no outline. The participants then wrote a summary with the outline still available, and a second summary without the outline or their first summary. Then all the participants read the main text presented on a computer, in blocks of 3–4 lines, during a fixed presentation time of 250ms per word. The procedure was chosen so as to control exposure time while allowing a rather "unconstrained" reading condition. After reading, the participants performed several tasks including a network drawing task. The task consisted in filling in each of five circles with "the most important things they had learned." The participants were asked to draw lines between those circles they felt were related and to indicate the strength of the relation between 0 and 2.

Networks were content-analyzed for the source of the concepts included. A distinction was made between concepts originally presented in the text (text concepts) and concepts originally presented in the outline but not in the text ("nontext" concepts). The participants in the different-outline condition included more nontext concepts in their network, and drew more links between text and nontext concepts. They also produced more elaborations (information from a different part of the materials) in response to text cues. Finally, only the participants in the different-outline condition included intrusions (i.e., information from the outline not present in the text) in their summaries of the text. The results suggested that participants in the different-outline condition had used a reinstatement-and-integration strategy in order to bring together new information from the text with previously acquired information from the outline.

In the second experiment, Mannes used an online task in order to demonstrate that the effect of different outlines took place during the encoding of the main text, through the reinstatement-and-integration strategy, rather than at the time of recall. The participants were 20 undergraduate psychology students. They read either the same or the different outlines, and the main text. Then they were asked to judge the relatedness of 190 pairs of statements reflecting either the same or different perspectives on a six-point scale. The students in the different-outline conditions found different pairs more related than students in the same-outline condition. They also responded significantly faster overall, and especially for the different pairs. This was interpreted as reflecting their more integrated situation model, that is, a representation that included more connections between ideas originally presented in different perspectives. In the author's view, these results indicated that when reading challenging expository texts, students engage in a goal-directed comprehension strategy that leads them to generate high-level integrating inferences that they may not generate when reading simpler texts, or reading in less challenging contexts (see also Murray & McGlone, 1997).

Interestingly, the quality of an introduction also affects expert evaluation of text quality, as evidenced in a study by Townsend, Hicks, Thompson, Wilton, Tuck, et al. (1993). One hundred and fifty-four undergraduates wrote an essay on genetic and environmental influences on IQ. Then a group of 10 judges were presented with essays that included good or poor introductions and conclusions. The quality of the introduction had an important effect on the overall evaluation of the essay, whereas the quality of the conclusion had a smaller influence. Townsend et al. proposed an interpretation in terms of communication acts: When reading an argument, the reader has to understand the meaning of the text but also the intentions of the author. Introductory statements are important for three reasons: First, they communicate the overall organization of the text; second, they allow the reader to activate relevant previous knowledge; and third, they indicate a possible interpretation frame.

Do readers possess global schemata for more complex texts such as book chapters, literary essays, or scientific articles? This issue has been far less studied so far. Dillon (1991) investigated the case of academic articles in the area of ergonomics. He hypothesized that experienced article readers may possess an introduction–methods–results–discussion schema. In the first experiment, Dillon asked 12 human factors specialists to sort a series of paragraphs extracted from two published journal articles. The articles were new to all the participants. One of the articles was presented with the original headings and subheadings, the other was not. The participants were able to replace paragraphs within their original section even in the absence of headings. Paragraph order within sections, however, seemed more difficult to retrieve. Most confusions occurred between the introduction and discussion paragraphs (40% of errors), or between the results and the discussion sections (30%). The discussion section seems the least specific, which makes much sense considering that it often serves as a summary of the article, among other things. The second experiment replicated the same results, with eight participants working either with printed or computerized paragraphs. Experienced scholars thus seem to possess a high-level organizing framework that allows them to categorize passages from scientific articles that they have not read before. Because no control group was included in the study, however, it is hard to decide how much of this knowledge is gained through experience in a particular discipline, as opposed to general experience in academic work.

Another issue open for investigation is the knowledge and use of high-level content description devices, like indexes and tables of contents. A study by Rouet, Vidal-Abarca, Bert-Erboul, and Millogo (2001, experiment 2) suggests that a table of contents may help readers appreciate the top-level structure and the complexity of a lengthy expository text. Undergraduate students were more willing to revise text sections after their initial reading if the text included a table of contents than if the text merely contained embedded headings. And efficient information searchers spend more time studying a table of contents or an index, as opposed to searching content pages (Dreher & Guthrie, 1990; see chapter 4). Thus, it seems that the benefit of text organizers depends on the amount of knowledge readers possess about these devices. Consequently, it is important to examine when and how such knowledge is acquired throughout secondary, higher education and/or occupational training.

2.3. LEARNING ABOUT TEXT ORGANIZERS

Most educators and parents are aware that reading texts for comprehension is often a problem for children as they begin secondary education. And many researchers have pointed out that college students vary a great deal in their awareness and actual use of comprehension strategies (Lonka et al., 1994; Nist & Simpson, 2000). Some, but not all, of students' difficulties can be related to their insufficient mastery of basic processing skills, for example, decoding. Other problems, however, seem to have more to do with students' lack of explicit knowledge of the role of text organizers. In this section I review evidence for individual differences in the knowledge and use of textual organizers. I also examine the issue of when and how students acquire knowledge about text organizers.

2.3.1 Individual Differences in the Use of Organizational Devices

Adult readers vary in their ability to set up effective reading strategies. For example, Fischer and Mandl (1984, experiment 1) asked college students with little prior domain knowledge to study a 1,700-word social sciences text for recall and comprehension. The students were identified as poor or good readers based on a combination score of recall, comprehension, and reading time. After reading, subjects were asked to explain their reading strategies. Good and poor readers reported different types of strategies. Good readers more often sought to identify the main goals and issues dealt with in the text; they performed a fine-grain diagnosis of reading difficulties and described flexible and adaptive strategies. Poor readers were not as specific in their descriptions; they reflected on their general capacities as learners, and expressed concerns about their comprehension performance. Poor readers metacognitive control seemed to be little more than some fuzzy awareness of their likely failure. The authors concluded that it might be worthwhile to train poor readers to use specific "preventive" strategies rather than general "summative" strategies (see also Pressley & Afflerbach, 1995).

Do organizational signals equally affect any reader of an expository text? Early researchers argued that they should be especially beneficial for students with poor learning skills. For instance, Meyer, Brandt, and Bluth (1980) found that content organizers could improve the performance of "comprehension underachievers" (i.e., students with relatively low scores on a reading comprehension test, and higher scores on a vocabulary test). Loman and Mayer (1983) argued that signals helped poor comprehenders use a meaningful strategy instead of a rote learning strategy. Kardash and Noel (2000) argued that organizational signals help readers switch from a list-learning strategy to a topic structure strategy. The latter strategy consists in identifying the main ideas and their conceptual relations, thus forming a more integrated and durable trace in long-term memory. Whether readers spontaneously use either of these strategies, however, may depend on a number of individual variables. For instance, Mayer (1984) suggested that more mature readers may readily employ a topic structure strategy, thus making the presence of explicit signals less necessary. Kardash and Noel focused on another personality variable, "Need for Cognition" (NFC), that was defined as "an individual's tendency to engage in and enjoy effortful processing" (Cacioppo, Petty, & Kao, 1984). NFC was shown to influence how much argument students recall from written or audio texts and their ability to acknowledge uncertainty and inconclusiveness after reading texts dealing with controversial topics (Kardash & Scholes, 1996).

Kardash and Noel (2000) asked 92 undergraduate psychology students to read the "energy problems and solutions" text previously used by Lorch, Lorch, and Inman (1993; see also section 2.2.2). The participants answered the 18-item version of the NFC scale by Cacioppo et al., as well as a vocabulary and a prior knowledge test. A six-topic, 1,701-word (unsignaled) version of the text was used in the experiment. The signaled version used an introduction to energy problems, a topical overview, six numbered headings (one for each proposed solution), and a topical summary. The participants read the text for memory. Immediately after, they free-recalled the text and answered a recognition test. Both organizational signals and NFC accounted for small but significant portions of variance in topic recall (7% and 4%, respectively). Need for cognition and organizational signals also predicted overall recall, and so did prior knowledge and vocabulary knowledge. As regards conditional recall, a signals x NFC interaction was found. In the nonsignaled condition, high NFC students recalled more subordinate information for each recalled topic. NFC did not influence conditional recall in the signaled condition.

The results confirm that organizational signals help readers encode and retrieve the top-level topic structure of expository texts. Furthermore, Need for Cognition seems to be positively associated with topic recall and overall recall. Finally, signals seem particularly beneficial for those students who do not spontaneously employ a structure-building strategy, for example, students with a low Need for Cognition.

2.3.2. Schooling and the Acquisition of Metatextual Knowledge

Schooling allows students to acquire more explicit knowledge about texts and text organization. Research studies demonstrate, however, that metatextual knowledge develops gradually through the elementary and secondary grades. Myers and Paris (1978) found that 8-year-olds are aware of basic features of texts (e.g., that sentences are organized into paragraphs), but that they ignore specific functions of paragraphs, as well as the function of initial and final sentences. Their study found, however, that by Grade 6 most children can define these features. Children's ability to tell whether or not a sentence fits within a particular text structure also improves with age. Englert and Hiebert (1984) asked 9- and 11-year-old children with good versus poor reading skills to read short series of sentences illustrating simple expository structures (Meyer, 1985, see section 2.1, this chapter). In half the passages, the last sentence introduced a shift in rhetorical structure (e.g., from description to sequence). The participants were asked to decide whether the last sentence was an appropriate continuation of the paragraph. Eleven-year-old children rejected 75% of inconsistent continuations, but 9-year-olds rejected only 50% (children at both age levels rejected less than 20% of appropriate continuations). "Collection" and "sequence" passages were easier to evaluate than "description" and "comparison" passages. Garner, Alexander, Slater, Chou Hare, Smith, and Reis (1986) observed that 12-year-old students could order sentences within paragraphs using cohesion marks (e.g., anaphora). They often failed, however, to discard partially irrelevant sentences, and they seldom used the "thematic sentence first" heuristic frequently employed in expository English.

Children also vary in their ability to define what makes a good reader, and what are the constraints of specific reading tasks. Yuill and Oakhill (1991) pointed out individual differences in the way 9-year-old good and poor readers define skilled reading and the origin of comprehension problems. When asked to define what makes a good reader, both good and poor readers mentioned speed and accuracy. For poor readers, however, "not knowing the words" was a frequent issue, whereas good readers referred to more global aspects of text processing such as comprehending the main points. Lovett and Pillow (1995) found that 9-year-olds are able to make a distinction between different reading objectives (i.e., to memorize vs. to comprehend). However, they need concrete purposes (e.g., comprehend in order to build a game). In the absence of such concrete objectives, even 10-year-olds seem less able to adjust their strategies (Lovett & Flavell, 1990).

Students' effective use of text organizers during reading also seems to improve with age. Lorch, Lorch, Gretter, and Horn (1987) examined the comprehension of well-structured expository texts in fourth-grade, sixth-grade, and college students. The main issue was to find out if children identify topics online, as they go through the text. The materials were two expository texts with a clearly marked hierarchical and comparative structure. One text compared two fictitious writing systems, the other one compared two fictitious countries. The texts contained 66 and 72 sentences, respectively. Each text contained an introduction and 10 content paragraphs. The paragraphs discussed five main features for each of the two countries/languages (e.g., geography, climate). Each paragraph contained a topic sentence (always paragraph-initial) and a series of elaborations. In one version of the texts, each paragraph was preceded by a transition question (e.g., "What is the weather like in Lambeeda?"). Each participant read a text with questions and another one without questions. The texts were presented one sentence at a time on a computer screen, in a self-paced timed procedure. The main dependent measure was reading time for topic and elaboration sentences.

Reading time for topic sentences was faster for texts with transition questions. Transition questions did not affect reading time of elaborations. In addition, topic sentences were read more slowly when they introduced a major shift (i.e., a shift in both countries or languages, and in features) than when they introduced a minor shift.

Reading time decreased with age, and there was an age by transition questions interaction (Fig. 2.4). The decrease in reading time when transition questions were present was significant only in sixth-grade and college students. In other words, transition questions seemed more effective for mature readers.

An interesting issue is to find out how much students know about textual organizers at various stages of schooling. Even though this issue

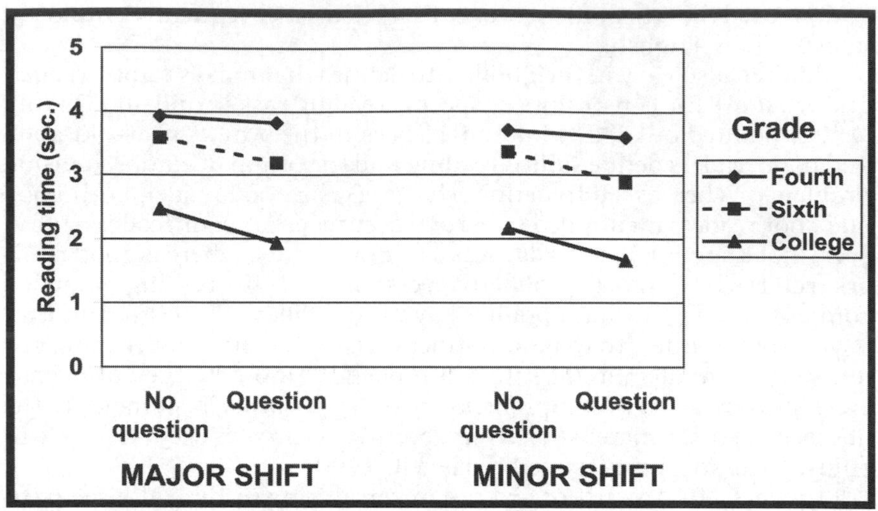

FIG. 2.4. Reading time for topic sentences as a function of grade, type of shift, and the presence of transition questions (adapted from the data presented in Lorch, Lorch, Gretter, & Horn 1987).

has been addressed for some basic organizers (i.e., headings, paragraphs; see Garner, Alexander, Slater, Chou Hare, Smith, & Reis, 1986), few data are available concerning the knowledge of more complex organizers (i.e., tables of contents, indexes) and their use in specific reading situations (i.e., scanning a text for specific content). Eme and Rouet (2001, see also, Rouet & Eme, 2002) investigated metatextual knowledge in 8- and 10-year-old students. The study aimed at providing evidence of the differential development rate of various aspects of metatextual knowledge. Eme and Rouet also examined the relationships between several dimensions of metatextual knowledge, on the one hand, and children's reading comprehension performance on the other hand.

The materials included a metatextual knowledge questionnaire and a text comprehension task. The metatextual knowledge questionnaire was built according to the distinction between three metacognitive dimensions of comprehension (Jacobs & Paris, 1987; Paris & Jacobs, 1984), namely *evaluation, planning,* and *regulation*. Items representative of each dimension were formulated or borrowed from previously published questionnaires (Ehrlich, Kurtz-Costes, Rémond, & Loridant, 1995; Myers & Paris, 1978; Paris & Jacobs, 1984). In addition, Eme and Rouet added a fourth subset of items aimed specifically at evaluating metatextual knowledge, that is, knowledge about structural or functional properties of written discourse (e.g., "What is a table of contents? What is it used for?").

In the first experiment, Rouet and Eme (2002) asked 42 third-grade and 42 fifth-grade students to answer their metatextual knowledge questionnaire, which was presented orally by the experimenter. The results showed a significant increase in knowledge of text features, planning, and regulation activities between the third and the fifth grades. As regards text features, Rouet and Eme reported that 33% of third-graders could not define a paragraph (7% of fifth-graders); only 19% of third-graders and 41% of fifth-graders could tell the function of paragraphs when reading for comprehension. A majority of children acknowledged the specific role of initial and final sentences in text passages, but a minority could mention a specific rhetorical function (e.g., to introduce a new topic, summarize, or conclude). Finally, 38% of third-graders and 67% of fifth-graders provided an acceptable definition of a table of contents, and only a minority (12% and 35%, respectively) could do so for an index. Significant development trends were also observed for the questions about planning and regulation of comprehension. For instance, less than a third of the children could mention an activity that may facilitate comprehension before one starts reading at school. Examples of preparatory activities were picking up a ruler, a dictionary, seeking the presence of an adult, discussing the contents to be read, and previewing the contents (e.g., pictures, headings). The latter category was mentioned by 7% of third-graders and 17% of fifth-graders. Importantly, the amount of metatextual knowledge was positively related to children's performance on the reading comprehension task.

In the second experiment, Eme and Rouet used a similar procedure to investigate college students' metatextual knowledge. Most participants displayed elaborate knowledge about basic text features: titles (100%); paragraphs (76%); table of contents (85%). A striking result, however, was college students' apparent lack of knowledge about higher level organizers. As much as 58% of the participants could not define an index as an alphabetic list of words along with page numbers. And a significant proportion failed to define the functions of first and last sentences accurately (25% and 49%, respectively).

Some, but not all, college students were aware of study strategies. For example, most participants cited skimming as a means to deal with time constraints; they also mentioned underlining, taking notes, self-questioning as comprehension-fostering activities. However, only a third of the students cited specific ways to get prepared to study or to improve recall. Finally, few participants mentioned elaborate regulation behaviors. Less than 50% cited the use of context or syntax as a means to understand difficult words or difficult sentences.

Thus, children in elementary grades have limited knowledge of text features and study strategies. Basic text features are easily defined by college students, but the study did find gaps in college students' knowledge of high level organizational devices and specific comprehension enhancement strategies. Furthermore, poor metatextual knowledge is related to low comprehension performance. Eme and Rouet's findings corroborate other studies of metatextual knowledge in young and older students (e.g., Hacker, 1998; Nist & Simpson, 2000). It must be pointed out, however, that their conclusions are based on declarative data, rather than on the actual observation of students' strategies. Thus, they are dependent on the participants' ability to reflect and communicate about reading-related matters. More direct evidence might be obtained by looking at how students concretely deal with text-based study tasks. The high cost associated with collecting and analyzing such complex behavioral data may explain why most studies conducted so far have relied on survey-like investigation techniques. Examples of studies investigating specific study strategies such as document search are provided in chapter 4.

In summary, there is a close relation between what people know about texts and the way they cope with complex comprehension tasks. Even though current scientific knowledge about the acquisition and use of expert comprehension strategies by adults is still scarce, it may be suggested that when dealing with complex textual materials, expert readers also rely on their knowledge of complex textual organizers such as paragraphs, headings, sections, table of contents, and indexes. Knowing these devices and how they work allows one to shift from basic linear reading to more elaborate forms of interactions with texts. These elaborate comprehension strategies are critical when dealing with complex documents.

CONCLUSIONS

When looking at naturalistic texts, such as a newspaper article, a textbook chapter, or a Web page, it is easy to see that texts are much more than linear series of natural language statements. Naturalistic texts come with a variety of text organizers that shape and structure content information. In this chapter, I reviewed the role of text organizers in expert comprehension. Text organizers may be categorized as visual or verbal. Visual organizers include the position and spacing of presentation of information on a page. The position of information is strongly associated with a hierarchy of importance. Information presented on top or at the beginning of a text tends to be considered important, even though position alone does not overrule the intrinsic semantic importance of information. Paragraph marking helps readers identify thematic transition within lengthy texts. When encountering a paragraph mark, readers generally slow down and mentally integrate the information they have just read.

Verbal adjuncts, such as headings, overviews, and connectors, are used to make explicit the semantic structure of a text. The inclusion of such signals, when consistent with the semantic structure, also guides readers' formation of a mental representation of the text. Readers of well-signaled texts recall more of the gist content, write better summaries, and generally perform better on comprehension tasks. These findings extend to more complex verbal organizers, such as outlines and tables of contents, even though the research on such devices is still scarce.

Thus, the use of information associated with visual and verbal organizers seems to be an intrinsic part of expert comprehension. This does not mean, however, that any signal included in a text will be automatically noticed and interpreted by the readers. Research has also found substantial differences in how adult readers deal with text organizers. This is because the effective use of text organizers is dependent on the readers' learning about these devices and how to use them. Such knowledge is acquired gradually throughout elementary and secondary grades. For instance, a significant proportion of fifth-graders are not fully aware of what paragraph marks and tables of contents are for. Consequently, they cannot make use of these organizers when reading.

The broader picture that emerges from these studies is that expert comprehension involves much more than efficient low-level reading skills, even if such skills are related to comprehension (Haenggi & Perfetti, 1994). In order to become skilled comprehenders, people must acquire a great deal of knowledge about the rhetorical properties of texts and the visual and verbal devices that signal such properties. The knowledge of text organizers, combined with a greater awareness of the comprehension process, allows expert readers to build up efficient strategies, even though they may have limited cognitive resources, topic knowledge, or verbal skills.

Realizing the role of text organizers in expert comprehension sheds new light on the nature of expertise acquired as part of schooling. Content-area learning consists of acquiring knowledge about the theories, concepts, stories, and facts of a discipline. But content-area learning also provides an overlapping expertise in the information resources characteristic of the discipline. These include typical document types, their internal structure, and the way they may be used to solve problems typical of the discipline. For instance, college students are to a large extent aware of the demands of different reading tasks and situations.

In summary, naturalistic texts are complex artifacts that contain several layers of information. The expert use of these artifacts requires a thorough knowledge of each and every layer of information, including the visual and verbal organizers that contribute to a text's meaning. Even though little research has been conducted on experts' reading behavior, it is quite likely that their reading strategies are strongly shaped by their experiences with texts and documents representative of their discipline. I reviewed some evidence that many students have not yet reached a very high level of awareness of texts and text processing strategies when they reach college. College training, however, confronts them with even more complex study situations, including situations that require them to study and integrate information from multiple documents. Their ability to acquire knowledge from these situations is dependent in part on their mastery of the shape of elaborate discourse. I go deeper into this particular issue in the next chapter.

3

Comprehending Multiple Documents

OVERVIEW AND CONTENTS

When reading for real-life purposes, readers often have to get information from multiple texts. They must both integrate information taken from various texts, and remember where each piece of information comes from. This chapter investigates the cognitive processes that underlie our ability to build up memory representations of multiple documents. Even though multiple document comprehension is typically carried out by experts in professional activities (e.g., historians, architects, or computer scientists), it may also be used as a means to foster students' comprehension of complex topics. Thus, novice reading of complex documents requires specific cognitive processes, but it gives way to expert-like mental representations and forms of reasoning.

Contents

INTRODUCTION

From primary school until higher education, students find themselves confronted with an increasing variety of information sources. Learning from multiple sources begins with the traditional classroom teaching situation, where the teacher speaks, presents overheads, passes handouts with additional information, documents, and exercises. When studying at the school library, students also have to make their way through a large diversity of printed materials, including books, journals, magazines, newspapers, and so on. For many assignments such as poster making, essay writing, or personal research, students need to collect and make use of more than just a single text. Other forms of education such as distance learning, informal education, or online training also rely heavily on students' ability to learn from multiple documents. Furthermore, students' environment provides them with various ways to complement, enrich, and sometimes contradict information received at school. In the past few years, the advent of the Internet has resulted in a huge increase in the number and diversity of sources potentially available for learning.

Looking at educational materials from a closer point of view, the multiplicity of sources used in learning is even more obvious. In textbooks, for example, information is often presented in the form of a main text, along with figures, tables, diagrams, photographs, and other materials. Take, for example, the double page shown on the upper part of Fig. 3.1 (in reduced format). This document is drawn from an 11th-grade French history textbook. Even though the texts and pictures are blurred, a simple glance at the double page shows that it includes several information sources of different kinds. The main categories are shown on the lower part of Fig. 3.1: headings, content list and introduction, legends, supporting documents, and so forth. Such a salient visual structure provides a comprehensive illustration of the role of text organizers in complex documents (see chapter 2).

Let us assume that an 11th-grade student is using this page to work on a class assignment. The student will identify the contents of this section of the book thanks to the *title* and *content list* found at the top left corner of the page. Nearby, the general *introduction* presents an overview of the chapter's main points. In the lower left page, a *thematic chronology* may help categorize key events in the period considered (i.e., cultural life in the aftermath of World War I).

The right-hand page presents a series of documents and illustrations that introduce more specific aspects of the historical period covered in this section of the textbook. A *photograph* (upper right corner) shows the damages caused by bombings on a European city. A *painting* (lower right corner) shows an artistic representation of soldiers with mon-

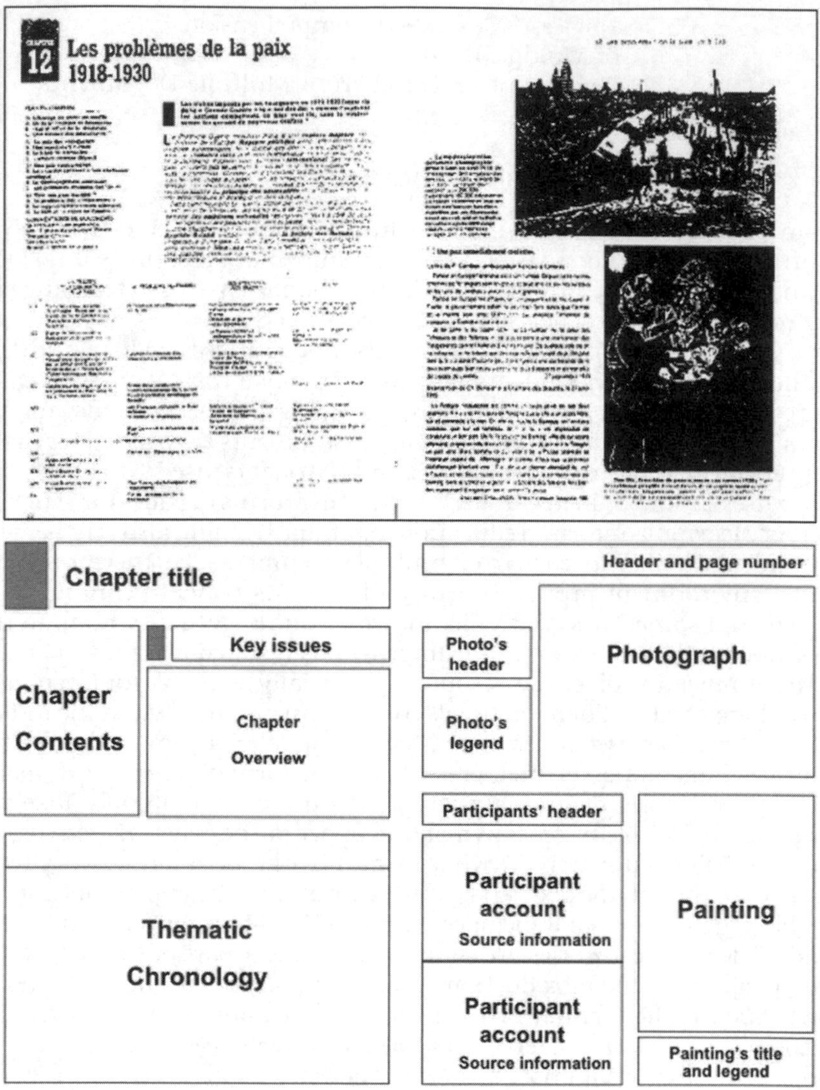

FIG. 3.1. Excerpt from a French 11th-grade history textbook (Marseille, 1988). Reprinted by permission of Nathan.

strous wounds playing cards, suggesting the deep psychological consequences of the violence and injuries they have suffered. Finally, two *accounts* by political figures at the time—one French, one British—discuss the consequences of war and the ambiguity of the Versailles Treaty. The following pages in the book, just like the first one, include both a "voiceless" lesson (in fact, that of the textbook author) and a large variety of documents. Such a diversity of sources is rather common in high school and higher education textbooks. It is also found in magazines and encyclopedia.

What are students supposed to do when they study multiple documents? And what kind of mental representation of such materials do they form? Learning from multiple documents requires one to decide on a study plan (given, e.g., time constraints and a study assignment), then to read and comprehend each document. The student must also understand the specific features of each source (e.g., whether it is important, credible, reliable, useful, and so forth). Finally, the student must integrate information from the various sources into a coherent whole, while assigning each contribution to the relevant source.

What kind of knowledge structures and cognitive processes are involved in these activities? A simple answer could be that they are essentially the same as the text comprehension processes discussed in chapter 1 (see also Kintsch, 1998; Otero, León, & Graesser, 2002). However, as I already suggested in section 1.4, there are several objections to this simplistic view. First, a set of documents such as presented on Fig. 3.1.does not meet the minimal coherence criteria required to construct a single propositional representation, let alone a situation model in the sense of contemporary cognitive theories of comprehension (see chapter 1). Second, there may be some differences or even discrepancies in the various "stories" told by these documents, preventing the construction of a single coherent representation (regardless of the underlying cognitive theory). Finally, there is no direct correspondence between any of the sources and the "situation" the student is trying to study. Each document may be used as a tool to build a representation of the situation, but none of them is a complete and reliable representation of the situation. Therefore, comprehension partly amounts to evaluating and selecting those aspects of the documents that may fit into a coherent whole, and assigning each of them a special status or role as descriptors of the situation.

For this reason, it seems likely that specific meaning-making processes are involved when reading multiple documents. There are also reasons to believe that the mental representation built from a set of multiple sources includes more than a representation of the situation described in the sources. Such a representation must also keep track of "who says what," that is, where and how the information presented in each document comes from. An integrated representation should also include the relationships between different documents, in order to account for explicit or implicit cross-references.

3.1. HOW EXPERTS INTEGRATE MULTIPLE INFORMATION SOURCES

Only recently has the issue of multiple document comprehension been acknowledged per se by psychologists and instructional scientists. Wineburg (1991, 1994) conducted one of the earliest empirical studies of multiple document comprehension in the area of history. In Wineburg's (1991) study, eight high school seniors (history novices) and eight graduate students and faculty from history departments (history experts) participated. They were asked to study a set of paintings and documents representing the battle of Lexington (one of the opening chapters of the United States' Independence War, at the end of the 18th century). The textual materials included witnesses' accounts (e.g., an excerpt from a soldier's diary), related primary sources (e.g., a court decision), and a variety of second-hand accounts (e.g., excerpts from historical essays, novels, and textbooks). The participants were examined individually and they were asked to think aloud while studying the documents. Wineburg examined the study strategies of experts and novices (i.e., how they read the documents, in what order), and their evaluation of each document (i.e., whether they found the documents useful and trustworthy, and why).

The expert participants demonstrated three study strategies not shared by novices. First, they focused on source information presented at the bottom of each document, even prior to reading the document. The experts used source information to evaluate and interpret the document content. For instance, one history expert dismissed information found in a historical novel because of the mixture of fiction and fact found in this type of text. The diary of a soldier directly involved in the event raised much more interest because it was firsthand testimony, even though this account was likely to be strongly biased. In contrast, high school seniors hardly ever consulted source information prior to reading. They generally paid little attention to source details, except for the textbook excerpt. Wineburg's study also found that experts and novices differed in the way they evaluated source information. The historians tended to find primary sources more useful and trustworthy, whereas high school students trusted the textbook as the most useful and reliable source.

Second, experts corroborated information across documents, especially for critical details such as time, place, or the participants' attitudes. The corroboration heuristic involved physical manipulation of the documents, in order, for example, to put them side by side so as to facilitate parallel reading. Expert students were sensitive to discrepancies, and they established relations between different versions of the events. For instance, one expert was able to notice a contradiction between the timing of the battle (dawn) and one report mentioning weapons "glittering in the sunshine." In contrast, high school seniors considered each source in isolation, and seldom noticed discrepancies across sources. They tended to "take it or leave it" without attempting to weight the contribution of the most complex or ambiguous sources. For instance, they accepted the textbook version even though some aspects were in contradiction to other documents (the contradiction was noticed by most historians, who dismissed the textbook).

Third, the experts contextualized document information using their prior knowledge of the situation. They used contextual information to put the specific events described in the documents into a broad context of time, space, and conditions. For this, the historians brought to bear whatever knowledge they may have had about the period, the actors and political figures, and related facts and events. New information was readily integrated in a dense network of prior knowledge and contributed to its development. The contextualization heuristic is an illustration of the role of content area knowledge in comprehending new information (see, e.g., Spilich et al., 1979; Afflerbach, 1990). In a study similar to Wineburg's, Carretero and Limon (1995) also found that experienced historians were able to draw more elaborate conclusions from a set of texts and tables about a particular topic in Spanish history, compared to a group of undergraduate history majors.

Wineburg's (1991) study pointed out that "being an expert" in a discipline such as history does not only mean that one has a great deal of knowledge about facts, events, dates, or characters. Expertise also means having specialized knowledge about information sources and how to use them. Source knowledge is brought to bear at the time of reading, as illustrated by the sourcing and corroboration heuristics. It is also used at the time of evaluating and using content information found in the documents.

Is expertise about discourse styles, sources, and rhetorics bound to the discipline of history? Even though few studies have been conducted in other areas, there are reasons to believe that it is not. A case study by Rouet, Deleuze-Dordron, and Bisseret (1995) provided evidence that both general and project-specific knowledge is brought to bear as expert software designers search, select, and write comments about software modules. Dillon (1991) found that human factors specialists possess detailed knowledge about the structure of scientific articles, which allows them to guess the likely location of any paragraph excerpted from an article, even though they have not read the article before (see chapter 2, section 2.2.3.).

These studies suggest that expertise in any discipline includes both *content area knowledge* and *document knowledge*, that is, knowledge about how knowledge is represented in documents, characteristics of various types of documents, and so forth. Document knowledge pertains to the broader category of metatextual knowledge discussed in chapter 2. It may take various forms, including generalized schemata that represent typical documents normally found in a given area of knowledge and/or activity. Document knowledge, whether general or domain-specific, is most likely used to encode, store, and retrieve information from multiple sources, as part of learning or other specialized activities. The nature of document knowledge and how it affects expert comprehension strategies is the subject of a new and fast-growing research area that has important implications both for discourse comprehension theories and for the teaching of literacy skills.

3.2. A THEORY OF MULTIPLE DOCUMENT REPRESENTATION

In this section, I present some theoretical notions concerning the mental representation of multiple documents. A mental representation of multiple documents is formed as the person reads several independent documents that refer to the same situation or topic, during a continuous time interval. Such an activity may require elaborate strategies, such as skimming or corroborating information across texts (Wineburg, 1991). It may also involve rereading, taking notes, or consulting adjunct sources such as a dictionary. Defined in those terms, comprehending multiple documents differs from comprehending single texts in at least three ways.

First, each text or document has a proper identity, which is represented by explicit or implicit *source information*. Source information includes the authors' identity, his or her credentials, and other details helpful in assessing the author's authority (e.g., previous publications in the domain). Source information also includes the conditions surrounding the publication of the document: whether it is private or official, the date of publication, whether it was reviewed, and so forth. Source information is relevant for comprehending single texts, but it plays a more prominent role in comprehending multiple documents. When studying multiple documents, source information simply cannot be ignored. This is because source information allows the reader to differentiate documents, and to evaluate the respective contribution of each document to a global representation of the situation.

Second, multiple document comprehension emphasizes the *distinction between texts and situations*. In Table 1.2, for instance, reading the second passage about the protest allows one to appreciate the relativity of the first report as regards, for example, the number of people wounded. Thus, reading multiple documents may promote the updating of previous knowledge or beliefs (Johnson & Seifert, 1999; van Oostendorp, 1996). This is important because updating previous knowledge is a central aspect of text-based learning.

Finally, *documents may complement each other* in various ways. A document may provide support in favor of the arguments presented in another document. It may fill in the gaps left over by the other document, thus confirming or disconfirming the inferences generated by the reader in order to fill in those gaps. When reading two scientific papers, two newspaper editorials, or two reports about a company's activities, the reader has to decide whether and how the texts are compatible or contradictory, whether one prolongates, responds to, or turns down the other one. The most common case is probably one in which each document contributes to representing one part or aspect of the situation, as in Fig. 3.1. In such a case, the reader has to identify global relationships between documents in order to integrate them into a coherent whole. Representing multiple documents thus includes, in addition to the semantic relationships described in the text-processing literature, higher level discourse relationships that connect and organize the sources into a coherent whole.

3.2.1. Describing the Organization of Document Sets: An Example

In a series of studies conducted together with Britt, Perfetti, and other colleagues at the Universities of Pittsburgh and Poitiers, we have proposed a number of theoretical principles in an attempt to account for the mental construction of global intertextual relationships (Britt, Rouet, Georgi, & Perfetti, 1994; Perfetti, Britt, & Georgi, 1995; Perfetti, Rouet, & Britt, 1999). In these studies, we used documents sets dealing with controversial historical events such as the 1903 acquisition of a canal in Panama by the United States. This is a controversial chapter of American history, due in part to the ambiguous role played by the U.S. armed forces during the revolt that started in Panama City in November 1903. The rebels wanted Panama (then a Colombian province) to secede from Colombia. The U.S. armed forces present in the harbor of Colón prevented the Colombian regular troops to travel to Panama City in order to suppress the revolt. This allowed the rebels to declare the independence of the Republic of Panama. Soon after, the United States and the Republic of Panama signed a treaty that granted the United States full control over a piece of Panamanian territory, a provision that allowed the United States to build and control the Panama Canal until its restitution to Panama in the 1990s.

The U.S. intervention in Panama has generated an abundant, colorful, and highly conflicting literature. Among other controversies, two opposed interpretations have been proposed as regards the rights of the U.S. army to intervene in Panama. According to one interpretation, the intervention was justified on the grounds of the Bidlack-Mallarino Treaty signed in 1857 between the United States and Colombia. The treaty granted the United States the right to intervene to maintain order in Panama (the United States had just completed the construction of a railway in Panama, to facilitate westward emigration). The second interpretation claims that the intervention was illegal based on a different chapter of the same treaty that guaranteed the sovereignty of Colombia over Panama. Both interpretations also make use of participants' accounts and various other sources.

In order to understand the story of the Panama Canal, one has to build up a mental representation of the situation: characters, places, goals, actions, influences, and the rich set of temporal and causal relationships among them (Magliano et al., 1999; see also chapter 1). One must also understand the similarities and differences among the various versions of the story available. In other words, one must bear in mind "who said what" and whether the different points of view are compatible or not. What would this type of representation be made of? Let us consider the set of documents presented in Fig. 3.2.

Figure 3.2 offers a simplified representation of a set of documents about the Panama revolt and their relationships. Each document is shown as a card with some basic information about its source and contents. For instance, the document by "Professor Norman" argues that "the U.S. military intervention in Panama was not justified on legal grounds." The document set includes two main types of documents: primary sources (e.g., military correspondence) and second-hand accounts (e.g., historical

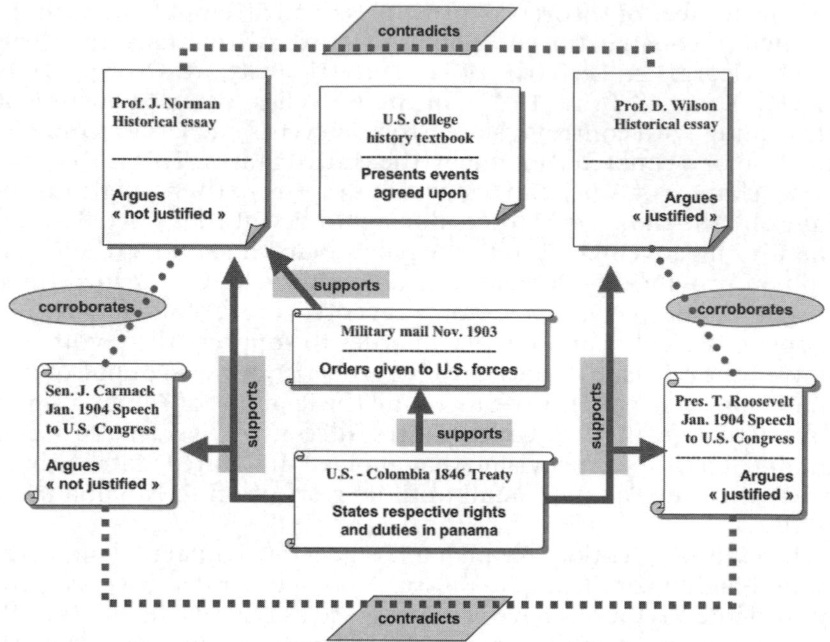

FIG. 3.2. Example of a document set dealing with one of the Panama controversies. The arrows indicate explicit (full lines) or implicit relationships (broken lines) between documents (adapted from Britt, Perfetti, & Rouet, 1996).

essays). Primary sources are written by characters directly involved in the events, for example, diplomats, politicians, military, and other participants. Secondary sources are written by characters commenting on the events, sometimes much later. All the documents contribute to a global representation of the situation in Panama in the Fall of 1903. Some documents, however, provide a rather neutral view, whereas other documents argue in favor of specific interpretations of the events (e.g., the U.S. intervention in Panama was/was not legally justified). The neutral/biased dimension is independent from the primary/secondhand dimension.

Relationships between documents are shown as arrows in Fig. 3.2. "Support" relations are represented by solid lines. They indicate that a document is used by another document to support the latter's view or claim. Primary sources are typically used to support secondhand accounts. An example is the arrow between the 1846 United States–Colombia treaty and President Roosevelt's 1904 speech. President Roosevelt explicitly cited this treaty in his speech. A second example of a "support" link is the arrow from the 1846 United States–Colombia treaty and Professor Norman's historical essay. In his essay, Norman cited the treaty to support his claim that U.S. intervention in Panama was not justified. Other, implicit relationships are shown in Fig. 3.2 by broken-line arrows. These include *corroboration* and *contradiction* relationships. An example is the contradiction between Prof. Norman and Prof. Wilson's claims. Finally, some documents may be related by more than one type of relationship. For instance, Roosevelt's speech and Wilson's essay are related by a "support" arrow, because the latter explicitly cites the former. The two documents also corroborate each other, in that both come to the conclusion that the intervention was justified.

An important issue is to find out how readers will manage to construct a coherent representation based on such multiple and partly contradictory accounts of the situation in Panama. Clearly, a theory assuming that comprehension is achieved by simply integrating the information found in a document to knowledge previously acquired from other documents would not work because the documents do not make up a single coherent story (see chapter 1). For instance, some documents contain conflicting semantic propositions, for example, "the military intervention was legal " versus "the military intervention was not legal." Conflicting propositions can hardly participate in a single coherent representation of a situation. Assuming that the reader will update the representation by replacing prior knowledge with new information would not work either because there is no way to decide a priori if the information found in the latter source is any more valid than information found in the previous one(s). Thus, specific integration mechanisms must be involved when comprehending multiple documents.

3.2.2. The Components of Multiple Document Representations

When reading a set of multiple documents, competent readers encode both source and content information from each document. Thus, a description of the mental representation of any single document must include a "source" component and a "content" component. Both components take the form of conceptual networks that integrate prior knowledge and knowledge newly acquired from the document. Source and content components are connected through source–content links, for example, "*according to* source S, event E occurred." Multiple sources are connected through higher level connections that integrate the sources into a coherent "source model." Figure 3.3 summarizes the main components of such a representation.

Two documents (A and B) are represented to the left of Fig. 3.3. Each document gives birth to two representation components or "nodes": a *source node* (rs) and a *content node* (rc). The source node includes any information available about the source, as well as any information that may be added based on the reader's prior knowledge of the source. The content node is a representation of the situation as it can be drawn from the document, that is, a situation model (see chapter 1). The nodes are connected through source–content links (S-C), for example, *attribution*. Furthermore, sources A and B are also connected through source-to-source links (S–S). For instance, source A may cite source B (reference), or the reader

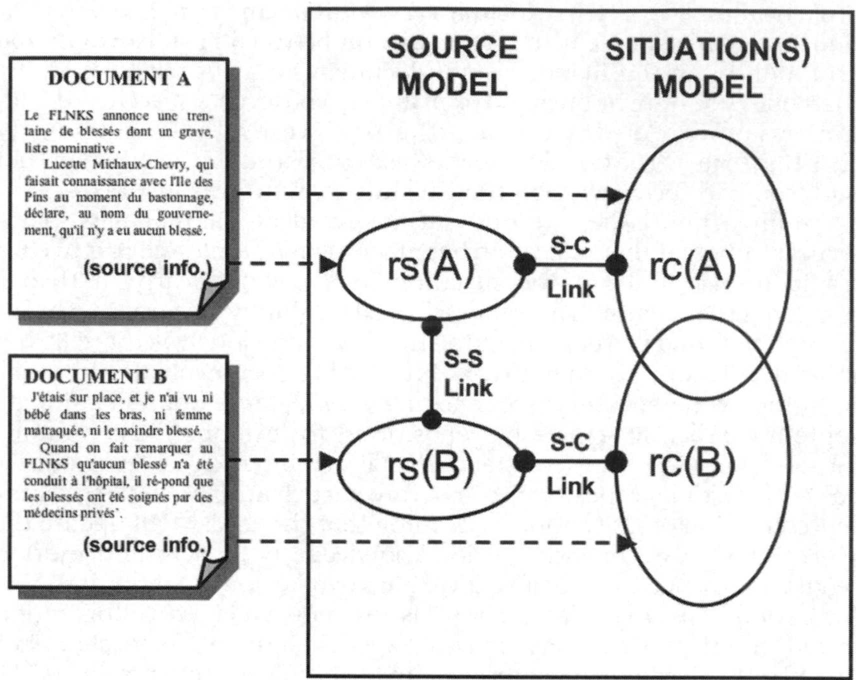

FIG. 3.3. Elements of a mental model constructed from multiple documents. rs(A) = representation of source A; rc(a) = representation of content found in document A.

may find that they corroborate each other. Conversely, the two sources may oppose or contradict each other to some extent.

The Semantics of Source Representations. What kind of information is included in a source node? This question is complex and largely open. Common sense would predict that the author's identity (name, credentials) is likely to be encoded, provided that it is mentioned in the document. Other important information such as the type of document, date of publication, language, and length are also likely to be identified as characteristics of a source. Chances are that the amount and type of information identified and stored from a document will vary as a function of the reader's expertise and the situational constraints. Perfetti et al. (1999) proposed that an expert source representation includes information about the author, setting, and form of the document. Author identification variables include the name of the author (whether an individual or an organization), his or her credentials (e.g., status, experience, reputation), and means as regards access to the information reported (e.g., witness, participant, student-of, individual, or teamwork). Information about the author also includes his or her motivations in conveying the content (e.g., career, profit, posterity), intended audience (students, colleagues, customers), and communication purposes (e.g., to inform, persuade, sell).

Information about a source is not bound to knowing the author. Source information also includes the setting or context of production (i.e., place in which the document is created, date and historic period, economic, political, or cultural context). In addition, document form variables characterize the type (e.g., treaty, letter, textbook, magazine, essay, and so forth) and the language style (e.g., legal, diplomatic, conversational) of the document. Source information might even include some content information, for example, the topic or main point in the source. This information is merely a summary or rough description of what the document is about. It pertains both to a description of the document and to the situation model that can be drawn from it.

It should be noted that source characteristics may be explicit in a document, or they may have to be inferred by the reader. For example, the rhetorical goals are not always explicitly stated, or explicit statements about them may not be complete or accurate. The actual goals have to be inferred by the reader based on prior knowledge. Wineburg (1994) refers to these goals as a *document's subtext*. Whether a slot in the source node will be filled in or not depends on a number of factors, among which are the availability of the information at the time of reading, document specificity, task requirement, and the reader's expertise. For instance, a novice history student with little prior experience of document-based learning may only be able to identify and memorize salient attributes (e.g., author name, text type), or familiar values of these attributes (e.g., document type is a textbook). A more knowledgeable reader will be able to add more subtle attributes, for example, the author's reputation, experience in the topic, the document's publication date or intended audience. Moreover, it is likely that various "source models" are available to expert readers, in the form of preexisting schemata or memory packages. An experienced historian may possess a schema for a "press release," "private correspondence," "official document," "research report," or "novel."

Finally, the expert representation of a source node may vary from one knowledge/discourse domain to another. The source characteristics studied by Perfetti et al. (1999) pertain to reading history documents. In other areas (e.g., science, literature, business, engineering), however, other source features may have a more prominent role. In computer science, for instance, the version of a document describing a project or software component is often a critical parameter (see Rouet et al., 1995). In literature, the status of agents (e.g., says, like, wants, knows) with respect to the actions or speech acts stated in the story can also be encoded (Graesser et al., 1999). The framework does not make any systematic prediction as regards the centrality or importance of these parameters. The hypothesis is merely that sources are represented as a structured set of parameters that are used by the reader when reading and evaluating content information.

The Role of Source Information in Document Comprehension. When reading multiple documents about a situation, the reader may come across different accounts of the same event. The accounts may agree on many aspects of the situation, but they may also differ on other aspects. This is because the authors want to emphasize different aspects of the situation or because they disagree about the facts, their respective importance, and/or the causal relationships among them.

Consider again the two newspaper accounts presented in Table 1.2 (chapter 1). The two excerpts describe the same controversial protest, but with quite different viewpoints. Furthermore, each of them uses a distinct set of sources. The first report mentions three sources (i.e., the protesters, city physician, and government spokesperson), two of which support the view that there were at least some people injured during the protest. The third source (spokesperson) is dismissed because she did not witness the events, and because she speaks on behalf of the government, who is interested in minimizing the degree of police brutality. On the other hand, the author of the second report introduces himself as a firsthand witness and claims that no one was injured during the protest. Furthermore, the second excerpt tends to dismiss the protesters' party because they only offer unverifiable evidence (i.e., that all the wounded were helped "by private physicians," the latter expression between quotation marks in the original).

In these two excerpts, the sources play an important role in understanding the events. In fact, there are almost as many sources as there are facts being reported. A full interpretation of those texts can only be achieved if one understands why the different sources would give different versions of the story. The FLNKS, a party in favor of independence, is interested in emphasizing that the ruling government has a brutal attitude against the local people. The government's spokesperson is interested in emphasizing the opposite. And L'Humanité, a newspaper opposing the government at the time, is interested in criticizing the government policies. On the other hand, Le Figaro and their reporter, who support the governing political party at the time, are interested in showing that the protest did not turn violent.

Knowing the identity and motives of the sources helps a lot to understand the content of these two accounts. The benefit is even greater if one considers that information about the sources allows one to reconcile the two versions. If no such information were available, the reader would be left with two discrepant accounts of the same event: There is no way to believe at the same time that people were wounded and that nobody was wounded. With the help of sources and source information, the reader can encapsulate each version into an independent mental space: that of the reporter telling each story. When later telling about these events in an essay or in a conversation with friends, the reader will be able to use source-to-content predicates such as "*according to* L'Humanité, there were several people wounded" or "Le Figaro *claims that* no one was wounded."

Text variables affect the way source information is stored in memory. Graesser et al. (1999) examined readers' ability to remember the source of statements after reading literary stories. They assumed that there would be differences in the salience of agents (including the narrator and story characters) as a function of whether they are introduced explicitly or not. They proposed that stories written in the first person would increase the salience of the narrator (in this case also a character) in memory. The first-person narrator would also be more salient than other, nonnarrator characters. In the first experiment, 120 undergraduate students read one of 10 short stories (9–18 pages long), five of which were in the third person (i.e., "invisible narrator") and five in the first person (i.e., amalgamated narrator and character). Each story contained two prominent characters. Immediately after reading, the participants were presented with 36 statements taken from or derived from the stories. Nine statements were spoken by the narrator, nine were spoken by each character, and nine were foils obtained by modifying the meaning of a text statement. The participants were asked to identify the source of each statement. Four answers were proposed: narrator, character A, character B, or neither. For stories in the first person, mean proportion of correct answers were higher for the narrator (71%) than for other prominent characters (61%). For stories in the third person, answers were less accurate for narrator statements (53%) than for prominent characters (64%).

Graesser et al. (1999) also analyzed the linguistic features that signal who the speaker is, in case of nonnarrator character's utterances. Five cases were identified: (a) the speaker is explicitly mentioned, for example, "Vicky said, 'Jim is now a baker'"; (b) the speaker is mentioned through a direct reference ("Vicky") or through a pronoun ("she"); (c) speaker is mentioned in the same versus in a different sentence; (d) the speech act is a direct quote versus an indirect form (e.g., "Vicky said that Jim is now a baker"); (e) speaker is identified before or after the speech act (e.g., "'Jim is now a baker,' said Vicky"). None of these linguistic surface features was found to have an impact on source recognition.

In the second experiment, Graesser et al. (1999) studied the effect of retention delay on source memory. The underlying hypothesis was that source retrieval from memory could rely on the use of literal memory for discourse. They also tested whether sources for story statements could be guessed based on reading an abstract of the story. One hundred twenty-eight participants read one of four first-person stories in one of four conditions: full story–immediate test, full story–delayed test, abstract–immediate test, and abstract–delayed test. Reading the abstract did not allow the participants to make accurate source attributions. This ruled out the possibility that source memory could be based on sophisticated guessing or reconstructive inferencing. Source memory was overall less accurate after a 1-week interval. The decay rate, however, was more steep for nonnarrator characters (72% and 50% at immediate and delayed tests, respectively) than for the first-person narrator (85%

vs. 72%, respectively). According to the authors, this result demonstrates that first-person narrators are a salient source of information that is slow to decay in memory.

Thus, when reading literary stories, readers construct agents at various levels. One level is the story line, with characters as agents; another level is the discourse, or pragmatic level, with the narrator, narratee, author, and reader as agents. Graesser et al. suggest that the ability to identify and keep track of these agents may vary as a function of the reader's training or level of instruction. For instance, students in literature would be more apt to pay attention to the narrator or author as an agent; or readers who have more knowledge of the world depicted in the story may be more able to examine critically the facts and claims stated in the story.

The findings by Graesser et al. (1999) suggest that a complete model of document comprehension should include source parameters as an integral part of readers' memory representation. Such a model of document comprehension helps reinterpret the results from past research on the updating of text-based mental models. In their experiments (already discussed in chapter 1), both Johnson and Seifert (1994), and van Oostendorp and Bonebakker (1999) used lists of messages, not texts, as materials representing evolving situations. Had the messages been presented as connected texts, the information would have simply been inconsistent. In addition, the researchers suggested implicitly that several sources were telling the same story by arranging the messages chronologically and by using fuzzy source references such as "the police report." Even though there is no direct evidence for this, it is tempting to suggest that with no further information about who says what, the reader is left with some confusion as regards which account they should trust or remember. Hence the high rate of answers based on the initial information generally observed. It would be interesting to check whether updating mental models is made easier when one uses a clearer marking of source differences across "messages."

Establishing Connections Across Sources. How are multiple sources connected to each other? The schematic representation in Fig. 3.3 assumes that the reader builds up links that convey any relationship between sources. These links may be very general (e.g. "talk about the same thing"), or more specific. Table 3.1 presents a few examples of "predicates" that convey source-to-source relations in the context of the Panama Canal story previously outlined.

Each example is taken from a text passage. In the first example, the passage is a presidential address in which the president (source A) cites a treaty (source B) to justify a military intervention. In this example, the source-to-source connection originates from one of the documents. It serves the purpose of supporting the claim made in this document. In the next example, the passage is an essay written by a student after reading a set of documents. The student cites two sources (president, historian Norman) and mentions that these sources agree as to the legality of the intervention. In this case, the connection did not originate explicitly from one of

TABLE 3.1
Examples of Source-to-Source Connections in the Context of Historical Problem Solving

Example	*Sources connected*	*Origin of connection*	*Type of connection*
(excerpt from Presidential address) "According to the treaty, the intervention was absolutely legal."	A. President B. Treaty	Source A	Reference (rhetorical support)
(excerpt from student essay) "The President at the time and historian Norman agree on the legality of the intervention."	A. President B. Historian Norman	reader (student)	Corroboration, agreement
(excerpt from student essay) "The senator challenges the president's claim that the intervention was justified."	A. Senator B. President	reader (student)	Opposition, conflict

the documents. It was built up (inferred) by the student after reading the documents. Finally, the third example shows a similar case, but with a different type of connection. The student acknowledges a discrepancy between the information acquired from two sources (i.e., senator, president).

There is currently no full grammar to describe the many connections that can be established between two documents or more. Scientific reports, press releases, and literary essays (to cite only a few genres) contain a very large variety of intertextual connections. Some of them are unidirectional (e.g., source A cites source B, but source B does not cite source A); others are symmetrical (e.g., source A and source B both corroborate each other). Furthermore, some source-to-source connections may have a complex structure. For instance, the "rhetorical support" connection may take different forms: community of opinions, reference to authority, or new facts provided by an external source that feed one's reasoning. Rhetorical support can also vary in intensity (e.g., partly vs. fully agree) and scope (e.g., citing an external source globally or only parts of it).

The type of links that typically connect sources may also vary across knowledge domains. In the case of historical controversies, the dimension of "solidarity versus opposition" often dominates. Common types of links include "agree/disagree," "support/oppose," "provide evidence for/against," and so forth. These links are not unique to historical discourse, though. They also appear in elaborate scientific discourse and virtually any form of argumentative discourse. There are probably many more types of intersource relationships that play a role in more specific areas of knowledge or intellectual activity. For instance, verbal protocols from computer scientists using a library of software components bear the trace of elaborate discourse models, in which parameters such as the date, author, and production context are used to compare the relevance of various objects (Rouet et al., 1995). More generally, intertextual connections can refer to any incremental relationship ("based on ..."), temporal or genetic ("after the work by ..."), intellectual or aesthetic ("in the spirit of ...," "in the style of"), or even unspecified relationships ("relevant for ...").

In scientific discourse, bibliographic citations are the most common expression of intertextual relationships. The expert reader will often want to check the bibliographic references found in a paper in order to assist his or her interpretation of the situation described in the paper. Document types play a major role in this process. Depending on the domain, peer-reviewed journals, edited books, conference proceedings, monographs, or unpublished reports are associated with various levels of credibility. Bibliographic references allow the reader to represent both the situation model and the source model proposed by the author of a paper. When bibliographic references are missing, the reader must infer the influences or sources used by the author (see parameter "access" already mentioned) based on his or her own knowledge of the domain. Scholarly works often include a large number and variety of references. Other types of works (e.g., inexpert students' essays) often lack references, cite inappropriate references, or make inappropriate use of references. Examples of inappropriate citing strategies are citing a very large number of references to support a mundane assertion, or making a highly specific claim without providing any bibliographic support. Another inappropriate strategy consists in not citing any source at all, which amounts to overemphasizing the author's own contribution to the idea presented in his or her text (plagiarism). In any case, the pervasive use of bibliographic references in scholarly texts further demonstrates that forming multiple document representation is an intrinsic part of elaborate discourse.

3.3 CONDITIONS ON LEARNING FROM MULTIPLE DOCUMENTS

So far I have discussed the construction of multiple document representations in fairly general terms. An implicit assumption was that the reader has enough knowledge and skills to perform the required operations. This is not to say, however, that complete and coherent document models are constructed any time a reader comes across various accounts of the same story. Constructing document models is an expert activity that can be achieved only under certain conditions. In this section, I summarize the available evidence about the nature of these conditions and the effects of studying multiple sources on student's ability to reason about complex events.

3.3.1. Novice Versus Expert Comprehension of Multiple Documents

Two general assumptions underlying the multiple document comprehension theory just presented are that (a) mature readers can, to some extent, read and understand events presented in the form of multiple sources, and (b) that expertise in a content area greatly facilitates the comprehension of and reasoning from multiple documents.

There is mixed evidence about younger readers' ability to integrate materials that present different points of view. Stein and Miller (1993) found evidence that children as young as 7 can participate in an argumentative dialogue, provided that the topic refers to personal values. Golder and Coirier (1994), on the other hand, showed that some 12- to 14-year-olds have trouble using counterarguments, which are typical of controversy accounts.

There have been few studies examining directly teenage students' ability to understand multiple documents. Golder and Rouet (2000) conducted an experiment in order to find out whether 6th- and 8th-grade students understand texts presenting conflicting accounts of a controversial event. They hypothesized that a text organized by arguments (i.e., comparing directly the two versions of the same event) would be easier to understand for 8th-graders because the argument structure would be apparent. They used a text describing a fictitious protest, based on several newspaper accounts like those presented in Table 1.2. The text described five episodes of the story: The reason for the protest, the number of protesters, their attitude, the attitude of the police, and the number of people wounded. For each episode, two different sides or interpretations were provided: the "government's side" versus the "protest organizers' side." Moreover, Golder and Rouet wrote two versions of the text. In the *source version*, the two interpretations were given separately, as two subsequent paragraphs (e.g., the protesters' version followed by the government's version). In the *argument version*, the two interpretations were given for each episode, for example, "According to the government, there were only a few superficial wounds. However, the organizers claimed that many people were seriously injured."

The participants were 63 6th-grade students and 52 8th-grade students from a semi-urban middle school. They participated collectively as part of a regular language class. In the first session, the students read silently one of the four versions of the text. Then, they answered two comparative questions (e.g., "According to the text, what can be said about the number of wounded?") and one integrative question (e.g., "According to the participants, what happened during the protest?"). One week later, the students answered the same questions again. The order of sources within a text and the content of the questions were counterbalanced.

The results indicated that the text was rather difficult to understand, especially for 6th-graders. Students' answers to the comparative questions ranged from one argument (e.g., "that is too much (wounded people). The police are too violent.") to a complete counterargumentative structure (e.g., "the government says there were only a few people slightly wounded, but the protesters say there were many wounded, many of which badly.") with all the intermediate levels represented (see Table 3.2).

TABLE 3.2

Examples of Answers to Comparative Questions by 6th and 8th Graders in the Golder and Rouet (2000) Study. The Participants' Answers Are Adapted From French

Answer categories and examples	*6th Grade (%)*	*8th Grade (%)*
Complete structure "Government says there were only a dozen of slightly wounded, however the protesters claim that there were many wounded among which many seriously [sic]."	16.7	56.7
One argument only "It is too much. The police are too aggressive."	33.3	8.7
Partial structure	17.5	23.1
One source, one argument "The number would be of only a few people slightly wounded, a young woman said it."		
Only sources "We do not know because the protester say a figure and the police say another."		
One source, two arguments "The government is lying because there were many wounded."		
No answer	32.5	11.5

Only 17% of the 6th-graders were able to provide complete argument structure in response to comparative questions. The percentage rose to 57% at the 8th grade. One in four 8th-graders provided incomplete source–content structures, with either one source and one argument, only two sources, or two sources and one argument. Most 6th-graders either did not answer (33%) or only mentioned a single argument (33%). Scores on the integrative question also rose sharply from 6th to 8th grade, with an average of four out of five topics recalled by 8th-graders at the immediate test (versus an average of two out of five at the 6th grade). Furthermore, a qualitative analysis showed that many answers to integrative questions included intrusions from the other side, as if the students did not keep track of the source-to-content connections. Thus, keeping precise track of what the two sides said about each episode proved a daunting task for 11- to 12-year-old students. It might be, however, that the students did not feel particularly motivated in studying this type of event, which involved characters and motivations that do not belong to their everyday environment (see e.g., Stein & Miller, 1993). Whether or not they would better recall two-side stories dealing with more familiar topics remains to be found.

How about older students? Can they learn about a complex issue by studying from multiple documents? And to what extent do they appreciate differences across sources in terms of usefulness and trustworthiness, with respect to the issue at stake? Rouet, Britt, Mason, and Perfetti (1996) conducted a study in order to examine these questions in the context of history learning. More specifically, they wanted to determine whether letting students read primary documents (e.g., treaties, correspondence) would influence their representation of complex historical stories. Rouet et al. used four controversies related to the history of the Panama Canal (e.g., "Was the U.S. military intervention in the 1903 Panamanian revolution justified?"). For each controversy, they prepared a chronological list of the main facts, and a "study set" made of seven documents:

- *Two historian essays*. These accounts were written by historians or politicians commenting on, but not participating in the events. Historian essays argued opposing interpretations of the controversy, citing other documents as support (see Fig. 3.2).
- *Two participant accounts*. These were accounts written by characters directly involved in the events, and arguing opposite positions on the controversy.
- *Two primary documents*. Primary documents were defined using three criteria: First, primary documents were written before or during the events (e.g., the 1846 treaty between the United States and Colombia). Second, they did not contain arguments nor did they take a position regarding the controversy. Third, primary documents were explicitly cited in the historians' essays and in some of the participant accounts to support their arguments.
- *One textbook-like excerpt*. The textbook-like excerpt was written by the experimenters, but it was introduced as an excerpt from a college-level textbook. The textbook-like excerpt gave a factual description of the major events. It did not contain any argument pertaining to the controversy.

In order to assess the influence of primary documents on students' reasoning, Rouet et al. also selected two additional historians' essays to replace the primary documents in the control condition. The additional essays were selected according to the guidelines previously described for the historian essays. One essay argued for one side of the controversy and the other argued for the opposing side.

The subjects were 24 college students with varying experience in history. However, none of the students was a history major. In the first session, students were tested for their history and geography knowledge and then given a background text. Subject assignment to the primary group or to the secondary group was balanced for gender, history knowledge, and reading ability. In the second session, the students were asked to study each controversy for about 20 minutes. Half the participants received a study set containing the primary documents ("primary group"), and the other half received a study set containing the additional secondary documents ("secondary group"). At the end of the study period, the students were asked to write a one-page essay expressing their opinion about the controversy and to evaluate the documents' usefulness and trustworthiness.

The ranking and justification results showed that students were aware of the properties of different document types. In the secondary condition, students trusted the textbook most. However, when given relevant primary documents, the students trusted those documents as much as the textbook. Furthermore, the students' justifications of their trustworthiness rankings varied across groups and document types. Content characteristics were critical for evaluating textbooks and historian essays, whereas source characteristics (document type, author) were critical for primary documents and participant accounts.

Rouet et al. also counted the number of explicit references to the sources in students' essays. The data showed that source information was selectively used to recall the story (Fig. 3.4).

Figure 3.4. shows the frequency of mention of each type of source. For most types of documents, there was less than one reference per essay on average. For the primary documents, however, the citation rate was

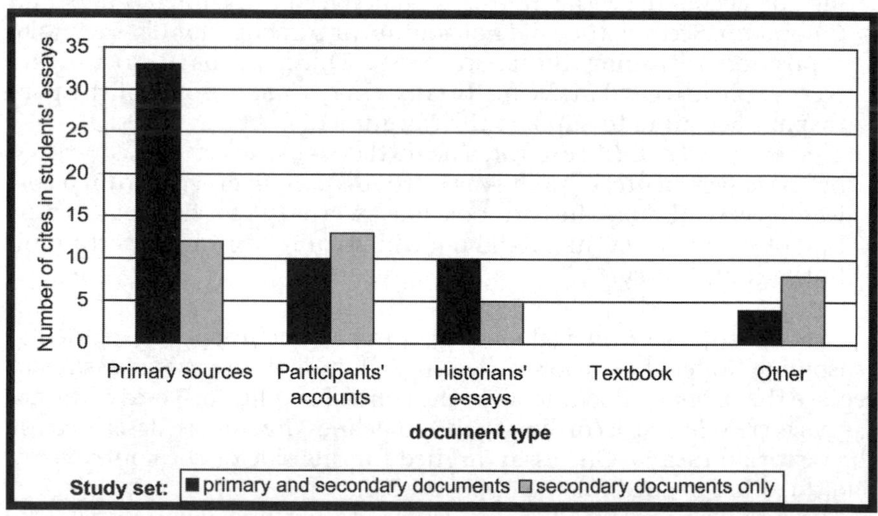

FIG. 3.4. Number of references to documents by type of document, collapsed across problems (adapted from Rouet, Britt, Mason, & Perfetti, 1996).

much higher, especially in the group that actually got a chance to study those documents. As a result, two thirds of the essays written by primary-group students included at least one reference, compared to only 39% in the secondary group.

Rouet et al. (1996) concluded that inexperienced students' were able, to some extent, to reason about various types of historical documents. More specifically, they concluded that readers of multiple documents use information at two levels, the discourse level and the content level. At the *discourse level,* students recognize the document as belonging to a certain discourse category (e.g., textbooks). They also notice some features of the source. At the *content level,* students identify the facts and events stated in the document, as well as the claim or position stated, if any. These features are used to determine the document's usefulness (e.g., whether the document contains information relevant to the issue) and the document's trustworthiness (i.e., whether it contains a biased position, a partial selection of evidence, or even a misrepresentation of the story).

Does discipline expertise increase students' ability to learn from multiple sources? Academic training allows students to build up expertise in specialized content area knowledge. An interesting question is whether training in a discipline also develops students' awareness of document properties, and their document comprehension strategies. This question is a rather difficult one because document comprehension skill is not easily separated from domain knowledge. Rouet, Favart, Britt, and Perfetti (1997) attempted to circumvent this problem by comparing students of comparable academic level—two groups of graduate students—who differed primarily in their area of specialization. They recruited 11 psychology graduates and 8 history graduates from a French university. The students were asked to study two of the Panama controversies, presented as sets of primary and secondary documents in a way similar to that of Rouet et al. (1996). After studying the documents, the participants were asked to evaluate the usefulness and trustworthiness of each document on a seven-point scale, and to write a short statement justifying their evaluation.

Both the history and psychology students found primary documents most useful. Contrary to the psychology students, the history students also found participants' accounts useful. Conversely, the psychology students, but not the history students, rated the textbook as useful. History and psychology students tended to use different criteria to justify their evaluations. The psychology students mostly justified their rankings using the document content as a criterion, for example, "(the document) presents the agreement with Colombia and the reasons for intervention" (60% on average). In contrast, the history specialists used a roughly equal proportion of content, source, and task justifications. Source justifications were based on at least one parameter of the document source (e.g., "The author is a senator opposed to Roosevelt."). Task justifications mentioned or alluded to the problem statement (e.g., "This is a key document of the controversy."). Furthermore, the justifications used by the specialists varied across documents. They used both content and task for the textbook and historians' essays, and mainly source for the participants' accounts.

As regards the essays written by the two groups of students, several interesting differences appeared. Seventy-three percent of the essays written by psychology students included straightforward claims (e.g., "I believe that the intervention was/was not justified"), compared to 31% in the historians' essays. History students tended to make restricted claims or no claim at all. Furthermore, the specialists tended to make more extensive use of contextual information and firsthand accounts. In a reanalysis of some of these essays collected as part of this study, Rouet, Favart, Gaonac'h, and Lacroix (1996) categorized the students' statements in four broad categories:

- *First hand information:* Statements based on official documents (e.g., citing or paraphrasing a Treaty provision).
- *Secondhand information:* Statements based on participants' accounts or historians' essays. Most often the students would endorse the interpretations proposed in the documents.
- *Subject's opinion:* Any statement expressing the subject's personal view on the issue (e.g., "I think that the Hay-Buneau-Varilla Treaty was a bad deal for Panama.").
- *Other sources.* Statements that referred to external sources of information such as general historical context ("Obviously the US wouldn't have intervened militarily without an interest at stake.").

A frequency analysis of the pool of idea units found in the essays showed that novice and specialist students made different uses of information sources. About 75% of the statements made by the psychology graduates were drawn from secondhand accounts or from their own opinion. In contrast, history graduates used official documents or contextual information in 55.4% of their statements. In other terms, they tended to build up their own arguments based on primary evidence and contextual knowledge, rather than adopting or challenging other writers' opinions. To further illustrate this contrast, consider the two texts presented in Table 3.3.

The texts in Table 3.3 are excerpts from essays written by two graduate students: a psychology student (excerpt 1) and a history student (excerpt 2). In order to emphasize the differences between these texts, I have underlined references to documents (single line) and to the main story characters (double line). Essay 1 contains many references to the participants (the United States, Columbia, and Panama) and related concepts (Isthmus of Panama, Colombian territory). It starts with a comment on the treaty, and then provides an interpretation of U.S. motives and actions. The facts are evaluated against the writer's own opinion (e.g., "The Colombian army did not threaten free transit.").

TABLE 3.3

Excerpts From Two Opinion Essays About the November 1903 U.S. Military Intervention in Panama. (Adapted from French)

Excerpt 1. (French psychology graduate student)

It seems that most of the controversy rests on an ambiguity in the Bidlack (1846) Treaty. Article 35 grants the *U.S.* the mission to protect free access to the *Isthmus of Panama* as well as the sovereignty of *Columbia* on the *Isthmus*. The *U.S.* took advantage of the ambiguity to prevent the *Colombian army* from intervening. One must bear in mind that at the time, *Panama* was a *Colombian province*. Thus, this was *Colombia's* internal affairs. It was, however, the *U.S.'s* interests to favor the revolution (…). The *Colombian army* did not threaten free transit on the *Isthmus*, since it was headed toward *Panama City* (…).

Excerpt 2. (French history graduate student)

The *U.S.* intervention in *Panama* gave birth to two radically opposed theses: One defending the intervention, the other one not supporting it. (…) However the arguments proposed in each thesis do not "weight" the same. The U.S. President as well as historian Wilson seem to consider [past events] as a unique criterion. (…) Whereas the thesis which does not defend the *U.S.* intervention is supported by arguments selected in the very text that rules the relations between *Colombia* and the *U.S.*: the 1846 Treaty. It is on the basis of a text of international law that they argue; and they consider that there was a violation of the Treaty.

Note. Underlining signals references to documents; italics signals references to story characters.

The second excerpt starts with a presentation of the global structure of the controversy, that is, two interpretations of the events opposed to each other and supported by various kinds of evidence. No attempt is made to provide a single, author-based story or interpretation. Instead, there are many references to the sources (e.g., "the thesis," "President Roosevelt," "Wilson"), and a clear effort to present the contribution of each one. This essay fits the description of a documents representation presented in Fig. 3.3.

These data suggest that extensive training in history allows students to develop more complete source representations. This is apparent in their use of multiple criteria when evaluating the documents' usefulness. History specialists' greater document expertise is also shown in their ability to reuse primary sources directly, whereas novice students, despite being at the same level of academic training, tend to rely on ready-made interpretations. More generally, the comparison of novice and expert students suggests that studying multiple documents can result in various types of representations, which vary in the extent to which connections between content and sources of information are established.

The data summarized here suggest that discipline experts are also more likely to identify source information, to develop connections between situations and text sources, and to construct a more interconnected document representation. A study by Strømsø and Bråten (2002) found similar results in a different domain. They examined the type of elaboration and connections made by law students as they read lengthy texts for the purpose of preparing for class or the final exam. Seven students participated in three meetings at a 1-month interval. At each meeting, the students were asked to bring a text that they had planned to study, along with any supporting literature. During the first meeting, they were trained to think aloud while reading, and they were recorded as they read while thinking aloud in a 20–30-minute period. They were allowed to take notes, to consult notes taken previously, and to consult additional materials. In the second and third sessions, the students repeated the same procedure with new materials (sometimes taken from the same source, e.g., their textbook). Strømsø and Bråten established a typology of the associations or "links" made by students while reading (Table 3.4.).

Primary endogenous links involve sources located in the sentence, passage, or section of a book currently being studied. Secondary endogenous links involve sources located in other sections or in documents directly supporting the text being read. Exogenous links involve sources located in other texts or documents, as well as sources pertaining to the reader's prior experience.

TABLE 3.4

Typology of Links to Sources Made by Law Students as They Are Reading

Type of link	*Definition, examples*
Primary endogenous	Source located in current sentence, passage, or section
Secondary endogenous	Source located in other section of current text
	Source located in main supporting literature (i.e., code of laws) mentioned in the text
	Source located in other supporting literature (e.g., case descriptions) mentioned in the text
Exogenous	Source located in other, unmentioned supporting literature (e.g., lecture notes, other books of interest)
	Source related to other student's activities, lectures, or prior experience

Note. Based on Strømsø & Bråten (2002).

Content analysis of verbal protocols showed that most of the links expressed by students were of the "primary endogenous" type (62%). The percentage of exogenous links, however, increased from one session to another, to reach 32% on average during session 3. Concretely, the students made more references to their own notes and previous readings. They sometimes completed or modified their notes during these episodes. The shift in the type of sources mentioned by students was attributed to their getting prepared to take the final exam, which required them to review and integrate knowledge acquired during the term. Interestingly, the authors observed a relationship between students' success at the final exam and the frequency of their exogenous comments during the last reading session. Despite the small number of students involved in the study, the data support the view that, in naturalistic reading contexts, students normally establish connections between what they are studying and various other sources of information from the same text, different texts, or their own experience. These data corroborate the findings by Rouet et al. (1997) that students specializing in history tended to connect the materials currently read to other related materials or background information.

In conclusion, discipline experts are more likely to develop a detailed document model from a collection of texts in their area of expertise. This is, of course, largely due to their greater knowledge of the content area (Afflerbach, 1990; Perfetti, Britt, & Georgi, 1995). But the research summarized here suggests that discipline experts' better performance in document-based tasks also comes from their knowledge of the properties of different document types. Each new reading episode involving a document that pertains to a recognizable category activates generic knowledge of the document properties and conditions of use. This knowledge is used to evaluate and select relevant information from the document for further processing.

3.3.2. Benefits of Learning from Multiple Documents

Does studying multiple sources affect students' knowledge in the long run? Evidence from previous research supports the view that exposing students to multiple documents changes their perception and reasoning about a situation. Perfetti et al. (1995) studied a small group of college students over an 8-week period as they sequentially read lengthy excerpts from scholarly and popular books describing the U.S. negotiations to build the Panama Canal. Each week, the students read an average of 30 pages about the Panama Canal and then produced written summaries and answered knowledge and reasoning questions about the materials. Perfetti et al.'s analysis of students' responses revealed two interesting findings. First, students initially learned the basic narrative. They identified the main characters and major events, but little else. After reading subsequent texts covering the same subject, they learned other, less central, events and details. Second, as students acquired more events and details, they engaged in more complex reasoning. They began to give more supporting reasons for their claims, more qualifiers, and they used longer causal chains. It is possible that the increased quality in students' reasoning was due to students' acquisition of new domain-specific knowledge as well as to their exposure to multiple documents.

Does learning from multiple documents encourage students to think in the way experts do? Wiley and Voss (1997) proposed a distinction between document learning and document understanding. Document learning would require the identification and memorization of information, whereas document understanding would require the students to produce their own reasoning based on the available information. Wiley and Voss hypothesized that presenting information in the form of multiple, clearly separated and identified sources would foster students' understanding, compared to a more traditional single-text presentation. They asked 60 undergraduate students to study the 19th-century Irish potato famine either from a list of sources (e.g., legal documents, map, demographic data) or from the same information presented in a textbook-like single-text format. Moreover, they gave the students three types of study directions: One third of the students were asked to write a historical account, one third wrote an argument, and the last third wrote a narrative. Memory for text was assessed through a recall task, and understanding was assessed by analyzing the content of students' essays.

The students in the "source–argument" condition wrote more critical essays than students in the other conditions. Moreover, the students in the source condition included more transformed information (compared to borrowed and added information; see Scardamalia & Bereiter, 1987) than students in the textbook condition. The argument condition increased their use of causal connectives. Finally, recall was higher in the "source–argument" and "textbook–narrative" than in the other conditions. Wiley and Voss concluded that both the use of multiple sources and the argument production task promote deeper understanding of the events.

In another study, Wiley and Voss (1999) also tested the prediction that an argument production task would promote students' deep comprehension of a historical event. In the first experiment, 64 students read a series of documents about the potato famine. The data were presented either in the form of a single (long) text, or in the form of multiple sources presented through the Web. Four tasks were compared: write a narrative, an argument, a summary, or an explanation about the famine. Students were given 30 minutes to study the information and write up their essays. Then they had to perform a paraphrase recognition task, an inference judgment task, and an analogy task. Again, the argument writing task and the online source presentation format increased the rate of transformed information. Moreover, participants in the "argument–sources" condition made more accurate inference and analogy judgments. Thus, the increase of transformed information seemed the result of a deeper comprehension.

Are younger readers sensitive to voice and authorship when they study textual materials? A study by Paxton (1997) suggests that they are. Paxton asked six secondary school students to read two texts about ancient Egypt while thinking aloud. Then the participants answered questionnaires and participated in a retrospective interview. One of the texts was taken from a textbook chapter, whereas the other was more "visible": the author used first-person narrative, expressed commitment, used modal expressions, and so forth. Paxton observed that readers of the visible version were more engaged in their activity, and that reading seemed to promote a deeper level of reasoning. Beck, McKeown, Sandora, Kucan, and Worthy's (1996) Questioning the Author method also improved 4th-graders' comprehension of expository texts. The method encouraged children to visually represent the author and to question his or her purposes, motives, and methods. In other words, the author was made more "visible" to the reader, which may have stimulated interest and engagement in the comprehension activity.

It seems that, at the level of high school, students get a sense of "epistemic authority" and use it when evaluating document information (Otero & Campanario, 1990). García-Arista et al. (1996) examined the effects of study settings on high school students' comprehension monitoring. Study setting was defined as a combination of the class context in which reading took place (language or science class), and as the source attribution of the texts to be comprehended (newspaper or science textbook, respectively). In experiment 1, 76 10th-grade students (16 years old) were assigned to one of two settings: language class/newspaper article, or science class/science textbook. The students were asked to read a series of six short passages about unfamiliar science topics (e.g., superconductivity). Four of the six passages contained an obvious contradiction between two sentences (e.g., "Superconductivity has only been obtained by cooling (sentence 2) / increasing the temperature of (last sentence) certain materials"). The students were asked to read with an explicit purpose of evaluating comprehensibility and underlining conflictive sentences, if any. More contradictions were detected in the science than in the language study setting. The students were able to explain the contradiction in about half of the cases when detection was successful. In the second experiment, the same pattern was found with a larger sample and a reduced set of texts. García-Arista et al. concluded that high school students make use of the study context to set up standards and comprehension strategies for themselves. Contrary to what was expected, students were more likely to detect inconsistencies in the science class/science textbook setting. This was not expected because the science textbook is supposed to be more "authoritative" than newspapers. The authors suggested that students tend to increase their standards of coherence and comprehensibility when reading texts with a high perceived epistemic authority. Because of the confound between the source and setting manipulation, however, it is hard to know which of the two dimensions was the most influential.

In sum, the evidence so far suggests that multiple documents and/or authentic settings with visible authors seems to foster deep comprehension in students. There are, however, some limits to the process, at least with inexperienced students. For instance, if the task specifically asks the students to integrate information across two texts, then too much heterogeneity might hinder their ability to do so. Nash, Schumacher, and Carlson (1993) demonstrated the influence of linguistic characteristics of source materials on subjects' written essays. Eighty-four undergraduate students were asked to study two texts describing Native American tribes in order to write an essay comparing the two tribes. The source texts had either the same or different overall structures (one was organized by topic, the second one chronologically). The participants were influenced by the structure of the first passage they read. Moreover, subjects' essays were better organized when text structure was identical across sources than when the organization was different, even though they may be of a lesser linguistic quality. This finding can be related to the results of a study by Kieras (1980), where the initial sentence of a passage influenced subjects' representation of the whole passage (see chapter 2). Stahl, Hynd, Britton, McNish, & Bosquet (1996) also found that reading two documents about the Tonkin Gulf incident did improve high school students' mental representation of the story. Studying additional materials, however, did not cause any further improvement. The analysis of students' notes and essays showed that studying multiple documents did not make students depart from basic, copy-paste strategies. The authors suggested that high school students need explicit study directions in order to take advantage of reading multiple documents.

Mannes (1994) discussed the benefits of reading an outline and a main text with different perspectives. She pointed out the need for a reasonable compromise between the complexity of the materials and students' processing capacities. She noted that "(...) increasing comprehension difficulty (within the range of the targeted learners' abilities) by presentation of multiple perspectives, may be effective in producing a richer domain model and, consequently, a deeper level of understanding than is obtained with traditional advance organizers." However, she also warned that "(...) care must be taken to ensure that the perspectives presented are not so disparate as to preclude the identification of any relationships by the readers, nor so similar that the perspectives entail the same sets of relations" (p. 586).

Bearing these limitations in mind, the results of Wiley and Voss' (1997, 1999) studies are consistent with the expert comprehension framework presented earlier in this chapter. When reading from multiple sources, learners have to distribute their attention between the two major components of the document space, the source model and the situations model. The multiple documents space allows a source model to be constructed; and the argumentative task encourages the development of an integrated documents model—one in which the source and the situations components are interconnected, at least during the writing task. In contrast, narrative writing appears to encourage the construction of a single situation model.

In conclusion, there are apparent benefits in the use of multiple documents as part of high school or college teaching. But using multiple documents alone does not ensure that inexperienced students will come to a thorough understanding of the situation. A critical parameter seems to be the task setting that surrounds the reading activity. The best results were obtained in conditions where students were explicitly instructed to read in order to come up with informed opinions, and/or to use the information in order to reason about the situation. A difference between novice and more experienced students might then be their capacity to self-organize the study activity, which is consistent with the studies reviewed in chapter 2 (section 2.3).

CONCLUSIONS

In a large number of school and professional activities, people are required to use several information sources simultaneously. Evidence comes from a simple look at the shelves, desks, and, sometimes, chairs in people's offices or study rooms. Very often do we see not just one, but several books, journals or magazines, technical documents, and notes scattered around, obviously for the purpose of being used in parallel. Reading multiple documents requires specific comprehension strategies: One may need to *identify the source* of each document (e.g., who wrote it, when, for what audience and purposes); to *compare information across sources*, in order to corroborate the veracity and the accuracy of information; and to *integrate information* into a coherent representation. All these processes pertain to a comprehensive definition of reading literacy such as that offered in the introduction to this book. They have, however, been somewhat overlooked in theories of reading competence and reading instruction, possibly because the importance of such processes only appears when studying complex, naturalistic text-processing activities.

In this chapter, I have suggested a number of hypotheses as regards the processes that are brought to bear in multiple document comprehension. Based on earlier works by Wineburg, Britt, Perfetti, and others, I have suggested that the mental representation of multiple documents (or "documents model") involves two distinct but interconnected components: a source model and a situations model. The *source model* contains a representation of each source and rhetorical connections among sources. The *situations model* contains a representation of the situation described in the documents. The situations model may also contain several alternate representations for complex or controversial events, hence the use of the plural form of the term "situations." I have argued that, in the latter case, a powerful means for readers to maintain coherence in their knowledge representation is to maintain active links between source representations and content representations. In other words, the reader has to remember both what was said and who said it. This is a core characteristic of elaborate document models.

Constructing complete and coherent document models is not an easy task. Rather, it characterizes the behavior of expert readers studying documents that pertain to their field of expertise. Expert readers need to rely on surface and content cues characteristic of their familiar sources (see Dillon, 1991; see also chapter 2). Several experiments have shown, however, that even inexpert university students can use and evaluate multiple documents. They do need, however, to be provided explicit instructions about why and how to do so. When students are given appropriate materials and task contexts, they may benefit from studying multiple sources, compared to single "voiceless" texts.

Analyzing the mental processes brought to bear when comprehending multiple documents points out the role of readers' objectives and purposes. In naturalistic contexts, the point of reading documents is seldom to memorize information or even to achieve comprehension of the contents. Very often do people use documents for much more specific purposes, like searching information about a topic. Thus, functional literacy involves one's ability to make appropriate selections among vast repositories of information. I examine the relationships between comprehension, question answering, and information search in the next chapter.

As online technologies become more available, studying from a variety of sources is becoming a rather common way of acquiring knowledge in content areas. The studies on multiple document comprehension and learning also suggest that there may be some benefits of using the World Wide Web to design instructional tasks that require students to study and confront multiple sources of evidence. Instructional designers and policymakers should be aware of the opportunities, and also the constraints, that characterize learning from multiple online documents. I return to this issue in chapter 6.

4

Question Answering and Document Search

OVERVIEW AND CONTENTS

Reading often takes place in a purposeful context, in which people engage in interactions with documents in order to satisfy a specific need or objective, for example , to locate a piece of information, to answer a question, or to perform a concrete action. The materials available may or may not offer exactly the information that fits the reader's purpose. When they do contain such information, it is rarely accessible at first sight. Instead, in order to access the relevant information, readers have to engage in document search. Document search is the activity that consists in consulting, rather than reading extensively, a document or a set of documents. Document search relies on specific cognitive processes and strategies, quite distinct from those used when reading for comprehension or memory. Answering questions from texts requires one to make extensive use of text organizers in order to proceed quickly to the relevant passage. Furthermore, deep comprehension is not always needed in order to locate information. Finally, search and comprehension may interact, as searching a document influences the reader's mental representation of the document's contents. Executive control processes play a critical role in planning and conducting efficient document search.

Contents

INTRODUCTION

Current theories of text comprehension assume that comprehension results from the interaction between the propositional content of a text and the reader's previous knowledge (Kintsch, 1998; van Dijk & Kintsch, 1983; see chapter 1). In such a perspective, the reader is supposed to read the text entirely, with an effort toward comprehension that is homogeneous throughout the text. This view reflects the comprehension tasks classically studied in experimental research, which usually involve short passages and simple memory tasks. However, a complete theory of comprehension should account for the full range of materials, tasks, and objectives that motivate reading activities. When looking at such naturalistic situations, it is clear that the text–reader interaction is considerably influenced by contextual factors. Those include the reason, purpose, time, and physical conditions that surround the reading experience. Especially important is the nature of the purpose or objective for reading. In real-world situations, reading objectives are much more diverse than those typically used in experimental research. People do not always have to read texts entirely, from beginning to end, in order to achieve their purposes. In many situations, readers use texts in order to locate information that is relevant to their need. This involves searching, as much as comprehending, written information. Searching is a pervasive way to interact with texts. Guthrie and Greaney (1991) argued that locating information is the primary purpose in most occupational reading activities. Searching texts is also important in the context of learning activities (Lorch, Lorch, & Klusewitz, 1993; Symons & Pressley, 1993). Finally, search is important in various forms of leisure reading: Most people do not read newspapers, magazines, cooking books, or encyclopedia in a continuous and extensive way. Instead, people search these materials in order to find interesting or relevant information. There may not always be an explicit objective or task that governs people's actions in such settings. But neither is the search for information random or unpredictable. Instead, expert readers' purposes and objectives guide their reading behavior in a way that traditional reading research, but also reading instruction, has tended to overlook.

In this chapter, I focus on the cognitive processes of *question answering and document search*, and their relationships with text comprehension. In the first section, I examine the mental processes of question answering from memory, and I review the specific constraints of answering questions from documents. In the second section, I examine in more details the cognitive processes and skills involved in expert document search. I propose a cognitive model that takes into account the external and memory resources involved in document search, as well as the steps and strategic decisions characteristic of complex search tasks. I point out the relationships between memory skills, prior knowledge, and the ability to search documents. In the third section, I review the effects of inserted questions on text comprehension and memory for text. Reading with the purpose of answering questions affects what people actually remember from the text, and the influence of question answering varies with the characteristic of the question asked. I also examine readers' generation of questions while learning from text, and their relationship with prior knowledge and comprehension. I draw some instructional implications concerning the use of search tasks as a means to promote effective learning from text.

4.1. ANSWERING QUESTIONS FROM MEMORY OR FROM TEXT

This section provides a general overview of the processes that take place when people attempt to answer questions based on what they have previously learned or read in texts. This is a situation familiar to students, for instance, when they take tests based on previous reading assignments. Text-based question answering is also a common situation in other forms of training (e.g., distance education) and in corporate teamwork, when people use information from reports or technical documents in order to discuss situations and to make decisions. Two cases must be distinguished. In the first case, no external information source is readily available at the time of answering the question. The reader has to rely on his or her memory in order to retrieve and use information previously learned. This is typical of students taking final exams or engineers making decisions as part of their field work. In the second case, people may use one or more external sources in order to answer. They have to engage in a search strategy based on their prior knowledge of the text and on the task demands. This is the case, for instance, of students searching documents in order to prepare an essay, or a medical team discussing alternatives based on a patient's data.

Let us illustrate these cases using an example in the area of science learning, borrowed from Rouet and Vidal-Abarca (2002). Consider the passage on "atomic models" presented in Table 4.1. Suppose that, some time after reading the passage, an 11th-grade student is asked a question such as, "What did Rutherford find out about atoms?" Exactly what kind of processes will the student bring to bear in order to answer this question? Again, this depends on whether or not the student has access to the information source. If the student is required to answer from memory only, the process will consist of inspecting his or her mental representation of the text, retrieving relevant information, and constructing an answer (Fig. 4.1). If, however, the student is able to review an external information source in order to locate information relevant to the question, the process will consist of both memory search and text search. Thus, the mental processes of question answering depend on whether the search is conducted from memory only or from both text and memory.

In the next sections, I review each of these two cases in more detail, in order to show how both types of processes combine in naturalistic document search situations.

TABLE 4.1
Excerpt From an Introductory Physics Text on Atomic Models With Various Types of Questions and Related Information

Inserted question	*Passage excerpt*	*Related information*
What did Rutherford find out about atoms?	"In 1911, Rutherford conducted an experiment that was critical in challenging Thomson's atomic model. The experiment consisted in bombarding a leaf of gold foil with packets of alpha particles positively loaded, of much larger mass than that of electrons and launched at high velocities. Rutherford observed that most of the particles traversed the leaf, while some were deviated and a few others bounced back. Rutherford concluded that atoms had to be made essentially of empty space since most of the particles traversed the leaf without being deviated."	Thomson defined atoms as compact but penetrable spheres.
What type of particles did Rutherford use in his experiment?		In a solid body atoms are squeezed together.
How did Rutherford's atomic model differ from Thomson's?		The particles could not go through the gold leaf except through the atoms themselves.

Note. Adapted from Rouet and Vidal-Abarca (2002).

FIG. 4.1. An illustration of memory-based search vs. document-based search.

4.1.1. Dimensions of Question Answering From Memory

Let us start with the situation where a student is asked to answer a question based on his or her prior knowledge. A full presentation of the psychological processes brought to bear in such situation is clearly out of the scope of this book, as such a presentation would require a complete introduction to memory structures and processes. I introduce only a psychological account of question answering from memory, before I turn to the case of text-based question answering.

Psychological research suggests that answering questions from memory is a fairly complex activity (Graesser & Black, 1985; Reder, 1987; Singer, 1990, 2003). Graesser and Franklin (1990) proposed a model named QUEST to describe the mechanisms of question answering from memory. According to the QUEST model, question answering involves a categorization mechanism that identifies the *type* of question (e.g., "what," "why," "how" type of question), the question *focus* (e.g., "Rutherford found something about atoms" in the earlier example), and the relevant *information sources*. In the case of memory search, information sources are the episodic or general knowledge structures that may be tapped for answers to the question. If the search occurs after reading a scientific text that introduced unfamiliar or complex information, the student may have to decide whether to search from his or her text representation only, from other episodic structures if any are available, or from a broader knowledge base.

According to the QUEST model, questions differ in the size of the conceptual structure needed to build up an answer. The simplest questions focus on a single concept or semantic proposition. For instance, "What year did Rutherford conduct his famous experiment?" calls for just a number to be found. More complex questions focus on broader conceptual structures. For instance, "How did Rutherford's atomic model differ from Thomson's?" calls for two knowledge structures to be activated and compared: the knowledge structure of Rutherford's atomic model, and the knowledge structure of Thomson's atomic model. The size of the knowledge structure(s) required to answer a question is a factor of complexity, as all the relevant information must be held in working memory until the answer is constructed and expressed.

In the QUEST model, the actual process of answering a question starts with the *activation of a knowledge node,* either directly if the node matches a term in the question, or indirectly through the contextual activation of relevant knowledge structures. Search continues through a radiation mechanism called "arc-search procedure." Arc-search allows the *propagation of activation* through a knowledge network, based on constraints specific to each type of question. For instance, "how" questions call for the search of causal antecedents or subordinate goals. Arc-search reduces the search space by identifying those knowledge nodes that may be chosen for an answer. The search space is further reduced by constraints of propagation and pragmatic rules. For instance, comparing Rutherford's and Thomson's models may take a line, a paragraph, or several pages of text, depending on practical conditions and the type of knowledge one is expected to exhibit. Notice that, for complex questions, note taking while thinking about the question can facilitate the search process by decreasing the amount of information to be held in working memory as the search proceeds (Kiewra, 1989).

The QUEST model points out the complexity of the memory processes involved in retrieving information from long-term memory. Such processes extend the notion of inference making more traditional in text comprehension research (see chapter 1). The QUEST model also points out the need for the reader to be aware of the appropriate source of information to be tapped. When several sources are available, the reader must be able to weigh each potential source against the others in order to find out which is the most appropriate or effective.

4.1.2. Dimensions of Text-Based Question Answering

Let us now turn to a situation where the student is allowed to search for the answer in a text. Do the processes of question answering unfold in a similar way?

The processes of *parsing the question,* identifying the *question category* and *question focus* look very similar indeed because these processes require only a question to be read. The first obvious difference between memory search and text search occurs at the level of source selection. The student has to decide whether he or she can answer based on prior knowledge, or whether searching the text is necessary. The selection of a relevant source in memory may be a problem for novice learners. In a previous investigation of middle school students' question answering from text (Rouet, 1991), I asked 6th- and 8th-graders to read a biology text on sharks and to answer a series of comprehension questions. Quite unexpectedly, some answers reported dramatic (and irrelevant) details (e.g., sharks' huge size, intelligence, and vindictive temper). Informal interviews revealed that many participants had watched the movie "Jaws" on TV on the evening before the experiment. Only one 8th-grade participant asked whether it was "compulsory to answer from the text or whether they could use their own knowledge as well." The latter observation suggests that the selection of an appropriate source may depend on students' metacognitive skills, for example, their awareness that several sources exist and that not all sources are equally useful or relevant (see chapter 3; see also Raphael & Pearson, 1985). The decision-making process may also be affected by students' general level of comprehension skill (Raphael, 1984), their feeling of knowing (Koriat & Levy-Sadot, 1999), or their selection of a retrieval strategy (Singer, 1990).

Let us assume that the student acknowledges the text as a relevant source of information. The next steps are locating relevant information, and using the information to construct an answer. These processes differ notably from their counterpart in memory search (Table 4.2). First, the search for a relevant information source will not proceed through the activation of knowledge from long-term memory. It requires the evaluation and selection of relevant text passages, based on the use of signaling devices (see chapter 2). Next, the conceptual network that has to be searched (i.e., as represented in the text) does not preexist in memory; rather, it is constructed or reconstructed as the search goes on. And the knowledge base to be searched is not reduced automatically through "constraints propagation," but through deliberate reasoning about text information. Moreover, all the constituent processes of reading and, in most cases, text comprehension are involved in text-based search. An important consequence is that, contrary to memory search, text-based search is all the more resource consuming as more information is

TABLE 4.2

Similarities and Differences Between Memory-Based and Text-Based Search

Search processes	*memory search*	*text search*
Question parsing	microstructure formation, categorization, identification of question focus	
Locating relevant information source	selective propagation of activation (arc search)	selection of information categories (through, e.g., metatextual cues)
Content search	knowledge activation, matching with question focus	content processing, matching with question focus
Retrieval cues	only from prior knowledge and/or memory for text	from cues present in text integration with prior knowledge

available: It is more difficult to search a whole book chapter than it is to search a single paragraph.

The comparison between memory search and text-based search suggests that the latter involves more complex mental processes because it requires the reader to manage simultaneously two distinct information sources: the text and information present in memory. Text-based search, on the other hand, presents the advantage of providing explicit cues from which the reader can identify target information. Thus, the skilled reader can quickly parse a lengthy document in order to locate relevant content words without paying attention to the global meaning. Such cues do not exist in the case of memory search. For individuals with appropriate search strategies, content search may be greatly facilitated by using signaling devices such as content tables, indexes, headings, and so forth. The use of textual cues requires, however, that each cue be matched against the question focus, which may take some additional reasoning when the two sources do not exactly match.

Whereas memory search is basically dependent on the extent of one's knowledge of the topic, the complexity of text-based search is subject to a wider range of factors. Mosenthal (1996) identified four factors that influence text-based search:

1. *Document complexity* is a function of the amount of raw information included in the document, and the document's structural organization. It is presumably simpler to inspect a one-page text than a 200-page book. In the latter case, inspection is easier if the book is well structured in chapters and sections, and contains a detailed table of contents and one or several indexes (see chapter 2).
2. *Type of information requested* varies from the most concrete (e.g., identifying a person or a place) to the most abstract (e.g., identifying equivalence or difference between trends). The type of information requested is equivalent to the question focus in the QUEST model presented earlier. The ability to address complex or abstract question focuses depends on the searcher's prior knowledge or experience of the domain.
3. *Type of match* characterizes the distance between the requested information and the information actually found in the text. This distance depends on both the type of *search strategy* (e.g., locate a single piece vs. integrate several pieces of information) and the amount and type of *inferencing* required to match the text's content with requested information.
4. *Plausibility of distractors* depends on the presence and location of information that shares some features with the requested information. In some cases, the question will only match one information category (e.g., a section) in the text. All the other categories will be clearly irrelevant. In other, more tricky cases, several categories may

seem relevant, but only one of them will actually contain the requested information.

Based on the analysis of 217 document search tasks taken from five national surveys on adult document literacy, Mosenthal (1996) showed that these four dimensions accounted for 80% of the variance in task difficulty. Thus, when searching an external source, the subject's strategy is strongly influenced by the amount of information to be searched, its internal organization, and the relationship between the search question and the nature of the information found in the external source.

Mosenthal's typology suggests that, depending on the type of search task, text search may involve superficial or deeper processing of the text's content. Imagine, for instance, that a student is asked to search the text on atomic models (Table 4.1) in order to locate "the type of particles used in Rutherford's experiment." Based on the analysis of the question focus, and assuming minimal knowledge of the word "particles," the student may expect the target to be a name or a code that will most likely appear next to this word. This defines a rather precise criterion that can be met without engaging in deep reading comprehension processes (at least when the answer is explicit). On the other hand, using text information to "compare Rutherford's and Thomson's models" will require the student to reconstruct coherent representations of the respective properties of the two models by carefully rereading the relevant text passages. Moreover, as pointed out earlier, the student will have to establish connections between the two macrocomponents of the mental representation, which he or she may have failed to do while reading the text for the first time (Einstein, McDaniel, Owen, & Coté, 1990; see also Newell & Winograd, 1989). In the latter case, searching the text may improve the students' understanding of the content.

In the next sections, I examine in more detail the cognitive processes involved in text-based search activities. Then I review the effects of question answering and search on comprehension and learning from documents.

4.2. RELEVANCE-BASED TEXT PROCESSING: TOWARD AN INTEGRATED FRAMEWORK

Exactly what do people do when they use texts for specific purposes? It may seem difficult to provide a simple, general answer, considering the extreme diversity of search activities and contexts. Contrary to text comprehension and memory, text-based search has not been the subject of much attention on the part of cognitive scientists. One reason may be the implicit assumption that reading for comprehension and reading in order to find task-relevant information rely on the same underlying mental processes. There is, however, evidence that being assigned specific perspectives or reading objectives influences readers' encoding and retrieval of text information (Baillet & Keenan, 1986; Britton et al., 1985; see chapter 1, section 1.4). In addition, information search theorists have argued that locating information in text relies on cognitive processes distinct from text comprehension. Guthrie and Kirsch (1987) argued that locating information in text involves specific processes, such as analogical reasoning, which may partly depend on a person's general literacy and/or domain expertise. Based on qualitative and quantitative analyses of professional workers' performance on a range of typical document-based tasks, they found little or no correlation between tasks that required locating information, on the one hand, and tasks that required text comprehension and recall, on the other hand. Empirical evidence from national and international surveys does suggest that searching documents involves specific cognitive processes (Kirsch et al., 2002).

4.2.1. Process Models of Document Search

Several "models" have been proposed to represent the mental processes that go on as a person uses a document. As pointed out by Mosenthal and Kirsch (1991), they are often "exploratory" models in that they seldom refer to specific psychological variables or processes that may explain variations of performance. Guthrie (1988) proposed a general account of the cognitive processes involved in locating information from simple and highly structured documents such as flight schedules and pay stubs. According to Guthrie's model, searching a document requires five distinct steps (Fig. 4.2). First, the subject constructs a mental representation of his or her goal, based on the search question or assign-

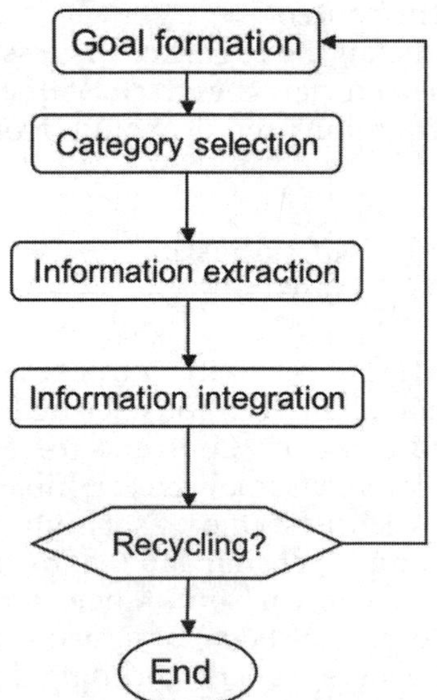

FIG. 4.2. A simplified representation of Guthrie's (1988) model of document search.

ment. Second, the subject selects a category of information, for instance, a column in a table. Third, the subject extracts a piece of content information (e.g., a number in a table). Fourth, if requested by the task, the subject integrates the new piece of information with previously extracted information; and finally, the subject recycles through the first four steps if further information is still needed.

Guthrie (1988) reported empirical evidence that people's performance in search tasks is specifically related to the effectiveness of those processes. In his first experiment, 26 undergraduates were asked to answer three questions about flight schedules. Several aspects of their search behavior relevant to the model components were recorded (e.g., search time and categories opened in the document). Then, variables assessing the last four steps of the model were entered in a multiple regression analysis of search time. The four variables accounted for 68% of the variance in search time. Experiment 2 showed a positive transfer from one task to another, as evidenced by large gains (between 50% and 342%) on the selection and integration components. According to Guthrie, the latter result suggests that the proposed model of document search is not bound to a particular task or domain. Instead, it is representative of how people generally perform search tasks in documents.

Mosenthal and Kirsch (1991) investigated further the variables that characterize document information, document-based tasks, and the processes required to achieve them. They proposed a model of document processing based on materials, tasks, and data collected as part of the National Assessment of Educational Progress (NAEP) young adult literacy assessment. Their model assumes that document use can be described in terms of *document variables, task variables* and *process variables*. Document variables allow one to characterize a document in terms of amount of information and complexity. Mosenthal and Kirsch proposed a grammar of document information that assumes that documents are made up of three levels of information: semantic features, specifics and organizing categories. *Semantic features* are similar to propositional components (i.e., they include arguments and relational terms). *Specifics* are groups of arguments and relational terms, forming propositional expressions. Finally, *organizing categories* are overarching terms or expressions that reflect a common feature of a group of specifics. Organizing categories may be explicit in the document, or they may have to be inferred by the reader. Along with their document grammar, Mosenthal and Kirsch proposed a document processing model that identifies five steps: identify a goal, establish a given information and new information frame, search the document to locate given information, identify new information, and verify the sufficiency of the new information. They analyzed 61 tasks taken from the NAEP survey and found that a selection of document, task, and processing variables accounted for 89% of the variance in the distribution of percentage correct scores. The variables were: the number of specifics in the document, the number of categories and specifics requested by the task, degrees of correspondence between the task and the document, and the type of process required to match the new information frame and document information (from literal match to high level inference). The authors argued that their model added explanatory power to previous studies of document use, because they could check specific assumptions within a single operational framework.

Simple process models apply for explicit search tasks that merely require the location of specific information pieces within readily available documents that possess a clear top-level structure. Text-based search, however, may depart from this basic situation in several ways.

First, there is not always a document that is meant to be the necessary and sufficient source of information, as assumed in Guthrie's model. In many search tasks, the subject has to rely on both internal resources (e.g., knowledge stored in long-term memory) and external information resources. For instance, when asked about Rutherford's experiment, the subject may first need to remember who Rutherford was, then look up an appropriate text to find out about the characteristics of his experiment. Whether the solution to the search problem may be partly or entirely found in memory or in documents must be thought of and decided by the subject.

Second, category selection and information extraction are not always as easily separated as in the case of timetables or pay stubs. In continuous texts, for example, the contents of a paragraph may be used as a selection cue or as a source of information. Thus, selection and extraction may occur simultaneously, as the searcher tries to assess the relevance of a text passage. In fact, some extraction is necessary before any relevance assessment takes place. Relevance, however, may be assessed either from descriptions of the contents (such as in headings and other text organizers), from the contents, or from other information characteristic of the document, such as its source, length, intended audience, and so forth (see chapter 3). The central process here is relevance assessment, a process that determines whether a piece of information is considered for further treatment, and if so, how it will be used in the resolution of the search task.

Finally, the relationship between the information contained in the document and the response to be issued is not always straightforward. Extraction of information may sometimes require the person to actually reason about the information found in the document, especially when the search question is complex or ill-defined. In such cases, the subject will gradually construct an internal model of the response (or solution) to be output on completion of the task. Such a construction may take several cycles, as already considered in Guthrie's (1988) model. It may also require a wide range of cognitive processes (e.g., construction, updating, and revision of the response model) until the model reaches a satisfaction criterion. Such processes are actually similar to the memory-based processes involved in text comprehension (see chapter 1).

4.2.2. The TRACE Model of Document Processing

In this section I outline a generalized model of relevance-based document processing. I use the phrase *relevance-based* to designate any situation where the reader's purpose is to gather information that fits a preexisting need. I do not make any assumption as to where the preexisting need may originate (i.e., through external directions or queries vs. the subject's own will). Furthermore, my goal is to account for the various ways in which a text (or set of texts) may fit the reader's needs: by containing a specific piece of information, such as a date or a name, or by being useful and relevant as a whole. According to this view, the central components of text processing are the *construction of a task model (or goal formation),* based on internal needs and environmental constraints; the *assessment of document relevance,* based on available information resources and search tools; and the cyclical *extraction and integration of content information,* in order to construct an internal response model (Fig. 4.3). This descriptive model may thus be characterized as Task-based Relevance Assessment and Content Extraction, or the TRACE Model.

The TRACE model represented in Fig. 4.3 takes into account the information and memory resources available to the subject. *Information resources* (left column) include (a) any material representation of the task requirements such as written questions, directions, or assignments; (b) the external sources of information available, such as texts, documents, or electronic information systems, along with the attached search de-

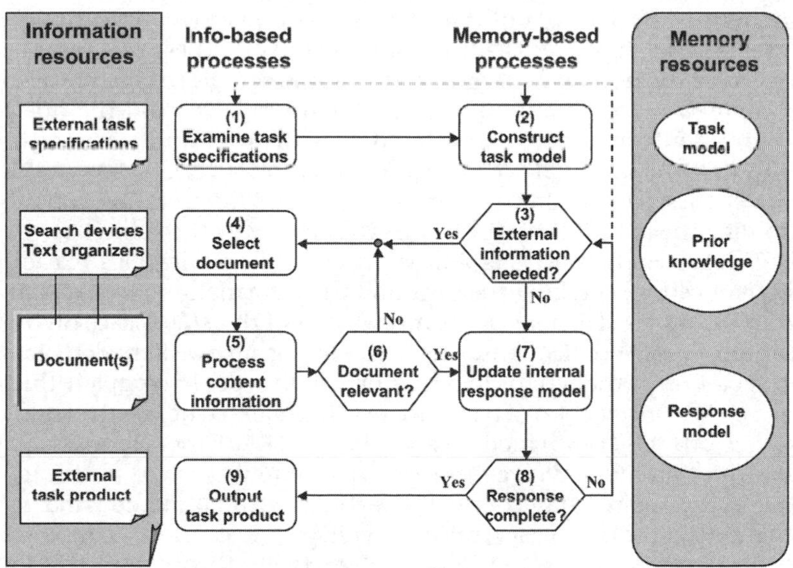

FIG. 4.3. The Task-based Relevance Assessment and Content Extraction, or TRACE Model of document processing.

vices and text organizers; and (c) the task products output by the subject as part of his or her completion of the task, such as notes, drafts, responses, or essays. Other contextual resources relevant to the search task, such as the time available or the possibility to tap additional information resources, are not represented in Fig. 4.3.

Memory resources (Fig. 4.3, right column) include the knowledge resources that may be brought to bear in connection to the search task. This includes the subject's prior knowledge of the content area, knowledge of the information resources, and prior experience with similar search tasks. Knowledge resources also include metacognitive processes such as one's feeling of knowing and executive control processes (see also chapter 1, Fig. 1.2). The memory resources represented in Fig. 4.3 also include memory representations that are built as part of the subject's activity: First is the *task model*, or internal representation of the search task to be completed; second is the *response model*, or internal representation of the response to be output.

According to the TRACE model, document search unfolds as a series of processes, as indicated in the central part of Fig. 4.3. The processes are represented in two broad categories: To the left are *info-based processes*, or processes that use information resources (documents) as primary input or output; to the right are *memory-based processes*, or processes that use memory resources as primary input or output. The specific information or memory resources that are used by each process are not represented in Fig. 4.3 because there is not always a simple term-to-term correspondence between a particular process and a particular resource. Furthermore, it must be pointed out that the distinction between info-based and memory-based processes is a fuzzy one, as most of these processes actually involve the two types of resources to some extent. For instance, when examining a search question, the subject must both read the question (i.e., use an information resource) and activate prior knowledge in order to interpret the question (i.e., use a memory resource).

Under these circumstances, step 1 of document processing consists of examining the initial set of constraints that motivate the subject's activity, which I represent here in a simplified way as "*task specifications.*" Reading a written question, checking the time and the information resources available are examples of actions performed as part of this step. Based on the acquisition of task specifications, the subject builds up a task model, that is, a representation of the actions to be performed in order to complete the task (step 2). The construction of a task model is similar to the "goal formation" stage in Guthrie's (1988) model. However, the TRACE model considers that goal formation may involve metacognitive actions, such as planning. For instance, the subject may consider a particular search method and/or information repository, if several are available. Task model construction may also proceed continuously and interactively throughout the search process, when the initial context does not contain an explicit and exhaustive definition of the search objective. The elaborateness of the task model may also depend on the subject's level of experience with search tasks in general, with the particular type of search task being performed, or with the content area being searched (see Lazonder, Biermans, & Wopereis, 2000; Marchionini, 1995; Rouet & Tricot, 1996).

Step 3 is a decision point, where the subject must decide whether some external information is actually needed (Fig. 4.3, step 3). This takes an examination of the knowledge already available, as well as a specification of the external information to be acquired, if any. If relevant information may be directly retrieved from memory, then the subject can build up an internal response model. At this stage, several memory-based strategies may be considered (see section 4.1.1; see also Reder, 1987; Singer, 2003). The TRACE model thus acknowledges that memory search and text-based search activities are frequently intertwined in naturalistic document use. If external information is actually needed, then the subject must select a document among those available (step 4). This may be done in diverse ways, which are not explicitly represented in Fig. 4.3. One way is to use the search devices and text organizers available, if any. Another way is to browse directly through content information.

Once a document or text passage has been selected, the subject must examine its content (step 5) and assess its relevance (step 6). If the document or passage is not relevant, then the subject must recycle through the document selection step. If the document is relevant, then its content may be used to update the response model (step 7). Steps 5, 6, and 7 lie at the heart of the search process. When search is performed in complex documents, these steps may involve complex subprocesses, such as reading from text and diagram, checking the accuracy, consistency, and importance of the information, incrementing, revising, or updating a mental model (see chapter 1). When a coherent model has been obtained from the document, the subject must check whether the model is satisfactory given the task specifications (step 8). This step requires the subject to consider both the initial task model (what was asked) and the current response model. It is thus a rather demanding step in terms of working memory resources. If the response is incomplete, the subject must find out whether additional external information can be found. The assessment of information needs, document selection, processing, and evaluation may thus recycle until a satisfactory stage has been reached. In some cases, however, the initial task model may be inaccurate. This happens, for instance, when the subject has not interpreted correctly the external task specifications. The subject may then decide to update the task model or even to reconsider the task requirements.

The process model represented in Fig. 4.3 extends prior representations of the search activity, in that it includes both memory and information-based processes, and places relevance assessment at the center of the process. It is still, however, a rather simplified representation, where important aspects of complex search tasks are omitted. For instance, in this representation the external task product is output at once at the end of the process. In naturalistic search tasks, the subject may have to return to the search assignments, or to reconsider his or her search strategies in an opportunistic fashion. In addition, it must be pointed out that in the current state of the art, the TRACE model is a descriptive rather than explanatory representation, as many of its features have not been empirically tested. The features of the model are nevertheless consistent with empirical research findings, as reviewed next.

4.2.3. Individual Influences in Relevance-Based Information Processing

How do cognitive skills and prior knowledge influence the effectiveness of document search? Differences between skilled and less-skilled searchers have been documented in many studies. THE TRACE model may be helpful in integrating and interpreting the evidence. For instance, the TRACE model distinguishes the examination of task specification, on the one hand, and the construction of a task model, on the other hand. This distinction is consistent with the classical human factors distinction between the prescribed and subjective task model. Domain novices and experts, for instance, may not interpret search questions in the same way (Marchionini, 1995; Rouet, 2003; Symons & Pressley, 1993).

The source selection step in the TRACE model also fits the finding that for inexperienced text users, choosing a relevant source of information is sometimes a problem (see section 4.1.2). Children often seem to have trouble knowing whether they can answer a question from memory or whether they should search an external source (Raphael & Pearson, 1985; Rouet, 1991).

Another important parameter in document search is the use of high-level textual organizers to accelerate the location of relevant categories. Dreher and Guthrie (1990) argued that efficient searchers devote more attention to the selection of relevant categories of information (Fig. 4.3, step 4). In their study, thirty-one 10th-grade students searched a textbook chapter presented on a computer screen to answer simple and complex questions. Content information was accessible through a table of contents, an index, or through page turning. Efficient versus less efficient searchers were identified based on their total search time. For complex questions, efficient searchers spent a larger proportion of time selecting information categories from the index or table of contents. Less efficient searchers spent more time extracting information from selected passages of the chapter. Dreher and Guthrie concluded that the mastery of text organizers and selection devices is an important component of document literacy. A study by Rouet and Chollet (2000) also found that elementary grade students frequently ignore the use of indexes and tables of contents when searching an encyclopedia. Mastering text organizers involves a declarative and a procedural component: First, the student must know about text organizers and their functions (Garner et al., 1986; Rouet & Eme, 2002; see also chapter 2). Second, the student must know when the use of each type of organizer is relevant, that is, they must possess efficient task-sensitive strategies (Cross & Paris, 1988; Garner, 1987).

Variability in search skill is also found in studies involving adult participants. Goldman and Durán (1988) examined the strategies used by college students in order to answer questions from a chapter-length oceanography text. They proposed a typology of solution strategies, which considers both the type of resource used during search (memory, text, memory + text, memory + text + computation) and the type of activities performed by students while searching (reanalyze question, text-based reasoning, process monitoring, product monitoring). Goldman and Durán found that students' use of strategy depended both on their level of prior knowledge, their native language (3 out of 7 participants were nonnative English speakers), and the type of question. The simplest strategies were found for verbatim questions, which had a high success rate for most students. The novices, especially nonnative speakers, had many more problems when the question required vocabulary conversion or paraphrasing. These findings illustrate the connection between a task model and the source selection step of the TRACE model (Fig. 4.3, steps 2 and 3). They also demonstrate the importance of memory resources (e.g., vocabulary and content area knowledge) in students' evaluation of document relevance (step 6) and in their assessment of response completeness or appropriateness (step 8).

Indeed, acquiring new knowledge in a content area improves students' search strategies. In a study by Symons and Pressley (1993), psychology students were asked to search a psychology manual in order to answer 10 questions. Five questions were related to the topics studied during the first semester, and five were related to the topics studied during the second semester. The students were also asked to search an earth science textbook in order to answer eight other (control) questions. Three groups of students were tested: One at the beginning of the school year, one in the middle, and one at the end. Search effectiveness (defined as the number of questions students could answer in less than 8 minutes) increased with exposure to the topic, regardless of verbal ability and academic success. A qualitative analysis of students' search strategies showed that the increase in search effectiveness was partly due to a decrease in students' need to review passages previously visited during the search. Subjects' background knowledge may facilitate the search activity in two ways: First, background knowledge facilitates the production of question related inferences. Such inferences, in turn, facilitate the selection of relevant information categories in a document (step 4). Background knowledge may also ease the process of updating the response model across cycles of passage selection, evaluation, and comprehension, that is, integrating relevant information from text sections (Afflerbach, 1990).

Thus, people are faster and more accurate at searching documents when they possess prior knowledge about the topic. However, one may wonder about the scope of this effect. Are people more efficient in general when searching about topics in their area of academic training or professional exercise? Or is this effect limited to topics that people have just learned about? For instance, are graduate psychology students faster and more accurate when searching documents in psychology? In other words, is general domain-dependent knowledge involved (e.g., text schemata, discipline expertise; see chapter 3), as opposed to more specific topic-related knowledge?

A recent study (Rouet, 2003) addressed this question by comparing the search performance of two groups of graduate students from two distinct areas: psychology and geography. The students were asked to search simple electronic documents in order to locate answers to four questions. Each student had to search a document dealing with a topic in psychology (i.e., anorexia), and a document dealing with a topic in geography (i.e., Peru). A pretest confirmed that students in each group outperformed the other group in answering content-related questions about their respective domain (e.g., "What type of vegetation is found in Peru?" "When were cases of anorexia documented for the first time?").

The document was presented online using a computer program. The text could be accessed through a hierarchical menu-based interface (see next chapter). The main menu included six categories (e.g., "a history of anorexia"), and each submenu contained between two and five topics (e.g., "earliest cases of anorexia in history"). The two documents were very similar as regards length (slightly over 2,000 words) and readability (Flesh index value of about 71).

The participants answered two specific questions and two more general ones. Specific questions targeted a piece of information located within a single document subtopic. General questions targeted information found in various subtopics. It was assumed that, provided that students formed an accurate task model (Fig. 4.3, step 2), general questions would result in longer, "integrative" search patterns because students would attempt to integrate various sources in their response model (step 7). These questions would also increase students' cognitive load (Sweller, 1994), due to the need to sustain prior solution elements in working memory. This might result in a decay in the initial task model, and to more en route reexamination of task specifications. Finally, students with more prior knowledge should be able to learn the structure of the document as they search through it, reflecting their better integration of information across trials and search cycles within trials. High prior knowledge students would thus exhibit a more accurate long-term memory representation of the document structure.

As predicted, the experiment showed a strong effect of question type on students' search patterns. General questions took more time (129 seconds vs. 76 seconds, on average), and resulted in more question lookbacks than specific questions. Furthermore, the question lookbacks did not occur during the same phase of search for general and specific questions. For general questions, students looked back more frequently when selecting a new topic in a menu or submenu, reflecting a difficulty at the level of information integration. Interestingly, the experiment did not find any main effect of students' major discipline on search time or search patterns. Students did tend to be faster in their area of specialization, but the within-group variance was too large to yield any significant difference. As predicted, however, students performed better on the document structure incidental recall task for the topic within their area of specialization. The lack of prior knowledge influence on the participants' search patterns may be explained by the fact that they were graduate students with a great deal of experience in document-based search tasks. Domain-independent search strategies learned through college education may overshadow more subtle domain-specific heuristics.

In short, information search may be seen as a complex process that unfolds as a series of processing cycles. Search is governed by subjects' goal representation and their ability to determine whether their current state of knowledge fits the requirements of the goal representation. Document search requires numerous control mechanisms, for example, assessing the relevance of information categories, making decisions, and holding intermediate information in mind while pursuing the search. Individual variables, such as the amount of prior knowledge one possesses about the domain, may facilitate search in lengthy documents.

4.3. HOW SEARCHING INFLUENCES TEXT COMPREHENSION

In the previous section, I emphasized that document search processes are distinct from those at work in continuous reading and text comprehension. In naturalistic contexts, however, the two activities are often interspersed. As noted by Armbruster and Armstrong (1993), for instance, reading assignments in elementary schools often involve reading, comprehending, and searching for specific information in texts. Searching for information influences the way students focus their attention while reading. As a result, question or search tasks inserted in texts may affect students' understanding of the materials they read. This section focuses on the complex relationship that exists between reading, question answering, and text comprehension. It is partly drawn from a series of theoretical and empirical studies I conducted with Vidal-Abarca and other colleagues from the universities of Poitiers (France) and Valencia (Spain). Our purpose was to better understand what happens when a student reads a text with the purpose of answering a question. Specifically, we wanted to find out how different types of questions (e.g., questions about general ideas vs. questions about specific details) influence both the reading behavior and the student's long-term memory representation.

4.3.1. Inserted Questions and Depth of Processing

The effects of inserted questions and adjunct tasks on the comprehension of instructional materials have been extensively studied in psychology and educational sciences (see Andre, 1979; Hamilton, 1985; Hartley & Davies, 1976; Rickards, 1979 for reviews). For Rothkopf (1982), questions are a means to stimulate and guide "mathemagenic" activities, or activities that promote learning. Questions help readers focus their attention on specific aspects of the materials to be learned, or to specific forms of reasoning or inferences. They play a role similar to other adjuncts such as study directions or instructional objectives. Indeed, there is ample evidence that study directions, adjunct questions, or instructional objectives deeply influence the processing of instructional materials. Moreover, the effect of instructional adjuncts varies qualitatively as a function of two main parameters (Rickards, 1979): The direction of the question (i.e., forward or backward in the text) and the kind of processing it triggers (i.e., specific or general information processing). Consequently, four types of inserted questions may be defined (Fig. 4.4). *Backward questions* encourage the mental review of the previously read text, whereas *forward questions* focus students' attention on specific information in the upcoming portion of the text (Rothkopf & Bisbicos, 1967). *Specific questions* focus on a single piece of information, whereas *general questions* may involve whole text passages.

General, or "higher level" questions facilitate deep comprehension, that is, the integration of text elements and the production of inferences (Andre, 1979). Andre argued that higher level questions encourage readers to pay attention to broader portions of the text, and thus help them structure their mental representation of the text. Wixson (1983) found that textually explicit, textually implicit, or schema-based questions each promoted the corresponding type of inferences in 10th-graders, as evidenced in a delayed recall task.

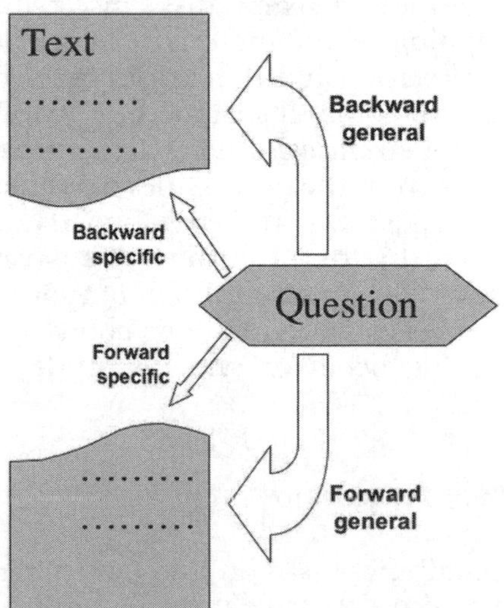

FIG. 4.4. A simple typology of inserted questions.

There is also evidence that searching a text in order to answer questions is a learning-effective activity. Andre and Thieman (1988) found that, after answering comprehension questions, students who reviewed the text in order to check their answers obtained better scores on the same questions repeated later, compared to students who received external feedback or no feedback on their initial answers. Younger or less able learners may need some guidance in order to articulate the questions and text information. Cataldo and Cornoldi (1998) observed that when 6th- and 7th-grade poor comprehenders were asked to locate and underline relevant information in the text before actually answering a set of comprehension questions, they later obtained better scores on a comprehension posttest. Students with poor learning skills may not engage spontaneously in the type of focused reading required to locate target information in the text.

An important condition for text search to be effective is that an explicit answer has to be constructed. Newell and Winograd (1989) compared the effects of note taking, question answering, and analytic essay writing on eight 11th-grade students' recall of 400- to 650-word expository passages on various topics. Compared to note taking and question answering, analytic essay writing fostered the recall of gist and relational information. They concluded that analytic essay writing "seemed to provide an occasion for the students to represent to themselves relationships that occurred in the connected discourse" (p. 211). The amount of relational processing may also account for the differential effects of various types of inserted questions. Vidal-Abarca, Mengual, Sanjose, and Rouet (1996) asked high school students to study a physics text, then to review it in order to solve either text explicit or inference questions. The students who received inference questions scored better on recall and inferential comprehension tests. However, these results were only partially replicated in another study (Vidal-Abarca, Gilabert, & Rouet, 1998), possibly because the latter study involved students with much more prior knowledge of the topic.

Exactly what are the processing differences between high level and low level questions? Although this distinction has been used extensively in the literature (see Andre, 1979; Halpain, Glover, & Harvey, 1985; Whilite, 1985), its precise definition varies from one author to another. In the context of text-based question answering, a distinction between high level and low level questions corresponds to at least three overlapping criteria: the raw amount of information relevant to the question; the fact that questions refer to the text's microstructure or macrostructure; and the fact that they refer to the textbase or to the situation model.

The first criterion is the most concrete and easily figured out: Some questions focus on single pieces of information (e.g., a date, a name, a figure), whereas others require a whole bunch of documents to be dealt with (e.g., complex historical controversies; see chapter 3).

The distinction between high level and low level questions is also partly related to Kintsch and van Dijk's (1978) concept of a text's microstructure and macrostructure (see also chapter 1). The microstructure is a hierarchized list of semantic propositions that are found in or drawn from a text. The macrostructure is made of a network of macropropositions, or propositions that condense and subsume detailed information. Part of the macrostructure is usually explicit in the text (through, e.g., introductions or summaries), whereas the other part must be constructed by the reader through the application of macrorules. High level questions are often implicitly defined as questions that focus on the text's macrostructure, whereas low level questions focus on a smaller group of semantic propositions, or even on a single proposition.

The third way to look at the distinction between high versus low level questions has to do with the amount of reasoning or inferences on the part of the reader. Some questions may be answered by using information found explicitly in the text, whereas others require the reader to draw on both textual information and his or her own previous knowledge. This fits van Dijk and Kintsch's (1983) distinction between a textbase and a situation model.

In practice, the terms of "high level" and "low level" questions are used to designate questions that differ as to the amount of information, type of information, and type of processing required, with no attempt to isolate one of these dimensions. More recent studies, however, tend to use a more specific categorization of questions. I return to this point in the next chapter.

High and low level questions differ in their respective attentional demands, that is, in the amount of mental effort required from the reader to deal with the question. Halpain et al. (1985) conducted five experiments in order to study the influence of question type on readers' allocation of attention during reading. They presented university students a 1,200-word expository text, in which high and low level questions dealing with the contents of each paragraph were inserted. Using a secondary task method, Halpain et al. found that reading paragraphs preceded by high level questions required more cognitive resources that reading paragraphs preceded by low level questions. The authors also found that when questions were presented after the corresponding paragraphs (i.e., backward questions), reading high level questions took more resources that reading low level questions. The difference disappeared when questions were presented before the relevant paragraphs (i.e., forward questions). Thus, when the students did not have the opportunity to read the text prior to the questions, the amount of resources devoted to high and low questions did not differ. These findings confirm the view that high level backward questions require the reader to review and integrate several text elements, creating more connections in long-term memory. According to this view, the process of answering text-based high level questions is more resource-consuming, but, as a counterpart, it promotes deep comprehension.

4.3.2. Investigating Text Search Patterns

Studies of inserted questions strongly suggest that high- and low-level questions trigger different types of memory processes. When question answering is based on reading or rereading a text, high- and low-level questions might also foster different patterns of text reviewing. This was confirmed in experiments looking at what students do while answering questions from text. Vidal-Abarca et al. (1998) conducted two experiments in which high school students (experiment 1) and university students (experiment 2) read a 2,500-word physics text presented paragraph-by-paragraph on a computer screen. The presentation was made using the Select-the-Text software (Goldman & Saul, 1990), which allowed the researchers to know precisely what paragraph the students were reading at a given point in time. In order to do this, the text was presented one page at a time on a computer screen (Fig. 4.5). Section headings and subheadings were directly readable, whereas each letter of the content paragraphs was replaced by an asterisk. Clicking on a paragraph with the computer mouse caused the whole paragraph to appear in a readable form (in the example shown in Fig. 4.5, the paragraph just below the heading "Le modèle de Dalton" [Dalton's model] has been selected using the mouse and appears in a readable form).

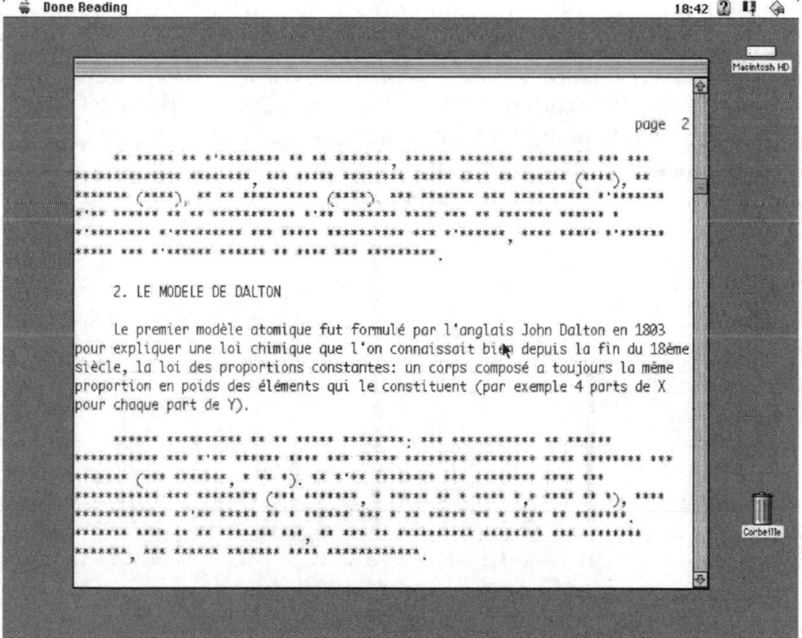

FIG. 4.5. The text presentation procedure used to record the students' review patterns (from Rouet, Vidal-Abarca, Bert-Erboul, & Millogo, 2001).

After reading the text entirely once, half of the students answered text-based explicit questions, whereas the other half answered global and inference questions. In both conditions, the students were allowed to search the text in order to locate answers to the questions. Answering both types of questions required the students to focus on the same textual information. Vidal-Abarca et al. (1998) found that students who answered explicit questions searched fewer number of paragraphs per question than those answering global and inference questions. Moreover, students who answered global and inference questions significantly spent less time searching information than students who answered text-based explicit questions. They concluded that the two types of questions promoted different types of text-based reasoning.

Using a similar procedure, Rouet, Vidal-Abarca, et al. (2001) asked undergraduate students to search a 35-paragraph text in order to answer high-level or low-level questions. Again, they observed that each type of question promoted specific review patterns. Figure 4.6 shows examples of search patterns for one high-level question and one low-level question.

The high-level question illustrated in Fig. 4.6. (light bars) required the students to compare Thomson's and Rutherford's atomic models. As apparent in Fig. 4.6, two subsections of the text were the most reviewed: the passage comprised of paragraphs 17 and 20, which presented the features of Thomson's atomic model, and the passage comprised of paragraphs 30 and 33, which presented those of Rutherford's model. Some paragraphs of the introduction (1–3) and the sections surrounding the critical ones were also reviewed. In contrast, the low-level question (dark bars) required the students to locate the type of particles used in Rutherford's experiment. This information was found in paragraph 21,

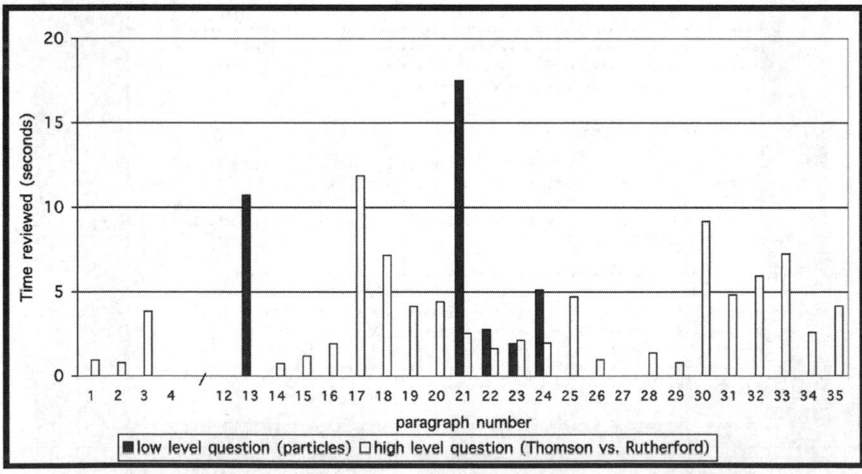

FIG. 4.6. Patterns of text review for one high-level and one low-level question (from Rouet & Vidal-Abarca, 2002).

which was the most reviewed by students in the low-level questions group, as shown in Fig. 4.6. Some students also reviewed the paragraphs following the target paragraph. The unexpectedly high review time on paragraph 13 was due to one student who mistakenly thought that the question had to do with radioactivity, the topic dealt in paragraph 13, which also mentioned particles. In this particular case, reviewing the wrong paragraph still allowed the student to provide the correct answer ("alpha particles").

The analysis of review patterns confirms that answering high-level questions is more demanding because the target information is less precisely located and must be integrated across different text paragraphs. But the higher demand probably contributes to making high-level questions more learning effective than lower level questions.

In sum, many empirical results converge on the notion that high-level questions promote deep comprehension, in part because they impose higher attentional demands on the readers. Graesser and Franklin's (1990) QUEST model accounts in part for the benefits of inserted questions on text comprehension. Because of the limitations in students' knowledge and processing resources outlined in the previous section, one single reading of a scientific text may not be enough for the student to establish connections between information distant in the text. Answering questions from memory allows the students to reactivate selectively part of the information (the question acts as a retrieval cue), and to reinforce connections between the information pieces needed to answer (through arc-search and coactivation in working memory). These processes also explain the differential effects of high- and low-level questions. Strictly speaking, only questions that require the reactivation of at least two pieces of knowledge have a chance to improve the integration of representational constituents in long-term memory. Questions that require the retrieval of a single piece of data may only strengthen the memory trace of target information. The effectiveness of high-level questions, however, is conditional on the student's ability to retrieve the various pieces of relevant information from memory, a process that requires that a minimal level of comprehension has been achieved.

4.3.3. Asking Questions About Text

The preceding sections addressed the issue of how people answer questions from memory or from text, and how answering various types of questions affects what a person comprehends from the text. In naturalistic reading situations, however, readers may have to generate their own questions, either as part of their effort to understand, or, precisely, because of their failure to comprehend the information. This section briefly reviews the relation between prior knowledge, question asking, and text comprehension.

In a seminal study of question generation, Miyake and Norman (1979) examined the relationship between readers' level of prior knowledge, the difficulty of the text, and the number and type of questions generated during learning. Sixty university students were assigned to either a high or low prior knowledge group. The high prior knowledge group (or experts) was trained to use a computerized text editor. Then, both groups were asked to learn about a new text editor by reading a manual that contained either simple or more difficult explanations. The simple version explained five text editing commands. A concrete example of each command was provided before the general explanation. The complex version presented seven commands and two special characters. Instead of an example, more details were given about the command. Novice learners asked more questions when using the simple version of the manual, whereas experts asked more questions with the complex version. Miyake and Norman (1979) concluded that prior knowledge is indeed needed for one to be able to ask questions about new information. They suggested that prior knowledge is needed for learners to know what they do not know, that is, what they should ask questions about.

More recently, researchers attempted to provide theoretical models of the process of question asking. Otero and Graesser (2001) introduced the PREG model in order to explain how students generate questions when reading scientific texts. The model is based on the general view that text comprehension rests on several levels of representation—surface representation, textbase, and situation model (see chapter 1). The PREG model assumes that questions are generated when the reader notices a discrepancy between the information found in a text and his or her prior knowledge, a state called *cognitive disequilibrium*. A specific prediction of the PREG model is that discrepancies at different levels of text representation and/or knowledge objects will trigger different types of questions. Otero and Graesser proposed a typology of the circumstances where readers may generate questions. The first category concerns discrepancies at the word level. This includes questions about unknown words (e.g., "What does asphyxia mean?"), or about referents. In the latter case, the question is about the concept referred to by the word. For instance, the term *bond* may be known in general, but its meaning in the context of "bonds that link hydrogen and oxygen" may not be known.

The second level of questioning involves discrepancies at the statement level. Two cases are considered: in the first case, the reader is unable to construct a mental representation for the meaning of a statement. For instance, students may not be able to represent the fact that "some gases are soluble in water," even though each word taken individually makes sense to them. In the second case, statements are discrepant with the reader's prior knowledge representation. For instance, students may draw inappropriate links between a situation described in the text and their own experience (e.g., water vapor in clouds vs. vapor from a pot of boiling water). Other situations include the construction of causal chains, the representation of negative statements, or the degree of specification of information in text. Finally, the PREG model also considers discrepancies at the level of links between statements. Just like statements, some links may be incomprehensible (e.g., "pollution causes a decrease in water oxygen"), or they may clash with the reader's knowledge (e.g., "turbulences slow down the falling of droplets from clouds").

Otero and Graesser proposed a production rule formalism to predict which questions should be generated from a text. They expressed a production rule for each case identified in their typology of text-reader discrepancy. The condition part of the production rule contained the discrepancy situation, and the action part of the rule contained a specific type of question. For instance: If statement X cannot be represented at the situation model level, then ask "what does X mean?"

They applied the production system to a set of text-based questions identified as part of a previous study. Based on teachers' evaluations of students' knowledge about concepts, statements, and links, they predicted occurrences of questions using the PREG production mechanism. They found that the model accounted for a vast majority of the questions actually asked by 8th- and 12th-grade students. Graesser and Olde (2003) provided further evidence that question asking may be explained in terms of a production rule system in which the learner adjusts the question to the type and level of cognitive disequilibrium. They found a correlation between college students' level of understanding of a mechanical device (e.g., a lock) and the type of questions they asked when confronted with breakdown scenarios. Better learners asked "good" questions, that is, questions that matched a predefined list of plausible faults that may explain the breakdown. Thus, the quality of questions generated by students as they are reasoning about incidents or breakdowns may be taken as a predictor of their capacity to understand the device's functioning at a deep level.

Empirical evidence and current theories of question asking suggest that merely encouraging students to ask questions while learning may not particularly help poor learners. Training students to ask "good" questions, however, may result in significant learning gains (Davey & McBride, 1986; Rosenshine, Meister, & Chapman, 1996). What matters is the type of cognitive processing induced by the question asking or question answering activity. In order to be learning-effective, questioning should promote the identification of important information, as well as the integration of information units into coherent long-term memory representations.

CONCLUSIONS

Reading documents takes place in a wide range of contexts and requires a diversity of strategies. In some contexts, like reading a single text in order to prepare for a memory test, the most efficient strategy consists of reading the text entirely, in order to understand the concepts, facts, and events presented in the document, as well as their coherence relationships. In other contexts, however, the reader needs to locate one or several pieces of information in order to answer a particular question or to solve a particular problem. In these contexts, the reader has to engage in a different strategy called *document search*.

Question answering from text and from memory share a number of dimensions. In both cases, the subject has to parse the question or problem statement in order to identify its focus. When performed solely from memory, the question focus guides the propagation of activation throughout memory structures until a match is found. Answering questions from documents is potentially a more complex activity, because it involves memory management, text selection, reading, and evaluation of content information. Well-designed texts, on the other hand, provide the reader with many content cues that may be quickly parsed in order to locate relevant categories (see chapter 2). But then again, the reader must be aware of those cues in order to use them in effective ways.

I have proposed a cognitive model of document search called the Task-based Relevance Assessment and Content Extraction model (TRACE), which takes into account the information resources and the memory resources brought to bear when searching. The model involves a series of steps and decision points, which take either the information resources or the memory resources as a main input. Some processes, however, require the use of both types of resources. At the heart of the search process is a step called *relevance assessment*, in which the subject checks whether a particular source of information (a document, or a passage within a document) matches the information needs as elicited in his or her task model. Other important processes are the selection of an appropriate source of information (i.e., knowing whether to search one's own long-term memory or an external source), and the updating of the response, which may require several cycles of document selection, evaluation, and integration. The TRACE model draws on earlier works on information location in technical documents, while taking into account the specific requirements of complex document-based search tasks.

The TRACE model helps understand why some search tasks are more difficult than others. When answering general questions, the searcher must complete several search cycles, evaluating, selecting, and integrating content information. A consequence is that the searcher must hold intermediate results in mind while searching for additional information. New incoming information may interfere with working memory content, causing the partial decay of the goal representation, which, in turn, may cause relevant topics to be neglected and irrelevant topics to be selected. Thus, searching for information requires the use of appropriate control mechanisms, that is, looking back at the question to make sure that one is "on the right track."

Students often search documents in order to learn new concepts. They may then be provided with different types of search questions. Research has found that using documents to answer questions influences what a person will eventually remember from the document. An important finding is that the extra effort needed to answer high-level questions pays off in terms of comprehension and learning from text. General questions foster an integration mechanism that allows the reader to review (either mentally or by rereading) relevant portions of the text, which may improve their memory for the text macrostructure.

Whereas prior research on text processing focused on tasks that promote "coherence-based" comprehension strategies, this chapter has addressed the text processing situations that emphasize relevance-based strategies. The key process is information evaluation, that is, confronting the information actually found with the information one actually needs.

Document search is now becoming the focus of more attention on the part of cognitive scientists. The research suggests that people need to learn in order to become efficient document searchers. The lack of explicit training of relevance-based comprehension strategies may explain why so many young adults fail in tasks that require not only comprehension and memory, but also the meaningful exploitation of text information. This points out the need to think about literacy skills in a different way, especially in a world that is being rapidly colonized by networks of electronic information systems whose core characteristic is precisely to confront people with opportunities to search huge repositories of information. How these systems affect our abilities to interact with document information, and whether they come with new demands in terms of document literacy are important questions for the future. I address them in the next two chapters.

5

Using Hypertext Systems

OVERVIEW LAND CONTENTS

Chapters 5 and 6 address issues raised by the recent advent of computerized information systems and the growing popularity of the World Wide Web as a means to acquire documentary information for purposes of education, training, or personal development. Chapter 5 focuses on the concept of hypertext, which forms the backbone of current online information systems. Hypertext consists of linking pages of electronic text in a nonlinear way, by means of semantic links. The concept of hypertext was invented in the 1960s, but it was not until the advent of the World Wide Web that hypertext emerged as a leading paradigm in electronic publishing. Early theorists saw hypertext as a means to facilitate access to content information to a wide range of users, by letting users freely "navigate" as a function of their needs and purposes. Empirical studies have found that navigating hypertext is a complex cognitive activity. Furthermore, the effectiveness of hypertext systems varies as a function of linking structure and content representation. The design of explicit and unambiguous hypertext organizers (e.g., content maps) has emerged as a key issue for the usability of nonlinear information systems.

Contents

INTRODUCTION

Over the past 25 years, the advent of personal computing has initiated major transformations in many areas of human activity. In particular, computers have deeply transformed information-related activities in professional contexts through, for example, office computing, process control, or intranets. Computers have also made their way into the sphere of education, supporting both general purpose tasks (e.g., word-processing, spreadsheet computing) and specialized learning activities (e.g., computer-assisted learning, distance education, Web-based learning). Finally, computers have become more and more present in the private sphere, where people use them both for leisure activities and personal management. The advent of the Internet and the explosion of general-purpose online services have consecrated the advent of an "information society," at least among the wealthiest social groups from the more developed countries.

The surge of powerful and versatile computer technologies has stimulated enthusiastic beliefs and expectations as regards the capacity of those technologies to accelerate the sharing of knowledge, culture, and entertainment. Many also think that computers will help resolve issues like unemployment, education, community involvement, and safety in western postindustrial society. There is, however, very little scientific knowledge concerning the effects—in terms of cognition, but also social integration and well-being—of widespread computer networking and intensive computer use. This is because research on the social and psychological impacts of information technologies has been somewhat overshadowed by technological development and innovation, combined with a rather positive stance toward technology on the part of policymakers, the media, and the general public.

I do not aim to cover such a large and complex issue here. Instead, I concentrate on hypertext as the core organizing principle of computerized information technology. This and the following chapter both address the effects of hypertext on document comprehension and document use. This chapter concentrates on the basic cognitive processes at work in hypertext perusal, whereas chapter 6 takes a broader perspective on the uses of Web-based hypertext in educational contexts.

In the following sections, I start with a brief review of the concept of hypertext (for related works see Conklin, 1987; McKnight, Dillon, & Richardson, 1993; Nielsen, 1995; Rouet, Levonen, Dillon, & Spiro, 1996;

Van Oostendorp, 2003). Then I examine the mental processes at work when using hypertext for various purposes. Hypertext was designed in order to promote not just reading, but sophisticated interactions with large bodies of texts and documents. I study the potential and limitations of the new medium for comprehension and information search, and review the issue of prerequisite skills involved in hypertext use.

A growing body of studies brings converging evidence that the hypertext user needs a great deal of support in order to navigate with a manageable mental cost, to locate information quickly and efficiently, and to make sense of the proposed networking of pages. Contrary to what many believe, such a need for support may be even greater than with printed documents (see chapter 2). Therefore, in the last part of the chapter, I focus on the role of electronic content representation (e.g., menus and graphical overviews) and their effects on hypertext comprehension and use.

5.1. AN OVERVIEW OF RESEARCH INTO HYPERTEXT USES

Where Does Hypertext Come From? The history of hypertext is rooted in the explosion of the publishing industry, in the emergence of modern librarianship, as well as in utopian undertakings aimed at creating universal knowledge repositories throughout the 19th and 20th centuries, such as Paul Otlet's Mundaneum (Rayward, 1991). The principle of nonlinear associative linking of information, which is the hallmark of hypertext, is generally attributed to Bush's (1945) article "As We May Think." Bush reflected on a major concern in the precomputer contemporary times, that is, the tremendous increase in the amount of scientific information available to scientists, with the correlative problem of retrieving and consulting information relevant to one's purposes. Bush noted:

> The summation of human experience is being expanded at a prodigious rate, and the means we use for threading through the consequent maze to the momentarily important item is the same as was used in the days of square-rigged ships.

He further diagnosed:

> Our ineptitude in getting at the record is largely caused by the artificiality of systems of indexing. When data of any sort are placed in storage, they are filed alphabetically or numerically, and information is found (when it is) by tracing it down from subclass to subclass (...). Having found one item, moreover, one has to emerge from the system and re-enter on a new path.

Bush went on describing the "Memex," a device that would allow its user to create associative trails by which any two pieces of information could be tied to each other. Later on, the retrieval of one such piece of information would allow the user to consult all the elements of the trail. This device, Bush argued, would let scientists, librarians, engineers, and so forth, develop applications tailored to their information needs.

The term *hypertext* was coined some 20 years later by Ted Nelson, who considered the possibility of constructing worldwide electronic information networks for the sharing of knowledge (for a historical summary, see Nielsen, 1995). It was not until the end of the 1970s, however, that the first prototype hypertext systems were actually developed as computer software. The Notecards® Software, by the Xerox Parc, was among the earliest, followed by several others. Hypertext as a research and development area was consecrated in 1987 with the first international conference on hypertext in Chapel Hill (Smith, Halasz, Yankelovich, Schwartz, & Weiss, 1987). The first European Conference on Hypertext took place in Versailles in 1990 (Rizk, Streitz, & André, 1990). During the 1990s, the industry of hypertext grew at a very fast rate, boosted by the advent of multimedia personal computers and the explosion of the Internet.

What Is Hypertext? From a technical standpoint, hypertext is a computer database that contains textual information (Conklin, 1987). The information is organized in files, and each file is connected to one or several others by means of software links. Hypertext systems also include a user interface that allows the user to search, display, and navigate the database using input and output interfaces (i.e., keyboard, mouse, screen, and printer). Nowadays, a large majority of Web sites and Web-based services actually include hypertexts.

The advent of hypertext has represented a significant breakthrough in the area of document design. Hypertext allowed the creation of networked arrangements of information units, challenging the traditional codex, that is, the linear arrangement of pages in a printed volume. More important, the advent of hypertext allowed writers and publishers to dissociate the contents of a database from its actual display. It was, therefore, possible to propose several representations of the same materials, without affecting the materials themselves. This is to be compared to the publishing process in the printed world, where any change in the presentation of information requires the reconstruction of an entirely new printed object.

Perhaps the most emblematic feature of hypertext is the use of embedded menus, or hyperlinks. Until the mid-1980s, database interfacing was dominated by the command line and hierarchical menus, separated visually and functionally from database contents. With the popularization of graphical interfaces and point-and-click devices such as the mouse, systems were created in which content information and command (or navigation) information were mixed up. In one of the earliest papers on the topic, Koved and Shneiderman (1986) defined embedded menus as follows: "In embedded menus, highlighted words or phrases within the text become the menu items, and are selectable using the commonly used touch screen, cursor, and mouse methods (…)" (p. 312).

Twenty years later, any Internet user may check that the embedded hyperlink was certainly a good idea, as millions of Web pages do implement this type of navigation device.

Is There Anything Psychological to Hypertext? One may wonder, though, whether hypertext technologies deserve a specific section in a book concerned with the psychology of comprehension. After all, readers remain readers and the general rules of language processing should apply, whatever the medium. However, many hypertext researchers and designers have claimed that the unique features of hypertext can qualitatively affect the cognitive processes brought to bear when reading and comprehending. For example, hypertext presentation of multiple documents, with embedded links to related sources and search tools, may promote students' reasoning at the intertextual, not just textual level. Hypertext features may also enhance the selection of relevant passages, the comparison of information, and the establishment of relationships between different types of information. Research on hypertext design and hypertext use during the past 15 years has shown, however, that augmenting people's ability to interact meaningfully with texts and documents is a subtle art, and that hypertext is by no means a magical solution to the problem of information access and information comprehension.

Independent from the still-vivid debate over hypertext promises and pitfalls, hypertext is important from a psychological standpoint because it gives way to new types of content representation and navigation tools. Those tools may not have any direct comparison with those available on paper. They raise, however, new issues as regards the nature of text comprehension and information usage processes.

5.2. COGNITIVE ISSUES IN USING HYPERTEXT

In this section, I focus on the issue of how people read and understand information presented in the form of hypertexts. This issue is part of a broader research area that investigates the use of electronic texts and information systems (see Dillon, 1994; Marchionini, 1995). Research studies dealing specifically with hypertext systems may be grouped into two broad categories, depending on the type of activity involved. The first line of research has attempted to study the impact of hypertext presentation on user comprehension of the contents. The second line of research has examined the impact of hypertext on people's ability to retrieve information. These two lines of research must be studied separately because, as I tried to show in earlier chapters, text comprehension and information search rely on distinct cognitive processes. I summarize only a few studies within each line of research, inasmuch as more detailed reviews have already been published elsewhere (Chen & Rada, 1996; Dillon & Gabbard, 1998; Rouet, 1992; Rouet & Levonen, 1996). I focus on the cognitive skills and abilities that have been found to be related to user performance in hypertext-based activities. The broader issues of whether and how students may take advantage of hypertext in the context of learning activities is addressed in chapter 6.

5.2.1. Hypertext Reading and Hypertext Comprehension

Ever since hypertext became a concrete technology, researchers have been eager to demonstrate that the use of hypertext systems may have beneficial effects on readers' comprehension and learning. Some researchers have tried a rather conservative approach that consisted of using hyperlinks only to present adjunct information within a linear online text. Others have attempted to demonstrate the benefits of "true hypertexts," that is, hypertexts that contain networked pages of information.

Hyperlinks for Online Definitions. An obvious application of hypertext is the provision of online definitions to readers of lengthy and unfamiliar texts. Checking the meaning of a word in a printed text is often a bother because one does not always have a dictionary at hand. Even with a dictionary, searching the word, reading the definition, and returning to the text can be quite disrupting. Hypertext links may provide a convenient means to provide definitions quickly and at little cost. In one of the earliest controlled experiments involving hypertext, Lachman (1989) hypothesized that the online definition of unfamiliar words may improve the comprehension of an expository text presented on a computer display, but only if the defined words are important to the meaning of the text. Lachman asked 32 college students to study a 6,522-word psychology chapter presented on 28 screen-pages. On each page, the definition of one word or phrase could be called for. Based on Kintsch and van Dijk's (1978) theory, Lachman parsed the text into a macrostructure and a microstructure. For half the subjects, the selectable words were part of the text macrostructure (i.e., important words); for the other half, the selectable words were not part of the macrostructure (i.e., less important words).

Overall, the participants selected 70% of the available definitions. Furthermore, the proportion of selected items as well as the time taken to read the definitions were greater in the second half of the text, but only in the "important definitions" group. Finally, the "important definitions" group obtained higher scores on a comprehension posttest.

Thus, in order to be efficient, computerized assistance has to do more than just provide additional information: This information must trigger effective comprehension processes. University students calibrate their use of online assistance as a function of the assistance effectiveness. More generally, this study illustrates the importance of a psychological theory for the design of user-centered information systems. The macrostructure theory of Kintsch and van Dijk (1978; van Dijk, 1980) led to accurate predictions of which definitions are likely to improve the comprehension of a long expository text.

The way inserted definitions are displayed may also influence the readers' willingness to use them. Wright (1991) reported a series of experiments in which online definitions of unknown words were inserted in a computer-displayed text according to various display options. When definitions could be read directly by clicking highlighted words, 93% of the available definitions were selected. Not highlighting the definable words caused this proportion to drop to 61%. Finally, an intermediate proportion (76%) was obtained with definitions grouped in a separate "glossary" instead of being directly selectable (Black, Wright, Black, & Norman, 1992).

Overall, the evidence suggests that online, optional definitions are most efficient under three conditions: when subjects are mature readers (for younger readers, compulsory definitions seem to result in similar or better performance; see Reinking & Rickman, 1990); when the definitions concern terms that are important for the particular text considered; and when the defined terms are clearly signaled and immediately accessible, to avoid harmful disruptions of the comprehension processes.

Comprehension of Linear Versus Nonlinear Text. During the 1985–1995 decade, the production of hypertext and hypertext browsers increased by large numbers, and so did the number of published studies providing empirical comparisons of linear text and hypertext for comprehension (Chen & Rada, 1996). As pointed out by Dillon and Gabbard (1998), however, many such experiments lacked a rigorous design and/or a sufficient level of control to provide interpretable data. Furthermore, due to the very versatility of hypertext, it is difficult to compare results across studies because one has to take into account differences in the participants, tasks, materials, directions, dependent measures, and so forth. For this reason, the actual impacts of hypertext on reader comprehension is still open to debate.

One of the earliest empirical studies of hypertext versus linear text comprehension was conducted by Gordon, Gustavel, Moore, and Hankey (1988). They selected printed magazine and technical articles, and converted them into hypertext using "informal subjective judgment." In the hypertext version, a summary of the document was presented first. The readers could access complementary information by selecting keywords (i.e., hyperlinks). The authors tested the linear and hypertext versions in order to find out which one would yield the best comprehension performance. Twenty-four students with little prior experience of hypertext reading participated in the experiment. They had to perform two distinct reading tasks: read a magazine article as they would do for leisure, then read a technical article in order to understand its content. In the "leisure reading" situation, the linear version yielded a better recall of the text's important information. Moreover, the participants preferred the linear version, and found the hypertext version harder to use. In the more demanding reading task, however, the participants did not find any difference between the two versions. The authors concluded that hypertext was probably not suited for reading situations that do not specifically aim at comprehension or learning.

One particular problem evidenced in the Gordon et al. study was the participants' feeling of uncertainty when reading the hypertext presentation. Some participants mentioned that, when using the hypertext version, they were bothered because they did not know "what was behind the door," that is, what information they would get by selecting the keywords. This finding suggests that better information about the destination of hyperlinks (i.e., labeled links) may have facilitated hypertext navigation. But it may also be suggested that when readers do not have any specific reading purpose, they cannot really take advantage of the "freedom" to choose or not to choose information categories present in hypertext. Reading a linear text is then as pleasant and as rewarding as reading hypertext (Charney, 1994). On the other hand, when asked to read more intensely the technical paper, the participants may have been encouraged to visit the hyperlink contents more systematically.

Early studies of hypertext found that navigating nonlinear document structures presented new challenges to the reader. Foss (1989, experiment 1) noted that hypertext readers tended to "loop" in the hypertext, and to flip through pages instead of reading them carefully. Self-reports indicated that looping and flipping did not reflect deliberate strategies, but resulted from a disorientation problem. Subjects reported difficulties in defining an optimal reading order, and in locating themselves in the network (see also Edwards & Hardman, 1989). Another study by Foss (1989, experiment 2) also highlighted the problem of managing a nonlinear reading task. Foss asked 10 adults to use a geographical hypertext database in order to perform a task involving the display and comparison of several cards. Foss reported two main types of problems: First, some subjects made too few comparisons and tended to lose track of their hypotheses or to forget how they had come to a conclusion. This was interpreted as a "search strategy" problem, or not having a good representation of the task requirements. Second, some subjects opened too few or too many windows at the same time, and/or positioned the windows in a way that did not allow easy comparison. This was interpreted as a "task management" problem, or not knowing how to perform the task. The two problems are not independent. For instance, poor task management (e.g., opening too many windows at the same time on the computer desktop) may prevent subjects from applying a good task representation (e.g., reasoning by elimination). In other terms, a coherent representation of the environment (what information is available and how to access it) is essential for effective access to the information of interest (see also Egan, Remde, Landauer, Lochbaum, & Gomez, 1989).

The navigation problem was also apparent in hypertext users' comments. Gray (1990) asked 10 students to read a 68-unit hypertext with the goal of answering questions. Think-aloud protocols were recorded during hypertext navigation and matched to the subjects' selections in the hypertext. The participants experienced several types of navigation problems: Some could not remember what they had read and not read, they missed organizational cues normally present in lengthy text, and they were not sure where to find the information they needed. When asked to draw a representation of the hypertext structure, subjects tended to reproduce conventional patterns: Sequences, simple hierarchies, or tables, rather than the actual hypertext layout. Gray concluded that novice hypertext users need analogies with conventional structures. She also suggested that with some training, hypertext users might become able to deal with loosely structured materials.

Hypertext navigation problems were observed even in very simple hypertexts. In my doctoral research work (Rouet, 1990, 1991), I asked French middle school students to read a hypertext made of six text passages connected to a single menu. Students were instructed to browse the hypertext until they had visited each unit at least once. Students' navigation patterns varied in the number and order of text selections. Some students read each unit just once, in an order that reflected semantic relations between topics. Other students went back several times to the same units ("looping"), and did not follow the relations between units ("jumping"). Results indicated that looping and jumping did not result from deliberate strategies, but reflected students' disorientation. Looping decreased when navigation was made easier by marking previous selections or making the relations between units explicit. Furthermore, in a second session, the students' selections followed more closely the relations across units, which suggests that familiarity did influence their navigation strategies.

These problems do not seem to be attributable to limitations or defects of early hypertext systems, as more recent studies have pointed out similar phenomena. For instance, Lee and Tedder (2003) found detrimental effects of a hypertext presentation of a history text, compared to a linear presentation, on students' factual comprehension of the contents. They suggested that hypertext reading creates a higher cognitive load on the reader and hence reduces the reader's ability to memorize content information. The reader must remember his or her location in the network, make decisions about where to go next, and keep track of pages previously visited (Wright, 1991). Given such constraints, it is hardly surprising that empirical comparisons between paper presentation (a familiar situation) and hypertext (a new, cognitively demanding situation) did not always favor hypertext (Dillon & Gabbard, 1998).

Hypertext and Relational Processing. How can we interpret the apparent "cognitive overload" that appears when reading and comprehending hypertext? Wenger and Payne (1996) suggested that the problem has to do with readers' comprehension strategies. To them, reading nonlinear materials fosters deeper relational processing on the part of the reader because the reader has to make a navigation decision after each page. The deeper relational processing causes an extra load on the reader's working memory, but it could be beneficial for texts that do not normally foster this type of processing. Hypertext presentation of descriptive materials could then force readers to establish connections between text units.

Wenger and Payne conducted two experiments in order to study the impact of hypertext on relational processing. In the first experiment, they used a secondary task technique in order to assess item-specific versus relational processing in hypertext. They compared the effects of two distinct secondary tasks. In the verbal-numeric task, the subject was asked to retain a series of six digits while reading each page of the text; in the spatial task, the subject had to hold in mind a configuration of six points on a four-by-four matrix. The latter task is assumed to require deeper relational processing, and thus it should draw more heavily on the subject's resources for relational processing. Twelve texts were prepared, based on scientific and technical publications. Six had a causal structure; six had a descriptive structure (following Meyer's 1985 typology; see chapter 2). The texts were divided into information "nodes" based on a thematic content analysis. The authors created semantic links between nodes. In the linear version, a unique link was drawn between each node and the next one, according to the basic rhetorical structure of the text. In the hypertext version, each node was linked to its superordinate theme, to its neighbors within the same global theme, and to other nodes in the text whenever this was justified. The presentation of the linear text started with the first passage in the source text; the presentation of the hypertext started with an alphabetic index where subjects could return during reading.

Forty university students read either the six causal texts or the six descriptive texts. Each subject read one text in each condition of presentation (linear, hypertext) and secondary task (numeric, spatial, or control). In the control condition, the series of digits was presented immediately after reading the page, just before the recall test. The analysis of subjects' free recall showed a better performance in the hypertext condition. Moreover, there was an interaction between presentation format, text type, and secondary task. Hypertext was better than linear text for descriptions, under a numeric secondary task condition. As regards the comprehension task, hypertext presentation was better for descriptive texts, whereas linear presentation was better for causal texts. Experiment 2 replicated experiment 1, using texts whose content was more familiar to the participants. Again, hypertext increased free recall of descriptions under the numeric secondary task.

Wenger and Payne's (1996) studies suggest that hypertext does not require more resources than linear text, but rather a qualitatively different type of resources. Hypertext may require more relational resources, which draw on Baddeley's (1986) "visuospatial sketchpad" in working memory. It should be noted, however, that these conclusions rest in large part on the analysis of free recall, which may not capture all the levels of processing involved in comprehension. Thus, hypertext reading may have simply encouraged the subjects to pay more attention to the materials, resulting in a better recall. Moreover, the experiments used a clearly structured text and an explicit linking scheme, mostly a hierarchical one. This may have greatly reduced the cognitive load and disorientation effects observed in other studies. In fact, other studies have found that hypertext linking with a predominant hierarchical structure does not harm comprehension, compared to linear chaining of the pages (Calisir & Gurel, 2003).

In conclusion, reading hypertext may stimulate the use of cognitive resources that are not used spontaneously when reading linear text, hence, maybe, a sense of greater effort, but also deeper processing of the materials. Thus, there is no simple linear relation between the amount of mental effort invested in the activity and the outcome in terms of comprehension. Even though there is no direct evidence for this, the data suggest an inverted U-shaped relationship, where either the lack of effort or an excessive level of effort both lead to nonoptimal performances. In all cases, the linking structure of the materials must reflect the actual semantic structure of the text. It should also be visible and readily interpretable by readers.

5.2.2. Searching for Information in Hypertext

In chapter 4, I argued that searching for information in documents is a complex activity that requires cognitive processes and strategies partly distinct from those involved in continuous reading. The construction of a mental model of the search task, and the management of the task requirements in working memory while searching, play a critical part in search effectiveness, just as does the efficient evaluation and selection of information categories, or planning (Dreher & Guthrie, 1990; Rouet, 2003). But search success is also tightly related to the quality of documents and content representation devices. Because hypertext came with new content representation and information search devices, many thought that hypertext may facilitate information search, compared to traditional, printed documents. In fact, hypertext was primarily designed to facilitate readers' interactions with large textual databases, that is, their selective access to relevant information.

Weyer's (1982) "dynamic book" may have been one of the earliest attempts to assess the effectiveness of hypertext for information search (Fig. 5.1). The principle of a dynamic book was to preserve the linear nature of the written text, while providing the reader with a set of tools to facilitate the retrieval and selection of related information. Weyer designed a prototype application based on a published high school history textbook. In addition to the contents of the textbook, Weyer's "Dynabook" included a variety of content representation devices and various search tools. The interface of the Dynabook included four major

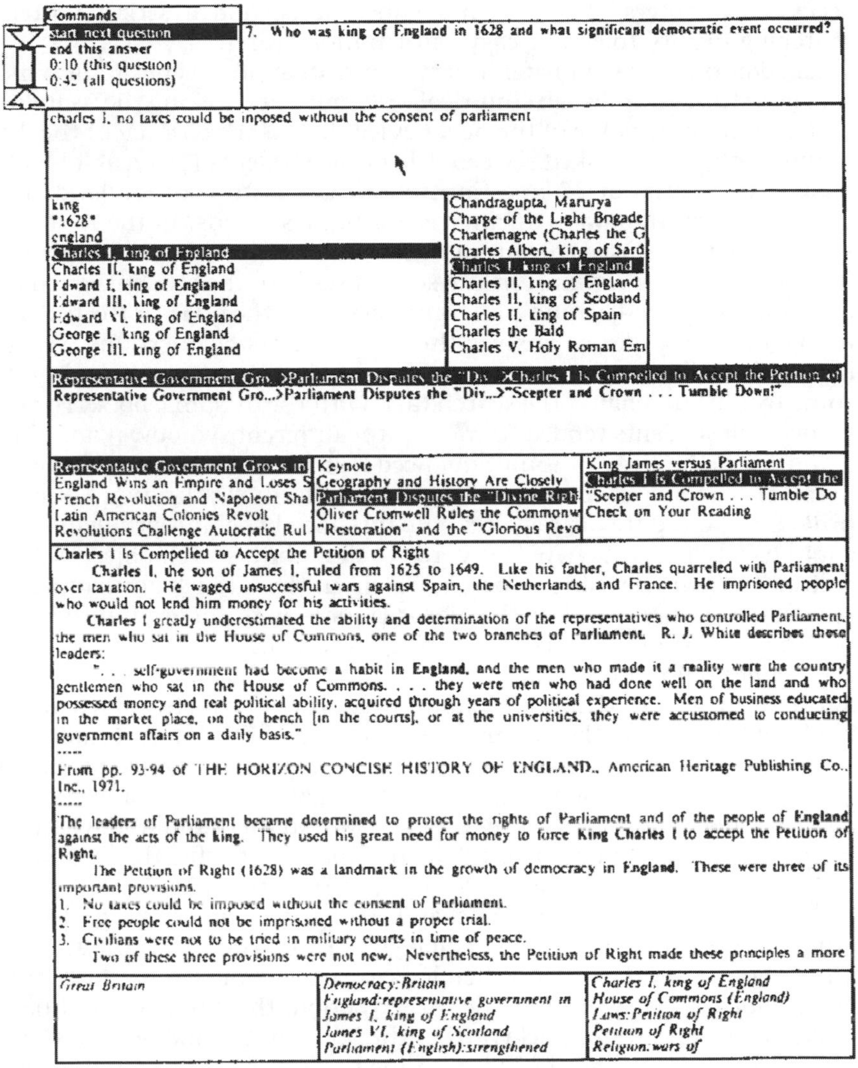

Commands
start next question
end this answer
0:10 (this question)
0:42 (all questions)

7. Who was king of England in 1628 and what significant democratic event occurred?

charles I. no taxes could be inposed without the consent of parliament

king
"1628"
england
Charles I, king of England
Charles II, king of England
Edward I, king of England
Edward III, king of England
Edward VI, king of England
George I, king of England
George III, king of England

Chandragupta, Marurya
Charge of the Light Brigade
Charlemagne (Charles the G
Charles Albert, king of Sard
Charles I, king of England
Charles II, king of England
Charles II, king of Scotland
Charles II, king of Spain
Charles the Bald
Charles V, Holy Roman Em

Representative Government Gro..>Parliament Disputes the "Div..>Charles I Is Compelled to Accept the Petition of
Representative Government Gro...>Parliament Disputes the "Div...>"Scepter and Crown . . . Tumble Down!"

Representative Government Grows in
England Wins an Empire and Loses S
French Revolution and Napoleon Sha
Latin American Colonies Revolt
Revolutions Challenge Autocratic Rul

Keynote
Geography and History Are Closely
Parliament Disputes the "Divine Righ
Oliver Cromwell Rules the Commonw
"Restoration" and the "Glorious Revo

King James versus Parliament
Charles I Is Compelled to Accept the
"Scepter and Crown . . . Tumble Do
Check on Your Reading

Charles I Is Compelled to Accept the Petition of Right

Charles I, the son of James I, ruled from 1625 to 1649. Like his father, Charles quarreled with Parliament over taxation. He waged unsuccessful wars against Spain, the Netherlands, and France. He imprisoned people who would not lend him money for his activities.

Charles I greatly underestimated the ability and determination of the representatives who controlled Parliament, the men who sat in the House of Commons, one of the two branches of Parliament. R. J. White describes these leaders:

". . . self-government had become a habit in England, and the men who made it a reality were the country gentlemen who sat in the House of Commons. . . . they were men who had done well on the land and who possessed money and real political ability, acquired through years of political experience. Men of business educated in the market place, on the bench [in the courts], or at the universities, they were accustomed to conducting government affairs on a daily basis."

From pp. 93-94 of THE HORIZON CONCISE HISTORY OF ENGLAND., American Heritage Publishing Co., Inc., 1971.

The leaders of Parliament became determined to protect the rights of Parliament and of the people of England against the acts of the king. They used his great need for money to force King Charles I to accept the Petition of Right.

The Petition of Right (1628) was a landmark in the growth of democracy in England. These were three of its important provisions.

1. No taxes could be imposed without the consent of Parliament.
2. Free people could not be imprisoned without a proper trial.
3. Civilians were not to be tried in military courts in time of peace.

Two of these three provisions were not new. Nevertheless, the Petition of Right made these principles a more

Great Britain

Democracy:Britain
England:representative government in
James I, king of England
James VI, king of Scotland
Parliament (English):strengthened

Charles I, king of England
House of Commons (England)
Laws:Petition of Right
Petition of Right
Religion:wars of

FIG. 5.1. The Dynamic Book (from Weyer, 1982). Reprinted by permission of Elsevier.

areas: the *command area* allowed users to read questions, keep track of time, and type in answers; the *subject area* displayed lists of subjects and subsubjects, and allowed users to type in their own keywords; the *title area* displayed topics and subtopics corresponding to the section of the manual currently displayed; and the *text area* displayed content information from the book. In addition, the prototype included two special navigation features: a hierarchical table of contents that enabled direct access to chapters, sections, and subsections, and a string pattern matching facility to enable easy information search.

In addition to introducing a very innovative prototype at the time, Weyer's study included an empirical test aimed at checking the usability and instructional value of the new device. To test the efficacy of the dynamic book, Weyer asked sixteen 8th-grade students (14-year-olds) to answer two series of 20 questions about the history of England. The students worked in pairs during two 2-hour sessions. In the first session, the students used a printout of the textbook in order to answer the first series of 20 questions. In the second session, the students used either a simple page-turning electronic version of the book or the full dynamic book in order to answer the second series of questions. Weyer reported qualitative observations showing that the students had quite some trouble managing the search task with the dynamic book. For instance, the students tended to mix up the different windows, and they could not make sense of some advanced features such as the addition of items to a table of cross-references. Furthermore, keyword search proved to be a difficult task, as students faced spelling problems and could hardly generate new keywords to describe a search objective. For instance, when searching information about the "French government," students insisted on finding the word "French" in the index, but they did not think of trying "France" or even "government." On other occasions they omitted important keywords, for instance, the keyword "holy" in a question about the "Holy Roman Empire," which led them to irrelevant sections of the manual (i.e., in this case, the Roman Empire).

When using the dynamic book, students also demonstrated problems due to their lack of knowledge of some high-level content representation devices. They tended to confound navigation in the text and navigation in the index, which could result in unexpected trouble. For instance, when trying to find out "who was king of England in 1628," a student performed a pattern-matching search using the phrase "king of England." As a result, the system displayed a list of kings that the student selected one after the other. When looking up sections about kings that ruled shortly before or after the target period, the student could have looked a bit forward or backward in the book, but he did not do so. Instead, the student continued to examine the list of kings until he found the correct answer (Charles I). Weyer also noted that searching the dynamic book to answer complex questions (e.g., questions that involved comparing information at various locations in the text) remained a complex cognitive task for high school students. The students seldom used high-level planning tools, such as the en route marking up of potentially interesting sections, for purposes of further reference.

The difficulties faced by participants may be interpreted in terms of the prerequisite knowledge and skills for document search (see chapter 4). First, middle school students are not fully aware of the role of textual organizers (e.g., tables, index), which form the backbone of the dynamic book. Next, the generation of appropriate search phrases requires a rich and flexible vocabulary, which typically students do not possess. Finally, information search imposes a heavy load in terms of memory management. Weyer's pioneering work showed that innovative information technology does not automatically eradicate those problems. In other words, although the dynamic book offered sophisticated search tools, it did not reduce the cognitive complexity of the search task. Weyer concluded that novice users might need some training before they become able to use the advanced features of the dynamic book efficiently.

A few years later, Shneiderman (1987) and his colleagues developed the Hyperties system, a hypertext system that was used for several applications, including a database on European history. In the Hyperties system, content information was categorized into a set of topics. Each topic was presented as a passage of text. Within each passage, several keywords were highlighted and could be selected, which led the reader to related topics in the database (see Koved & Shneiderman, 1986). A version of the database containing 106 articles was compared to its paper equivalent for question answering tasks. The paper version resulted in faster search for simple fact-retrieval questions. However, the users of the hypertext version performed equally rapidly for more complex items (Marchionini & Shneiderman, 1988; Shneiderman, 1989).

The Hyperties system was used in several other empirical studies. For instance, Wang and Liebscher (1988) asked university students to perform a series of search tasks using a version of the Hyperties system that included both embedded hyperlinks and an alphabetic index. The first experiment showed no difference in search effectiveness between the hypertext and a paper version of the document database. In their second experiment, Wang and Liebscher compared search using the index and search using the embedded hyperlinks. They found no overall difference. In the hyperlinks condition, however, search time decreased over trials, which suggests that the participants needed to get more familiar with this particular way of searching through a document database.

The lack of familiarity with hypertext search generally had negative consequences on users' performance. Gray and Shasha (1989) evaluated a database presenting information about sociology. They asked 60 university students to perform a series of five search tasks using one of three versions of the database: a version with a structured search facility, a version using the structured search facility plus a system of embedded links with categorized labels (e.g., "example," "comparison"), and a printed version with neither structured search nor embedded links. They found that the printed version allowed faster search for simple, explicit questions. For more complex questions, there was no difference across versions. They also noted that in the two computer conditions, search time tended to decrease across trials, suggesting again that search effectiveness could improve with the participants' familiarity with the system. McKnight, Dillon, and Richardson (1990) also reported evidence for disorientation problems in a hypertext search task. They asked a group of 16 adults to answer a series of 12 questions by searching a 40-card document. The document was presented in one of four formats: two hypertexts and two linear formats (paper and word processor). Search time was similar in the four conditions, but linear documents resulted in better answers. In the hypertext conditions, the subjects spent a greater proportion of time searching the menus, and they rarely used the direct links between cards. The authors concluded that inexperienced hypertext users face a task management problem, not knowing when and how to use the new navigation facilities.

To summarize the findings of both comprehension and information search experiments: Hypertext and related technologies have brought new means to represent and navigate complex information. The new technical tools did not, however, automatically result in observable benefits for the lay user. Instead, new problems were found, such as disorientation or poor task management. Very often, users seemed to lack the prerequisite skills or knowledge needed to take advantage of the system. This has resulted in an increased attention to the nature of the cognitive skills involved in using hypertexts and the factors underlying individual differences.

5.2.3. Prerequisite Cognitive Skills in Hypertext Use

Experiments on hypertext usage have often found large differences across individuals in terms of task management and performance. Such differences are attributable to a number of factors that have not been fully disentangled in the literature. Norman (1991) proposed a distinction between "inherent differences" (e.g., perceptual ability, memory capacity) and "acquired differences" (e.g., specific knowledge of the subject matter domain). Marchionini (1995) defined four factors of a person's ability to interact with computerized information systems: cognitive skills, domain knowledge, system knowledge, and searching knowledge. Empirical studies have confirmed the impact of both general cognitive dimensions and acquired knowledge and skills on people's use of hypertext (Marchionini, Dwiggins, Katz, & Lin, 1993).

Just like any complex mental activity, hypertext use depends on the efficiency of people's perceptual and cognitive processes. Particularly important are the processes that allow one to structure information received from the visual environment. Kim and Hirtle (1995) discussed the analogy between hypertext perusal and navigation in physical spaces. They argued that research on navigation in physical environments can be used as a reference frame to interpret the problems observed with hypertext navigation. Regardless of the specific task at hand, using a hypertext involves several cognitive activities, such as planning and executing a route through the network, processing content information, and coordinating the first two activities. Planning and executing routes in a hypertext network is in large part analogous to moving through a physical space. In both cases, routes may be based on one's knowledge of landmarks, on one's knowledge of familiar itineraries, or on one's learned map of the environment (survey-type of knowledge).

People vary in their ability to mentally construct and manipulate spatial representations, a skill called *spatial visualization*. Many studies have found an impact of spatial visualization on hypertext use (Chen & Czerwinsky, 1997; Lin, 2003; Westerman, Davies, Glendon, Stammers, & Matthews, 1995). Downing, Moore, and Brown (2005) found evidence for a relationship between spatial visualization and subjects' performance in a rather naturalistic bibliographical search task using the First Search online bibliographic tool. The time needed to access the first relevant article was shorter in participants with a high spatial visualization ability, independent from their expertise in the search domain. Freudenthal (2001) also found that a spatial ability measure predicted selection latencies at the deeper levels of a hierarchical menu. This relationship may explain older adults' lesser performances when using deep, as opposed to shallow, menu structures (see section 5.3.2).

Some researchers, however, have challenged the view that hypertext navigation relies on the same mental processes as navigation in physical spaces. Dillon, McKnight, and Richardson (1993) argued that the "space" metaphor is limited because hypertext is primarily structured according to semantic, not spatial dimensions. Farris, Jones, and Elgin (2002) argued that "hypermedia is inherently non-spatial" (p. 489), because it does not possess the qualities of depth and direction. They pointed out that there is no actual movement when using a hypermedia system. Thus, the exploration of hypermedia cannot result in the perception of spatial information. They deemed it unlikely that hypermedia users build a mental representation of the relative locations and depth of the pages that make up the hypermedia network. They designed several versions of a hypertext database of computer graphics that varied in depth (or the number of selection levels to be taken in order to reach a particular page) while sharing the same categorical arrangement. Forty university students explored the Web site for 5 minutes. Then they had to draw the structure of pages and links. The participants' drawings tended to reflect the categorical organization of the pictures rather than the connection structure of the hypertext. Farris et al.'s findings should be interpreted with caution since they are based on quite specific materials and on a task that is sensitive to people's generic schemata about information organization (see, e.g., Gray, 1990). They show, however, that it is not yet clear how spatial processes interact with other, semantic processes when exploring and using a hypertext system.

Be that as it may, the relationship between people's visuospatial ability and their performance in hypertext-based tasks is theoretically supported by text comprehension research. People tend to perform mental simulations of the "scenes" described in texts (see chapter 1). Furthermore, the use of graphical analogies helps people structure materials, even when the text does not have a strong spatial component (e.g., Glenberg & Langston, 1992). Robinson, Robinson, and Katayama (1999) demonstrated that the mental processing of graphical representations relies on the visuospatial component of working memory. Thus, spatial visualization skills might be related to hypertext use just as they are related to text comprehension in general (Graff, 2005).

Other cognitive dimensions also affect people's ability to use hypertext. Cognitive style, and especially field dependence versus independence, affects people's navigational style and efficiency. Field independence represents' people ability to reason independently from salient features in the perceptual environment. Kim (2001) found that field-independent students developed more efficient navigation strategies as they searched a Web site for specific information. However, the field dependence versus independence dimension was mostly significant for novice Web users (see also Chen & Macredie, 2004). Gillingham (1993) found a relationship between reading ability and hypertext search strategies. The more successful readers chose important hypertext nodes more often and read them relatively longer than unsuccessful readers. In addition to cognitive variables, the availability of prior domain knowledge, experience with search tasks in general, and experience with the particular search environment also improve people's use of hypertext.

Two major findings emerge from hypertext usage studies. First, the advantages of searching for information in hypertext are not immediately apparent in studies involving novice or inexperienced users. It was often noted that participants did not immediately understand how they could best take advantage of the system features. A training phase was necessary in order to assess the quality of the system properly. Second, some of the most advanced search or linking features available in hypertext may not be needed or even desirable. As Weyer (1982) noted, "Not having a feature may be better than using it badly" (p. 101). In fact, it seems that many of the prerequisites of effective search in traditional documents, such as knowing about metatextual organizers and how to use them effectively, are also present in search tasks involving electronic information systems.

5.3. REPRESENTING THE SEMANTIC STRUCTURE IN HYPERTEXT

From the early studies on, the history of hypertext systems has been that of a quest for *cognitive compatibility*, that is, a good level of match between the technical features of the system and the skills and needs of the users (Streitz, 1987). Cognitive compatibility can be achieved by selecting and representing relational information carefully (through hyperlinks), and by providing the user with structured top-level representations of the hypertext contents, or so-called *content maps*.

5.3.1. Link Labeling and Link Organization

Unlike printed documents, the top-level structure in hypertext is not made explicit through the linear arrangement of pages or chapters. Instead, structure is conveyed through semantic links that connect the hypertext nodes together. Hyperlinks allow the hypertext reader to move on from one passage to another. Critical issues in hypertext design are to find out what links should be offered with each hypertext node, how links should be labelled, and where they should be presented in the hypertext system.

What links should be included in a hypertext? Any content word or phrase on a hypertext page is a candidate for linking, provided that there exists another page dealing with contents related to that phrase. The number of potentially "linkable" items in a hypertext depends on a number of factors such as the amount of information contained in the hypertext, the way the hypertext is broken down into pages, and whether or not it is connected to other hypertexts. With the advent of Web-based hypertext, virtually any word or expression may be linked to either another page within the same hypertext (internal link) or to a page in another, external hypertext. Even though the concept of hyperlink is extremely seductive, the outcomes do not always live up to one's hopes.

Carelessly converting a linear text into a network of hypertext "cards" may decrease comprehensibility of the materials, especially due to coherence breakdowns at the local and global levels. Foltz (1996) pointed out that writers of traditional documents usually ensure local coherence by making contiguous sentences and passages share common referents. At the global level, texts and complex documents are usually arranged so that the reader can identify the overarching idea or theme (see also chapter 2). Foltz (1996) further pointed out that even though many hypertext designers have been aware of the need for local and global coherence, their approaches were rather empirical and a-theoretical. Foltz analyzed the paths followed by university students when exploring a 6,000-word hypertext for knowledge acquisition in introductory economics. The hypertext included both hierarchical and cross-section links. Using propositional analysis (see chapter 1), Foltz was able to identify those transitions that maintained textual coherence, and those that did not. Looking at how students with little initial knowledge explored the hypertext, Foltz reported that 80% to 90% of the transitions were respectful of the text's macrostructure. That is, the participants seldom used links that would lead them to remote parts of the hypertext. Foltz also observed that the more coherent the student's route was, the greater the amount of information the student was able to recall. In the second experiment, Foltz (1996) used verbal protocols to confirm that while browsing the hypertext, the students were busy keeping up with the text's macrostructure. He concluded that in order to understand a complex text, readers use a problem-solving approach that consists of building a route that will cause minimal disruption in their global representation of the text's content. Consequently, when linking information pages in hypertext systems, the designers should make sure that the subsequent action of jumping from the source page to the linked page will not cause excessive coherence breaks. This aspect of hypertext is especially crucial for information systems aimed at readers who are not experts in the domain.

Defining the global relations that may exist among portions of large documents is not an easy task, however. Holt and Howell (1992) called for rational methods to express semantic relationships between hypertext nodes. They designed a prototype hypertext generator, HyperNet, that allowed the authors to label all the links created among text nodes. In pilot tests, they found that authors did not have trouble linking text passages, but did have more trouble making explicit the semantic connections across passages. Therefore, they tried to gather a corpus of representative link types by asking university students to name the relationship between consecutive or unrelated pairs of paragraphs taken from a computer science manual. The students recognized a relationship in 79% of the consecutive pairs versus 19% of the unrelated pairs. Unfortunately, the students used rather vague and general expressions to characterize the relationships, for example, "how it works," "representation of," "example of," "description of." Thus, the provision of clear and explicit linking seems to require a great deal of expertise of the hypertext contents, in addition to careful consideration of the readers' needs.

Embedded Versus Explicit Menus. Embedded menus, or the integration of hyperlinks within the informational content of a hypertext, is one of the hallmarks of hypertexts. In their early discussion of the concept, Koved and Shneiderman (1986) argued that embedded menus may enhance navigation in computerized databases because they save screen space, and they preserve the semantic context in which a key word or phrase appears. They listed several applications of embedded menus in on-line databases, catalogs, spelling checkers, and programming editors. They briefly reviewed experimental results showing mixed but rather positive evidence in favor of embedded menus.

Subsequent empirical studies, however, failed to provide strong support in favor of embeddedness. Bernard, Hull, and Drake (2001) examined whether the location of links on a Web page had an influence on readers' performance at locating information, and on their subjective evaluation of document quality. They designed four 2-level hypertexts borrowed from *Scientific American* online. Each of the hypertexts used a different presentation of links. In version 1, the links were embedded within page 1 of the document. In version 2, explicit links were put at the bottom of the page. Version 3 placed explicit links at the top-left of the document, whereas version 4 placed the explicit links in the left margin, at the height of the corresponding content information (Fig. 5.2). Twenty volunteer students performed 10 search tasks with each version (content and presentation order were counterbalanced). There was no difference in search accuracy, time, or economy across versions. Embedded links received higher ratings in ease of navigation and ability to recognize key in-

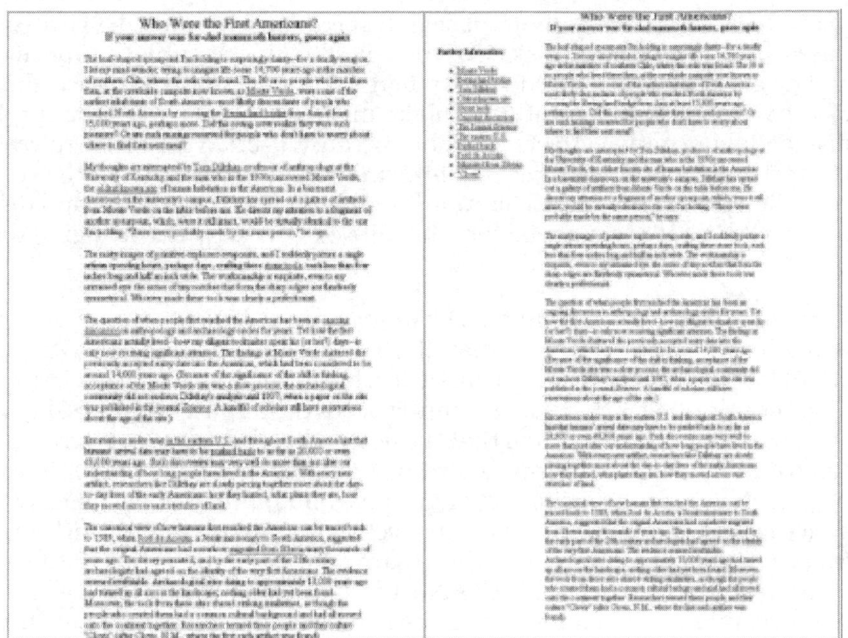

FIG. 5.2. Two versions of the hypertext used in the study by Bernard, Hull, and Drake (2001). To the left, a page with embedded links ("version 1"); to the right, same page with an explicit menu ("version 3"). Reprinted with the first author's kind permission.

formation, while bottom links had lowest ratings in comprehensibility and ability to follow main idea. Overall, embedded links were preferred most often, whereas bottom links were never preferred.

Link Density. Link density, or the optimal number of links that should be included in a page, is another important issue in hypertext design. Khan and Locatis (1998) examined the impact of link density and link display on high school students' retrieval of specific information in a Web-based hypertext system. The hypertext included the equivalent of 15 double-spaced pages organized in nine chapters, dealing with influence and suggestion. Four versions resulted from the combination of link density (low = 3 links per page, higher = 6 links per page), and link display (explicit links in the form of menus vs. embedded within paragraphs). Both the high and low density versions had links pointing to relevant subsections within each chapter, as well as irrelevant internal and extraneous links. Sixty-four high school students were assigned to one of the four versions. They had to locate the answers to six questions, whose wording was identical, similar, or different from the wording of links. List display facilitated all aspects of search performance, compared to paragraph (embedded) display. A lower density of links improved search accuracy (but not search speed) and promoted a strategy based on the ordering of tasks from simplest to most complex (implicit).

The authors conjectured that "when users have more choices, they also have more opportunities to make mistakes," whereas "paragraph display had negative effects probably because users were likely to read the text and/or had to extract the information in the links from the surrounding prose" (p. 180). They admitted, however, that paragraph display could be more beneficial for more difficult tasks by encouraging the user to connect links and content.

Hierarchical Versus Network Arrangements of Links. Some hypertext theorists have claimed that the networking of hypertext pages should favor a richer reading experience, by letting hypertext readers revisit the same pages from different perspectives. Empirical studies, however, have consistently found that the networking of pages was strongly related to the disorientation syndrome (Rouet & Levonen, 1996). In experiments where the linking structure was manipulated, evidence was generally in favor of simple, hierarchical structures. For instance, Mohageg (1992) manipulated the organization of a hypertext database containing information about six North African countries. The database was organized according to linear, hierarchical, network, or mixed formats. Sixty-four adult paid volunteers were assigned to one of the four versions. They used the database to answer questions involving two, four, or six nodes. The hierarchical version was searched faster than the network version. Mohageg noted that orientation was an obvious concern of most participants. For instance, they often preferred to backtrack along previously visited pages instead of using the "home" button to return to the cover page. Other, more recent studies concluded that a hierarchical organization was better, especially for senior users, due to the higher "spatial cognitive load" of network structures (Graff, 2005; Lin, 2003).

Thus, linking should preserve a coherent, explicit top-level organization. In addition, hypertext readers should be provided with content representations that help them identify the top level structure, their current position, and possible itineraries within the hypertext.

5.3.2. Content Representation in Hypertext

An important aspect of hypertext is the way contents are represented in the system. In printed documents, content representation is achieved through the use of tables of contents, indexes, and other signaling devices (see chapter 2). In electronic databases, contents are often represented in the form of hierarchical menus (Norman, 1991). The advent of the Internet has popularized the use of hierarchical menus in Web portals, providing access to hundreds of categories in potentially all areas of interest to the general public. Given a number of categories or pages to be represented in a menu system, several display strategies are available. The hierarchy may contain only a few categories at each level and several embedded levels of information. Alternatively, the hierarchy may contain more items per page and a smaller number of layers (Fig. 5.3). The former strategy results in "broad" menus, whereas the latter one results in "deep" menus.

Pages in broad menus are visually more complex, as in the main broad menu in Fig. 5.3 (left). On the other hand, broad menus allow the user to reach content pages more directly. Deep menu pages are visually simpler, but they force the user to make several selections in a row in order to reach the desired category (like, e.g., the submenu selection in the deep menu in Fig. 5.3, right).

In the current state of the art, menu design varies a lot from one hypertext to another. For example, some Web portals offer deep menus with only a few options available at each level, whereas others offer broad menus with many categories available at each level. In some cases, the items are listed alphabetically, whereas in other cases the items are grouped by semantic categories (e.g., finance, travel ...). Given the increasing importance of using the Web for information search activities, it is important to assess the effects of these design strategies on users' information-seeking performance.

Past research has found that selection in a menu can be facilitated if items are grouped according to semantic categories (Giroux, Bergeron, & Lamarche, 1987; Snowberry, Parkinson, & Sisson, 1983) and if the depth–breadth ratio is optimal (Kiger, 1984; Miller, 1981; Parkinson, Sisson, & Snowberry, 1985), with about eight items per selection level (see also Norman, 1991, chapter 8, for a review). Excessive breadth can cause visual clutter and prevent users from finding relevant items in the menu; whereas excessive depth causes a sense of disorientation and cognitive overhead.

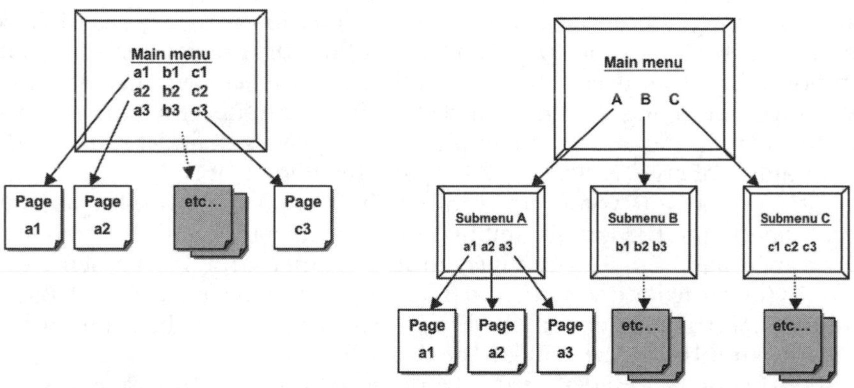

FIG. 5.3. Two types of menu organization: Broad menu (left), and Deep menu (right).

The need to compromise between breadth and depth appears to be independent from the technology, as studies conducted with recent, improved displays have essentially replicated the results of older studies. For example, Zaphiris, Shneiderman, & Norman (2002) compared traditional menus and "expandable" ones, in which subcategories appear in a pop-up area when the user selects a menu item. They found new evidence concerning the superiority of broad over deep menus. They also observed that search was generally faster with a traditional hierarchical menu than with an expandable menu, especially when the structure was deeper. The participants (21 university students) did not show any clear-cut preference for one type of menu. However, when the structure was deeper, they preferred the traditional menu over the expandable one. Zaphiris et al. concluded that expandable menus are acceptable only for shallow menu structures. Yu and Roh (2002) compared three types of menu presentation on university students' use and evaluation of a virtual shopping mall. They found that a pull-down menu that maximized visibility of intermediate categories was the most effective in terms of search speed for both specific and more global search tasks. Students' evaluation of design quality and disorientation, however, did not vary across menu types. Sears and Shneiderman (1994) pointed out the importance of ordering items within lists as a function of their selection frequency. "Split" menus, that present high-frequency items at the top, proved more effective in usability studies as well as a controlled experiment, compared to alphabetic menus.

Most of the empirical studies on menu search conducted so far have used students as participants. In contrast, there have not been so many studies of laypersons' use of menus in naturalistic activities. This was the purpose of a 2-year longitudinal study of Internet users' expectations, knowledge, and uses that my colleagues and I conducted in the urban area of Poitiers (France; see Rouet, 2005). As part of this study, Rouet, Ros, Jégou, and Metta (2003) examined the effects of menu design on younger and older adults' performance in a category search task involving various types of questions. Following previous studies, we hypothesized that deeper menus would decrease performance. We also expected that aging would negatively affect search performance, especially with deep menus and complex search probes (Freudenthal, 2001; Grahame, Laberge, & Scialfa, 2004; Westerman, 1995).

The participants were 50 volunteers from a panel of 100 laypersons participating in the longitudinal study. The sample included 9 men and 7 women aged 24–36 (younger adults); 5 men and 14 women aged 37–53 (intermediate adults); and 8 men and 7 women aged 54–80 (older adults). All the participants had been regular users of the Internet for over 18 months at the time of the experiment.

Rouet et al. (2003) designed a 400-item menu structure after existing Web portals. The menu structure presented a hierarchy of general interest categories and subcategories (e.g., education, travel, jobs, sports, and so forth). Three versions were developed: broad-categorized, broad-alphabetic, and deep. The broad menu versions involved a larger number of items per page (i.e., a maximum of 42), but only two levels of selection (main menu-submenus). The deep menu structure involved a maximum of only six items per page, but four levels of selection (Fig. 5.4).

In the categorized version of the broad menu, items were grouped according to semantic categories (e.g., "education," "travel," "jobs"; see Fig. 5.4a), whereas they were ordered alphabetically in the two other versions (Figs. 5.4b and 5.4c). The number and wording of target categories were identical across versions, as well as the visual characteristics of the display (e.g., size, color, etc.).

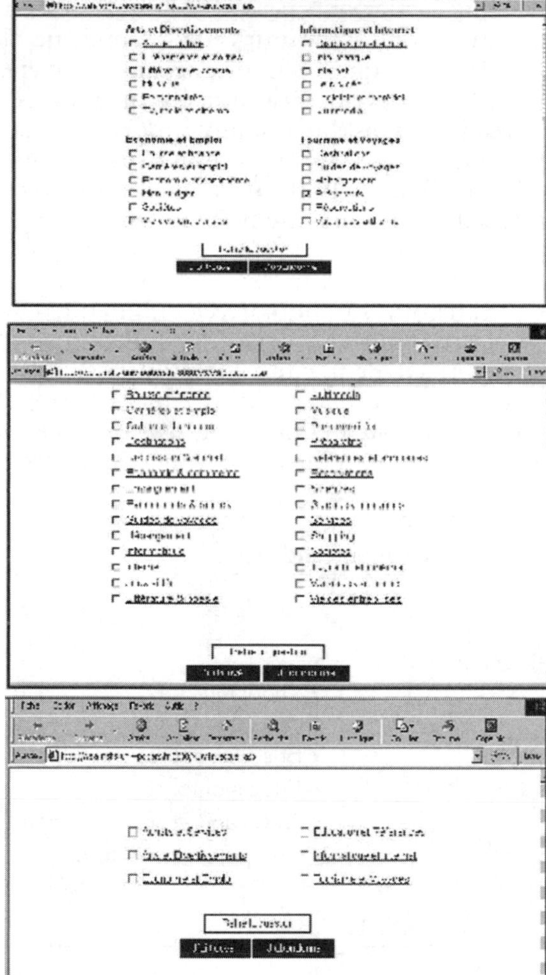

FIG. 5.4. The three menu organizations used in the study by Rouet, Ros, Jégou, and Metta (2003).

Twelve search questions were written based on keywords from the menu hierarchy, so as to be compatible with all three menu structures. For instance, the question "Find accommodation in a palace hotel" was written based on the hierarchy "tourism > accommodation > hotel > palace." Each question was written in four different versions in order to manipulate explicitness and length (Table 5.1). In the "implicit" versions, the original content words were replaced with synonyms (e.g., "Find lodging in a luxury inn"). In the "longer" versions, 2 or 3 content words were added to each question (e.g., "find temporary accommodation in a nice palace hotel in Paris"). Thus, for each question there was a short explicit, a short implicit, a long explicit, and a long implicit version.

All the participants were visited at their homes by appointment. They all possessed a standard PC with a 14-inch screen and a 56K modem connection to an Internet provider. The participants performed the 12 search tasks using each question presented in one of the four versions, and one of the three versions of the menu. For each question, the participants were asked to identify as accurately as they could the relevant subcategory using a check box. They could reread the question as many times as needed while searching. They were allowed to give up the search using a "give up" button. The categories selected, along with the selection delays, were automatically recorded and stored in the database by the Web server.

Despite the fact that all questions corresponded to a unique category, there was only a 52.5% average success rate. On 9% of the occasions, the participants selected another category in the correct submenu. On 38.5% of the occasions, they selected another category or failed to provide any answer. The broad categorized menu had a success rate slightly higher (57%) than both the deep and the broad alphabetic menus (50%). Both question explicitness and length had an impact on search success. Short explicit questions were answered in 67% of the cases, as opposed

TABLE 5.1
Example of Search Questions and Menu

Questions	Menu
Explicit, short:	
Find accommodation in a palace hotel	
Explicit, longer:	• Shopping
Find temporary accommodation in a nice palace hotel in Paris	• Arts and culture
	• Business and economy
Implicit, short:	• Education
	• Travel and accommodation
Find lodging in a luxury inn	• Computers and Internet
Implicit, longer:	
Find temporary lodging in a nice luxury inn in Paris	

Note. Based on Rouet, Ros, Jégou, & Metta (2003).

to 57%, 45%, and 41% for long explicit, short implicit, and long implicit questions, respectively. Finally, older participants tended to perform poorer when using the deep menus.

Rouet et al. also observed that participants reread the question less often with the broad-structured menu than in the other two conditions. Older adults also tended to reread fewer questions than the other groups, especially when searching the deep and broad-categorized menus. Looking back at the question may be interpreted as a measure of the cognitive load associated with searching a hierarchical document. Rouet (2003) found that the rate of question lookbacks increased when the question was complex or the domain was unfamiliar. The rate of rereading also increased with question length and complexity. The mental effort required to locate relevant categories seems influenced by the intrinsic complexity of the menu, as well as by the phrasing of the question.

A good way to help users retain a sense of orientation is to display the content representation permanently, at the left of the hypertext window. Jégou, Andréo, and Rouet (2001) trained 65 undergraduate psychology students to search a Web site in order to study course-related information. A third of the participants were novices in the use of Internet, whereas the remaining two thirds were occasional users. The Web site was designed so that two types of content representations were available: a table of contents and an index. Moreover, the content representation was always visible to the left of the screen, while content pages were displayed in the central area of the screen (Fig. 5.5).

The participants managed to locate relevant contents in more than 80% of the cases. The students reported positive feelings as regards their orientation and ease of navigation in the site, and they thought they would use this type of tool if it was made available as a learning resource. However, many students also reported that they had some trouble remembering the question while searching, and that they wished it was permanently displayed during the search. Thus, making available both the task representation (e.g., questions or study directions), a global representation of the information available, and the content information currently studied seems a condition for easy and efficient navigation in hypertext.

5.3.3. The Potential of Graphical Content Representations

Empirical studies emphasize the need to provide hypertext users with quality content representations. Because hypertext use resembles navigation in a physical space, many authors have recommended providing the user with metaphors (Hsu & Schwen, 2003) or content maps that represent the arrangement of nodes and links relevant to the user's purposes (Kim & Hirtle, 1995). Nilsson and Mayer (2002) defined content maps as:

> a graphic representation of a hypertext document, in which the pages of the document are represented by visual objects (whether simply the title of a page or an icon representing a page) and the links between pages are represented by lines or arrows connecting the visual objects. (p. 2)

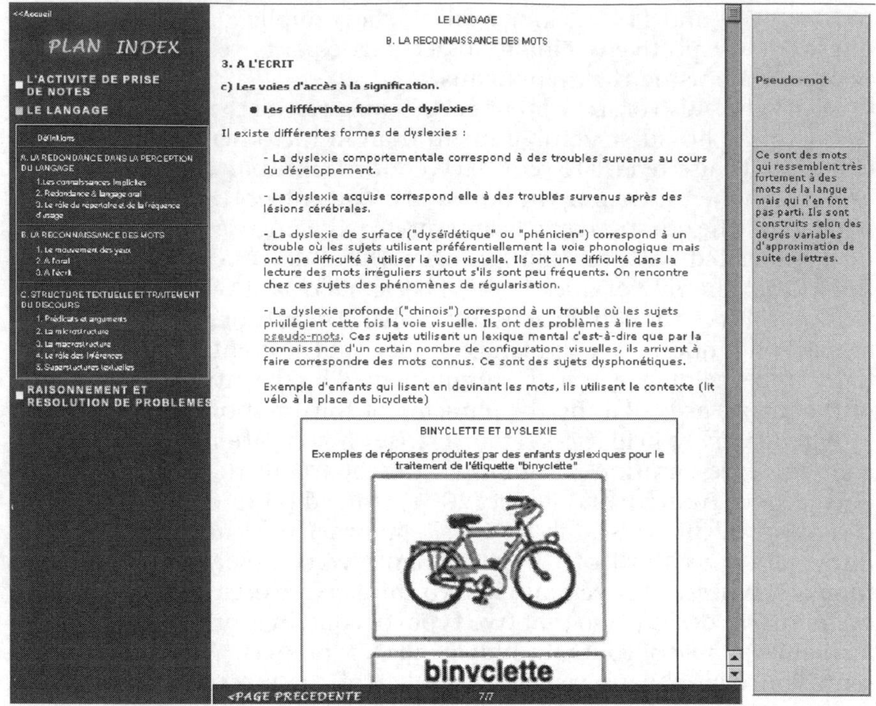

FIG. 5.5. A screenshot of the Web site used in the study by Jégou, Andréo, and Rouet (2001). The left side of the screen features the content representation (table of contents or index), the central part displays the current page, and the right-hand side area is for definitions or adjunct information that the user selects through hyperlinks.

In a concept map, each node represents the contents of a text passage by a thematic phrase. Links represent different kinds of relationships between concepts (Stanton, Taylor, & Tweedie, 1992). The reader accesses a hypertext section by selecting one of the nodes displayed in the concept map. Thus, concept maps serve two distinct purposes: They inform the reader about the contents of the hypertext, and they allow the reader to display information units on the computer screen.

Content Maps and Hypertext Comprehension. Empirical studies of the effects of interactive content representations on college students' comprehension of hypertext have had mixed results. Some studies found a beneficial effect of hierarchical content representations on hypertext comprehension. Dee-Lucas and Larkin (1995) hypothesized that hypertext presentation may facilitate the process of selectively reviewing a document because hypertext provides direct access to the document units. However, this would be the case only if the content map of the hypertext reflects the semantic structure of the domain. Dee-Lucas and Larkin compared three presentation formats of a nine-unit document on electricity: linear, unstructured hypertext (with an alphabetic index), and structured hypertext (with a hierarchical content map).

In their first experiment, 45 college students were asked to study the document in order to be prepared for a test on its content. The participants first read the document in a fixed order and then were allowed to review it. Compared to linear presentation, both hypertext formats resulted in more units being reviewed. However, the participants spent more time selecting units to be reviewed in the alphabetic index than in the hierarchical content map. There was no difference in the total amount of information recalled, but the two hypertext formats resulted in a larger "breadth" of recall: The subjects recalled more unit titles and ideas from more text units. Furthermore, the structured hypertext condition resulted in better memory for title locations in the index. In the second experiment, 63 college students read the same text in one of the same three conditions. However, they were given a specific reading objective—being able to summarize the document. The subjects reviewed more units than in experiment 1, and the differences between presentation formats were greatly reduced. The authors concluded that a hierarchical content map facilitates the construction of a text macrostructure, that is, a more integrated representation of the text content (see chapter 1). They also suggested that the demands of the task can override the effects of different presentation formats.

This study points out several interesting phenomena. First, hypertext presentation promoted the learning of the document structure, as evidenced by the larger "breadth" of recall in experiment 1. Happ and Stanners (1991) also reported that hypertext presentation led to a better learning of the structure of a relational conceptual system. Second, a hierarchical content map facilitated subjects' orientation in the hypertext. Students were faster at selecting the sections in the hierarchical than in the alphabetic index. This is consistent with Simpson and McKnight (1990), who observed facilitative effects of a hierarchical index compared to an alphabetic index. Subjects were also better at answering content questions and at reconstructing the hypertext structure. Third, the influence of different presentation formats varies according to task requirements. More demanding and/or more specific tasks may reduce the effects of content representation devices. For instance, in a study by McDonald and Stevenson (1996), undergraduate psychology students had to read a hypertext on the topic of human learning using one of three presentation formats (a linear text vs. a hierarchical map vs. a network map). Then, the students were asked to use the hypertext in order to answer 10 questions. The results failed to show any effect of the type of content representation on students' comprehension, as assessed by the number of questions correctly answered.

A potential drawback of rich external content representations is that they may decrease the user's effort to understand and memorize the hypertext's organization. Nilsson and Mayer (2002) discussed the potential effects of content maps in terms of two distinct theoretical constructs: the cognitive load theory and the active learning theory. According to the cognitive load theory, maps would help users locate relevant categories in a hypertext by providing an external representation of the structure, which saves the user the effort of building and retaining this representation in memory. According to the active learning view, however, using a map may reduce the amount of elaborative or constructive processes brought to bear by the learner while studying the document. This, in turn, may lead to a lesser learning of the hypertext contents.

Nilsson and Mayer designed a 150-page hypertext containing information about fish and other aquatic animals. The animals were categorized according to three different hierarchies: animal classification (e.g., rays and skates), area of habitat (e.g., Mediterranean open waters), and diet (e.g., omnivores). Three maps presenting each of the three hierarchies were included in the system. The maps could be accessed though explicit links displayed at the bottom of each animal page. The "No map" version did not include any such map.

In the first experiment, Nilsson and Mayer asked 53 undergraduate students to use the system either with or without maps in order to answer a series of 30 questions about aquatic animals (e.g., "How do ghost pipefish catch their food?"). The main finding was that even though participants in the map condition searched fewer pages during the initial trials, the number of pages searched in the no-map condition decreased more dramatically in subsequent trials. As a result, search in the no-map group was slightly more efficient in the last 10 trials. The authors also found that the participants in the no-map condition seemed to use a "task-based" strategy, that is, they considered the specific cues contained in each question, as opposed to a structural strategy based on their knowledge of the hypertext's overall organization. Nilsson and Mayer concluded that "any benefits from the structural information in the map was overshadowed by the negative effects of the map decreasing participants' involvement in the task" (p. 14). This experiment emphasized the importance of the reader's active involvement in a search task as a factor of success.

In the second experiment, Nilsson and Mayer replaced the content maps with a list of path-type expressions that showed the location of the current animal page, for example, "Habitats–Marine–Open waters–Mediterranean open waters–Common skate."

These expressions were "navigable," which means that the user could click on any of the component phrases (e.g., "open waters") to go directly to the corresponding group page. After a training period, path-type expressions speeded access to content pages, compared to a control condition. Spatial ability was positively related to search accuracy. Nilsson and Mayer concluded that the notion that any organizer would facilitate hypertext-based learning is inaccurate. They recommended that maps be used in systems aimed at one-time or occasional users, with no ambition of learning the system. The path-like organizer, on the other hand, seemed useful as a learning device, but only after a training period. Thus, depending on what the system is being designed for, different content representation and navigation tools are warranted.

Content Maps and Prior Knowledge. To further explain the effects of interactive content representations, other studies have considered readers' prior knowledge. Möller and Müller-Kalthoff (2000) showed that a hierarchical map facilitates comprehension only in low readers' prior knowledge. Undergraduate students with low prior versus high prior knowledge in psychology were asked to read a psychology text about cognitive models of writing, using one of two presentation formats (hierarchical content maps vs. no map) and to answer factual questions. The results showed a significant relationship between factual comprehension, hypertext organization, and prior knowledge. Only low prior knowledge readers gave better answers to questions with a hierarchical map.

Shapiro (1999) asked undergraduate students with low prior knowledge on ecosystems and high prior knowledge on animals' families to read a hypertext on these topics, with one of two learning goals: to learn specifically more about animal relationships in their ecosystem (goal A) or about similarities and differences between animals' families (goal B). The participants had to read the hypertext either using a hierarchical interactive map showing the categorical organization of species, or without the map. Then they had to answer explicit or implicit questions (i.e., questions about the textbase or on the situation model, respectively). The hierarchical map improved low prior knowledge participants' answers to implicit questions. The hierarchical map may have provided a conceptual aid to help low prior knowledge readers integrate new incoming information in their situation model. McDonald and Stevenson (1998) showed that navigation aids facilitate low prior knowledge (LK) readers' comprehension. Psychology students read a hypertext on the topic of discourse production. The text was presented either with a navigational aid (i.e., a network concept map or a simple list), or without such an aid (i.e., only as a set of hypertext nodes and links). Both types of aids lead to better comprehension, but only in LK students. Moreover, the time needed to answer questions was shorter when using a concept map than a list.

Another study, by Hofman and van Oostendorp (1999), tried to assess the effects of content representations on several representation levels as a function of readers' prior knowledge. Undergraduate students with high versus low prior knowledge were asked to study a science text on sun radiation and health. The text was presented either through a network concept map showing various types of relationships between ultraviolet radiation and skin cancer, or through an alphabetic topic list (i.e., without explicit high-level relations). Structural levels of text information (i.e., microstructure vs. macrostructure questions) as well as representation levels of text (i.e., textbase vs. situation model questions) were manipulated so as to produce four types of comprehension questions. Contrary to previous results, Hofman and van Oostendorp found that the concept map hindered LK students' situation model construction. They suggested that the concept map had diverted readers' attention from more appropriate levels of processing. For readers with little prior knowledge, simpler representations (e.g., content lists or hierarchical maps) may be more productive than complex network representations.

Thus, even though concept maps are usually thought to be beneficial, their actual effects vary across experiments. Potelle and Rouet (2003) suggested that the impact of content maps depends on an interaction between the features displayed in the map, on the one hand, and the user's prior knowledge of the domain, on the other hand. Hierarchical maps may facilitate the construction of the hypertext macrostructure in LK students (Dee-Lucas & Larkin, 1995; Shapiro, 1999) because they display basic global relationships among the topics dealt with in the text (Lorch & Lorch, 1995; see also chapter 2). Reading a hierarchical map may help LK students build a mental representation organized along categorical or thematic dimensions. On the other hand, a network map could hinder LK students' construction of the macrostructure because of its too complex semantic links (Hofman & van Oostendorp, 1999).

Potelle and Rouet (2003) designed a simple hypertext made of seven content cards about various aspects of "social influence," a core topic in social psychology studies. They designed three content representations of the hypertext (Fig. 5.6). The *hierarchical map* was organized with superordinate and subordinate links from the most general to the most specific topics about social influence. The *network map* was organized by connecting the main topics with semantic links. The relevant links were identified in a pilot study involving 10 PhD students who were asked to draw connections between two parallel lists of topics. Finally, the *alphabetic list* presented the topics in alphabetic order, without explicit connections.

Potelle and Rouet hypothesized that the hierarchical map would function as a structural cue for all the readers, which would improve comprehension, especially at a macrostructural level. The network map, however, was based on implicit semantic relations generated by expert students. Understanding these relations (e.g., "minority influence–innovation") requires some prior knowledge of the domain. Thus, having to study this type of overview might be detrimental to novice readers. Forty-seven students participated in the experiment. The participants were categorized as domain novices versus specialists based on the median split of a knowledge pretest. They studied the hypertext for a period of 20 minutes, with an explicit comprehension objective. Comprehension was assessed through a 16-item multiple choice questionnaire and a summary task. The participants were also asked to draw a map of the hypertext from memory.

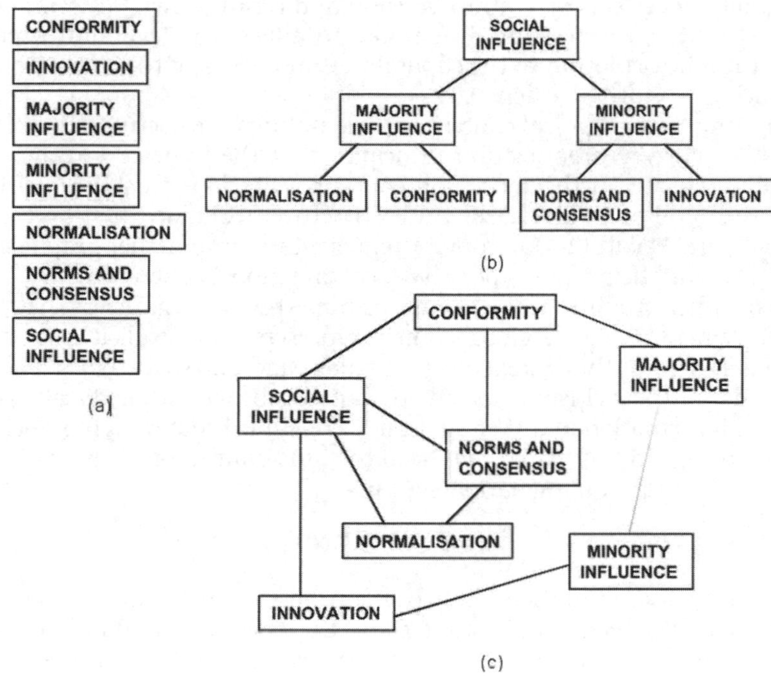

FIG. 5.6. Three content representations of the hypertext on "social influence" (based on the materials used by Potelle and Rouet, 2003); (a) alphabetic index; (b) hierarchical map; (c) semantic network.

Comprehension was positively related to prior knowledge, and microstructure questions were better answered than macrostructure questions. An interaction between prior knowledge level and the type of content representation was found. Low knowledge students had better scores when using the version of the hypertext with a hierarchical map than with the other two formats. For the more expert students, the type of content representation had no significant impact on comprehension. As expected, the effect was stronger for macrostructure than for microstructure questions, even though the three-way interaction failed to reach significance. Low knowledge students also included more thematic ideas in their summaries when reading from a hierarchical map. Finally, they drew more accurate maps of the hierarchical hypertext than with the other two systems. Again, no difference was found for high knowledge students.

Potelle and Rouet concluded that the effects of content representation depend in part on the reader's prior knowledge level. As for any text organizer (see chapter 2), the reader must be able to recognize and use the signals presented in a content map. If the map is ambiguous, or uses unfamiliar symbols, then the result will be an added burden on the reader, with dubious effects on comprehension and recall. When designing hypertext systems, care should be taken to adjust the level and type of structural information to the capabilities and needs of the user (see also Carmel, Crawford, & Chen, 1992).

In summary, graphical content representations are useful to the extent that they convey organization principles that the hypertext reader can readily integrate. Furthermore, content representations must be consistent with the hypertext's actual semantic structure. As pointed out by Dallal, Quibble, and Wyatt (2000), content representations, whether graphical or verbal, should help readers perceive local and global coherence links. This may be done through the use of various hypertextual organizers that play a complementary role: a global content representation, explicit links, indications as regards the context of a particular page, and so forth. Dallal et al. showed that the inclusion of such attributes improved students' ability to retrieve information in a Web site. They concluded that design guidelines based on cognitive research may lead to significant improvements in the quality of complex information systems.

CONCLUSIONS

Our ability to comprehend and use complex documents is partly dependent on the technologies that allow the production and dissemination of information. Since they were created, a few decades ago, hypertext technologies have had a deep impact in the area of document design and document publishing. Document writers and editors have gained much flexibility in the rules that govern the writing and displaying of large sets of texts. These new and exciting technical facilities have triggered optimistic expectations as to their potential role as facilitators of people's access to written information. However, so far hypertext has not always lived up to those expectations. A large number of experiments were conducted, and many have shown that novel ways of displaying and navigating information in hypertext had little or no impact on the readers' performance. Another form of evidence comes from the yet limited impact of hypertext in the publishing world. The explosion of multimedia technologies and the Internet did have a large impact on traditional publishing, especially in some specialized areas (e.g., science publishing). But it certainly did not cause any major drop in the production of traditional books, journals, magazines, and other printed materials. Furthermore, as the use of Web sites becomes more and more common in the general public, designers tend to rely on metaphors that are part of the users' background culture, instead of trying to force novel, artificial presentation formats into them (Nielsen & Tahir, 2002).

Powerful as it may be, hypertext is not always appropriate for presenting materials and tasks typical of the printed world. For instance, in many experiments the hypertext contents were adapted from printed documents, but the cues present in these documents were removed or replaced with less familiar ones. Moreover, initial hypertext studies were conducted with novice hypertext users, who were probably tempted to look for the type of cues they would normally rely on. Literacy skills are acquired through years of education and practice, and it is likely that people need a bit of time before they can adjust to profound changes in their information environment. So far, the research suggests that online and printed information each have their areas of applications. Whether in print or online, what matters is document quality, and document quality may be obtained only by paying a great deal of consideration to why and how people use documents.

Meanwhile, both print and online text technologies are evolving rapidly. Despite the large body of theoretical and empirical studies published in the past decades, any final conclusion concerning the intrinsic benefits and limitations of hypertext would be very much premature. The technology is fast evolving and, more importantly, a new culture of hypertext usage is slowly emerging from the technological big bang that characterized the end of the 20th century. The advent of general-public Internet and World Wide Web services has given information designers many new opportunities to apply hypertext concepts. Many more questions have arisen, and many more theoretical and empirical studies remain to be conducted in order to find out about the potential of hypertext.

Recent research suggests that the road to usable hypertext goes through a deeper analysis of the rhetorical processes involved in nonlinear writing. Hypertext writers need to be more considerate and to anticipate potential comprehension problems in their readership. In particular, the content representation of complex documents must be designed carefully, so as to allow hypertext users to build up appropriate comprehension strategies. Once again, this traces back to the issue of complex texts and the prominent role of content representation and rhetorical cues (chapter 2). This issue is all the more important when considering the increasing use of open, Web-based hypertext systems in educational contexts.

6

Learning From Multiple Online Sources of Information

OVERVIEW AND CONTENTS

In chapter 5, I discussed the concept of hypertext and its application in computerized information systems. The advent of the Internet has boosted the publication and use of online scientific and educational materials. Many institutions are offering innovative training programs that rely heavily on Web-based resources and services. The impacts of Web-based learning on the quality of training are not well known yet. This chapter discusses the consequences of Web-based materials for document-based learning activities. I discuss the new literacy skills needed for students to benefit from Web-based resources, and I suggest that education policies should consider programs specifically aimed at preparing students to think critically with and about the information resources they may find on the Web.

Contents

INTRODUCTION

Since the advent of the Internet, educational institutions in developed countries have started to offer online services that rely heavily on both the hypertext paradigm (chapter 5) and a multiple source approach to learning (chapter 3). Students are being offered new possibilities to study from various kinds of online resources. They are invited to exert their information search skills (chapter 4) in order to retrieve, study, compare, and make use of Web-based documents. This raises new, fascinating questions as regards the impact of these new learning situations on student motivation and knowledge acquisition. In this chapter, I address these questions from a psychological standpoint. First, I review the issue of integrating multiple documents from print and online sources; then I examine the specific learning processes involved in studying from multiple online sources. Finally, I address the problem of evaluating Web-based information sources.

Part of the difficulties observed in early experiments on hypertext use, as reviewed in chapter 5, were due to the fact that researchers tended to assess new hypertext systems using materials and tasks that were typical of the printed medium. Hypertext may be better suited to more complex materials and study tasks, such as those that require the use of multiple text passages that did not originate from a single source. As Mynatt, Leventhal, Instone, Farhat, and Rohlman (1992) suggested:

> Hypertext (...) is perhaps a more natural medium for non-linear information with many interconnections. By non-linear information we mean information that can be understood in isolation, and that does not assume that previous (non-general) information has been acquired. (p. 20).

For tasks that necessitate single texts of reasonable length, hypertext may not have much to offer. But for tasks that require the use of vast amounts of information, readers may benefit from advanced linking and navigation facilities. Hypertext may be used to connect related documents, and to facilitate cross-referencing between documents. According to some authors, hypertext is a suitable medium to support advanced learning activities, precisely because it allows multiple structuring of contents. For example, Spiro, Feltovitch, Jacobson, and Coulson (1991) proposed the Cognitive Flexibility Theory (CFT), a set of principles to account for advanced learning in ill-structured domains (e.g., biomedicine or social sciences; see section 6.2 for a more detailed presentation). Based on their analysis of students' difficulties when studying advanced knowledge, Spiro et al. (1991) claimed, "Revisiting the same material, at different times, in re-arranged contexts, for different purposes, and from different conceptual perspectives is essential for attaining the goals of advanced knowledge acquisition" (p. 28).

Meanwhile, another great technological step has been made in the area of computer networking and information superhighways. During the 1990s the fast and considerable growth of the Internet and the Web boosted the development of a multitude of hypertext-based services and information systems. Unlike the self-contained hypertexts studied in chapter 5, Web-based, open information resources can hardly be compared to any other publication medium. Web sites, portals, and search engines offer brand new ways to connect and to interact with information. Not only can Internet users find nonlinear hypertext organization of information within a Web site, but they can quickly gather and confront multiple sources of information, which originate from virtually any place in the postindustrial world.

Thus, the advent of the Web-based educational services has renewed the debate over the educational potential of hypertext. This is not to say, however, that the issue of information access and learning from hypertext is resolved de facto with the advent of the World Wide Web. Networked information systems bring both new opportunities and new challenges for education, and new potential difficulties for learners.

6.1. STUDYING WEB VERSUS PRINTED DOCUMENTS: USABILITY ISSUES

When considering new Web-based learning situations, one must first ask whether studying on a computer involves issues of usability and, especially, readability of the materials. This issue is particularly important in the design of online news and popular science materials. There are reasons to believe that the Web will be used more and more frequently as a medium for publishing science news in the future (Macedo, 2002). Among the factors that encourage the development of online science publishing are the speed, breadth, and cost of delivery (Eveland & Dunwoody, 2001). The Web is considered a "new space," where writers can guide readers through diverse information sources (Trench, 2000; Trumbo, Sprecker, Dumlao, Yun, & Duke, 2001). The general public may thus access a body of information that was previously "hidden" from them (Peterson, 2001).

Does the publication of popular science online rather than in print affect how students read and comprehend multiple document reports? On the one hand, hypertext may facilitate the identification of the intertextual rhetorics involved in science communication (e.g., the relation of claims to supporting evidence, and the comparison of different viewpoints). But on the other hand, because of limited screen size and poor design practice, the online presentation of popular science reports may lead the readers to overlook important information. The computer display area is bound by the physical size of the computer screen (currently 15" or 17" on most PCs). Moreover, text resources are represented by symbols such as icons in a file folder or links in a hypertext menu, as opposed to physical objects in the realm of print. When browsing through printed materials, contents can be scanned visually; when browsing a hypertext, the user must select links and use the scrollbar in order to explore the contents.

The physical and visual differences between print and online information have consequences on students' strategies in naturalistic study activities. O'Hara and Sellen (1997) asked 10 volunteer members of a research team to summarize a four-page science report. Five participants read the report in print and wrote their summary, while the five others read online and typed in their summary. The printed and online materials were designed so as to be as close as possible to each other in terms of page layout. Subjects in both conditions were asked to create a 200–300 word summary of the source article with the main points and ideas of the document. They were told that they could refer to the source article and take any kind of notes they saw fit at any point during the task. Based on videotapes and interviews, the authors found that note taking was a critical aspect of the activity, and that participants in the online condition found taking notes cumbersome and more effortful. One particular problem of note taking online was the difficulty to create notes that are "at a different layer," that is, perceptually distinct from the original text. Although taking notes on paper was frequently interleaved with reading, in the online condition the two activities were more distinct from each other.

The pattern of students' moves within and between documents also differed in print and online situations. Users of paper documents tended to lay out pages on the desktop space in order to get an overall sense of the structure of the document. Laying out and moving pages was fast and automatic. It did not disrupt the participants from other concurrent activities (reading, thinking ...). Furthermore, the participants learned the physical position of key information that was useful for further reference. In the online condition, navigation was found to be slower and more distracting, even irritating to some subjects. Furthermore, the limited display size prevented subjects from assessing document length and learning the location of information. In conclusion, the authors recommended that efficient annotation tools be developed, as annotation seems to be a key component of functional reading. Furthermore, they advocated the need for more flexible navigation techniques in order to optimize viewing and shifting through online document pages.

Macedo-Rouet, Rouet, Epstein, and Fayard (2003) compared the print and electronic versions of a popular science magazine report published by the Brazilian popular science magazine *Superinteressante* on the topic of "mifepristone," an abortive drug, and its effect on the debate over abortion. The report was formed by a set of documents: a feature (main text) and supporting documents (e.g., interviews, tables, infographics). Examples of supporting documents are: a list of countries where abortion is permitted or prohibited, a list of prolife and prochoice arguments, and an infograph showing different perceptions of the beginning of life (e.g., for Catholics, the conception). These documents synthesized and/or brought additional arguments to what was said in the feature.

They played an important role in the meaning and comprehension of the whole report.

The report happened to be published both in print and on the magazine's Web site, with similar contents but quite different presentation formats. In the print version, the complementary documents were displayed along with the feature, with explicit references in the main text, for example, "see table on the next page." The hypertext version featured the same content materials as the print version. Due to the constraints of the electronic medium, however, the hypertext version differed in the way documents were displayed and linked. Complementary documents were displayed by title, in a menu, before the initial paragraph of the main text. Infographics opened up in a pop-up window. One of them was animated and presented with a very small font. In order to read the captions on a 800x600 dot computer screen, the user had to activate a zooming tool (right mouse button).

Forty-seven Brazilian 4th-year journalism students participated in the experiment as part of a nonmandatory class assignment. The participants' prior experience with the technology and their prior knowledge of the topic addressed in the experiment were assessed in a pretest. The students were randomly assigned to a hypertext reading condition, a print reading condition, or a print control condition. In the hypertext and print reading conditions, the students studied the materials for 20 minutes for comprehension. Then they received a comprehension questionnaire, a perceived cognitive load questionnaire, and a satisfaction questionnaire. The comprehension questionnaire included questions about the main text and questions about the additional documents. In the print control condition, the students answered the comprehension questions first, then they read the materials in print, and finally they answered the other questionnaires.

Readers of the print and online version performed equally well on questions about the main document. For questions about additional documents, however, hypertext readers obtained lower results than print readers. Control readers obtained much lower scores on both subscales, which confirmed that reading the materials was necessary for comprehension, at least for the population involved in the study. Most students reported that they paid more attention to the main text than to the supporting documents. Furthermore, there was a significant correlation between the amount of attention paid to the supporting documents and the score on the document comprehension questionnaire. However, no difference was found in attention to the supporting documents between the hypertext and the print conditions.

Macedo-Rouet et al. reported that students' perception of cognitive load was generally low, but consistently higher in the hypertext than in the print condition. Despite the improved display quality and new publishing facilities (e.g., infographs), reading online is no less challenging than reading on paper. Online presentation of complex materials still poses the problem of making documents contents and structure visible to the reader. The "what's behind the door" syndrome mentioned by Gordon et al. (1988) in their early study of hypertext reading (see chapter 5) still seems to be a problem when studying online.

It is important to note that the results were not due to students' negative beliefs or attitudes toward computers. The satisfaction measure was high and did not differ across conditions. Thus, students seemed to enjoy reading hypertext just as much as they enjoyed reading the report on paper, but they found it more difficult in the former condition. The higher cognitive load in the hypertext condition was mostly due to the poor readability of tables and figures, the difficulty to appreciate the size and content of the documents, and the feeling of getting lost while studying the documents.

Martin and Platt (2001) interviewed 19 students about their reading habits on paper and online, in order to identify the reasons that cause so many students to print out documents that they could read online. Three types of reasons emerged. The first reason was practical: Students found reading online slower, more tiring, less practical than reading paper documents. For example, they mentioned that online documents cannot be transported easily, to be read, for example, on a bus or in a study room. The second reason had to do with learned habits. Students were more used to reading paper documents, they needed to take notes, and were not as comfortable with keyboards as with paper. Finally, students preferred paper documents because of their size and format. Printed documents were found more practical to study multiple documents in parallel, or to work in groups. Online documents, however, were preferred when they shared some characteristics with examination materials (e.g., quizzes), or when they included hypertext links to other resources or animations. It is interesting to note that these reasons have little to do with students' a priori beliefs or attitudes about print or computer technology. Instead, they are related to physical, time, and perceptual constraints associated with the act of reading. In many situations, the printed artifact is simply more practical than the computer screen.

Thus, in the current state of the technology, the advantages of reading online are not immediately apparent. However, many factors have to be taken into account, among which are students' experience with reading online, their motivation to engage in deep processing of the materials, and the quality of the Web site design (Nielsen, 1999; Nielsen & Tahir, 2002). Under optimal conditions, the features of hypertext technology are clearly beneficial to students, as illustrated next.

6.2. ADVANCED LEARNING IN HYPERTEXT ENVIRONMENTS

I have already pointed out that many studies of hypertext comprehension were based on rather simple comprehension or information search tasks, which may limit the possibility to generalize their findings. In fact, some authors have claimed that hypertext may be better suited for reading activities that require the comprehension and integration of multiple perspectives (Britt, Rouet, & Perfetti, 1996; Rapp, Taylor, & Crane, 2003; Spiro et al., 1991). The study by Jacobson and Spiro (1995) aimed at identifying under what conditions hypertext-based learning could lead to deeper comprehension of complex notions. Their approach rests on the cognitive flexibility theory, which states that five pedagogical conditions are necessary for advanced learning in ill-structured domains: (a) the use of multiple representations of knowledge; (b) the connection of concrete cases and abstract concepts; (c) preserving conceptual integrity at all levels of teaching; (d) learning conceptual links across concepts; and (e) assembling elementary pieces of knowledge in realistic situations.

Jacobson and Spiro (1995) implemented these principles into a hypertext that dealt with the influences of technology on society. The hypertext presented "cases" in the form of short texts (e.g., the French attempt to develop an electric car in the 1970s). Cases were discussed according to various points of views or "themes" (e.g., social networks, social nature of technology). Jacobson and Spiro hypothesized that studying the cases in a hypertext environment, with task conditions focusing on the interrelationships between cases and themes (i.e., "criss-crossing") would promote deep comprehension and learning, compared to a study context focusing on factual learning. They also predicted that the effect of criss-crossing may differ according to students' epistemic orientation, that is, the set of beliefs and preferences that determine the type and amount of cognitive resources devoted to learning.

Jacobson and Spiro designed an empirical study in order to test their predictions. Thirty-four undergraduate students participated in two experimental sessions. The participants answered an "Epistemic Beliefs and Preferences" questionnaire designed by the authors. They were divided in three groups (2 control groups, 1 "thematic criss-crossing" group). In the first session, all the students read the entire hypertext. Students in control group 1 were instructed to identify the most important theme for each case. Students in control group 2 and the experimental group were instructed to identify all the cases for which a theme was relevant. In the second phase, the control groups took a computerized drill on theme identification and factual information, whereas the criss-crossing group had to reread the cases in the perspective of multiple theme combinations. The purpose was to demonstrate conceptual interconnections that constitute the domain knowledge.

After the second session, all the participants answered a factual questionnaire and worked on two case studies, in which they had to identify themes relevant for the particular case, and to write up an essay. The main finding was an interaction between treatment (control, criss-crossing) and the type of posttest. The participants in the control conditions (i.e., study + drill) obtained better scores on the factual questionnaire. The students in the criss-crossing condition, however, produced higher quality essays (as evidenced by a blind holistic rating of the essays). The authors attributed this difference to the activities performed in the second study session. In the criss-crossing group, rereading each case under different angles (combination of themes) may have helped students map individual cases onto a network of more abstracts concepts.

Another interesting result is the interaction of treatment and epistemic beliefs. Students with "simple" epistemic beliefs who were placed in the criss-crossing condition obtained poorer performances on the essay posttest. In the control condition, students' epistemic beliefs had no impact on their performance. Thus, the "optimal" outcomes were the result of a combination of technology (hypertext), study conditions (reread and integrate information), and individual orientations (complex epistemic beliefs). The latter result highlights the need to take into account students' attitudes toward learning when assessing the effects of new instructional treatments.

Potential effects of hypertext presentation on deeper processing of document information were also reported in a study by Marchionini and Crane (1994). The study was based on the Perseus project, a hypertext database that presents works by classical Greek authors, in the original language and in modern English, along with iconography and supporting documents. Marchionini and Crane studied groups of students working with either the hypertext database or paper documents. The students were asked to write an essay on Greek theater. Students working with the hypertext version included more citations in their essays. The authors concluded that hypertext presentation facilitated the location of references (sources), thus promoting a higher level of intertextual integration in students' understanding. Providing easy access to definitions and cross-references is a clear benefit of the hyperlink paradigm (see also chapter 5, section 5.2.1).

Britt et al. (1996) examined the potential of hypertext for multiple document comprehension in history. The main purpose was to find out if a structured hypertext presentation would help students construct more elaborate representations of multiple historical documents. Students studying multiple documents covering a complex historical controversy have to figure out the structure of the "argument model," through source identification and integration (see chapter 3). Britt et al. hypothesized that hypertext could facilitate cross-referencing between documents and help students to build more coherent document models. More specifically, they argued that one advantage of hypertext linking over linear, piecemeal presentation is that in the former case, the argument model is "functional." The reader can use the hypertext navigating structure to access the documents by clicking on icons located next to the source. The relations between documents (both the source and content and the claim and evidence) should be more salient in the hypertext environment. Thus, structured hypertext presentation may help students build an argument model and hence, facilitate the understanding of the controversy.

Britt et al. used two sets of nine documents about two problems related to the history of the Panama Canal. Each problem included two parts or episodes (e.g., "planning" vs. "execution" of the Panama revolution, Fig. 6.1). Each episode featured a "textbook passage" that presented factual accounts of that episode. The problem was also discussed in four "historians' accounts" that presented conflicting interpretations of the episodes. For instance, Prof. Kelly argued that the United States helped plan the revolt in Panama, whereas Prof. Brown claimed the opposite. The historians' arguments were based on several types of available evidence. For each problem, three "primary documents" presented evidence used in the historians' accounts. For instance, revolutionary leader Bunau-Varilla's *Memoirs* mentioned a meeting with President Roosevelt. This document supported the "U.S. helped" interpretation.

Thus, for each problem, the documents could be organized hierarchically. Each textbook passage mentioned two opposite interpretations, and each interpretation was based on one primary document. The document sets were presented online using either a linear or a hypertext format. In the linear format, the system included a table of contents, the nine documents, and a "map" showing the hierarchical organization of the documents, each on a separate page. Students could go from one page to another by pushing "next page" and "previous page" buttons. In addition, students could access directly the first page (table of contents) and the last page (map) from any other page of the system.

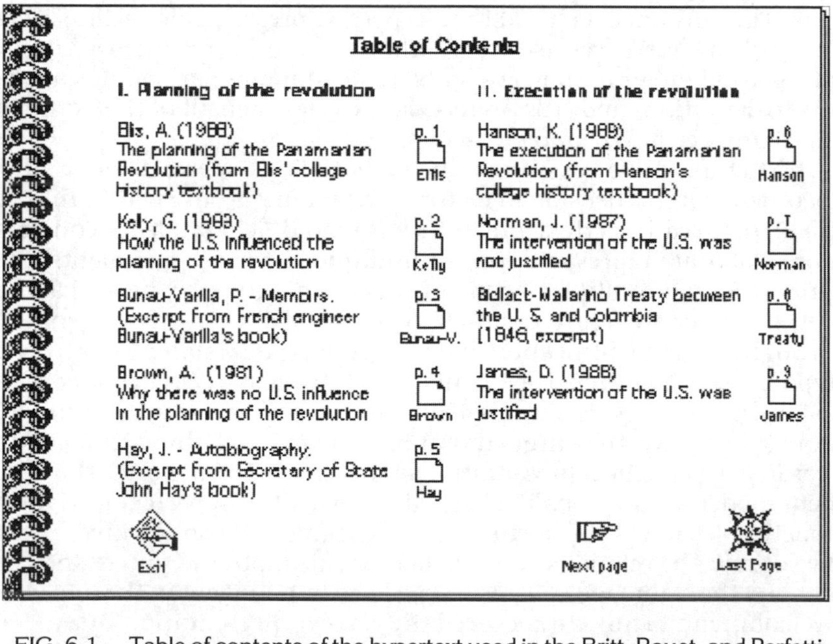

FIG. 6.1. Table of contents of the hypertext used in the Britt, Rouet, and Perfetti (1996) study.

In the hypertext format, the system included the same 11 pages as in the linear format: a table of contents, nine documents, and a hierarchical map. However, the tools for navigating the system were quite different. First, there was no "next page" button on the table of contents page. Instead, the icon next to each document was directly clickable, allowing direct access to the documents. Second, each document page included buttons that allowed the reader to go directly to referred-to documents. An example of a document page in the hypertext format is presented in Fig. 6.2.

The document presented in Fig. 6.2 (Brown) contains a reference to another document (Hay). The "Hay" icon in the lower right corner of Fig. 6.2 is a hypertextual cross-reference. The "Hay" icon can be clicked on in order to display the Hay document.

Both the hypertext and the linear formats contained a "map" showing the hierarchical organization of the documents (Fig. 6.3). The map page was very similar across formats, except for the navigation technique. In the hypertext format, the map could be directly called up from any page, whereas it was presented on the last page in the linear format.

In addition to the format, Britt et al. also manipulated the organization of the document set. In the structured condition, the documents were organized in a manner that corresponded to the hierarchical structure, with subproblem 1 on the left beginning with the textbook, followed by a secondary document, followed by the cited primary

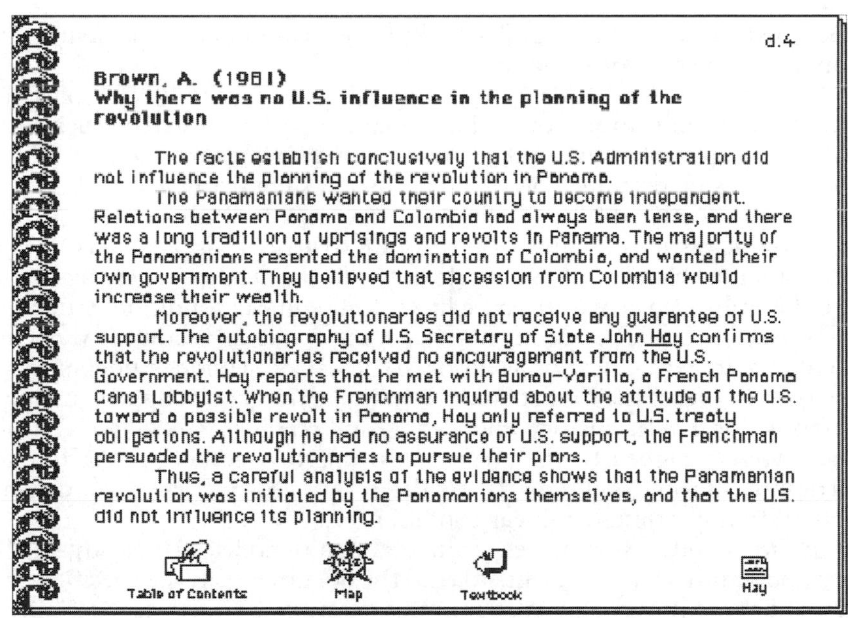

d.4

Brown, A. (1981)
Why there was no U.S. influence in the planning of the revolution

The facts establish conclusively that the U.S. Administration did not influence the planning of the revolution in Panama.

The Panamanians wanted their country to become independent. Relations between Panama and Colombia had always been tense, and there was a long tradition of uprisings and revolts in Panama. The majority of the Panamanians resented the domination of Colombia, and wanted their own government. They believed that secession from Colombia would increase their wealth.

Moreover, the revolutionaries did not receive any guarantee of U.S. support. The autobiography of U.S. Secretary of State John Hay confirms that the revolutionaries received no encouragement from the U.S. Government. Hay reports that he met with Bunau-Varilla, a French Panama Canal Lobbyist. When the Frenchman inquired about the attitude of the U.S. toward a possible revolt in Panama, Hay only referred to U.S. treaty obligations. Although he had no assurance of U.S. support, the Frenchman persuaded the revolutionaries to pursue their plans.

Thus, a careful analysis of the evidence shows that the Panamanian revolution was initiated by the Panamanians themselves, and that the U.S. did not influence its planning.

FIG. 6.2. A document with hypertext links. The Hay icon is a hypertextual cross-reference.

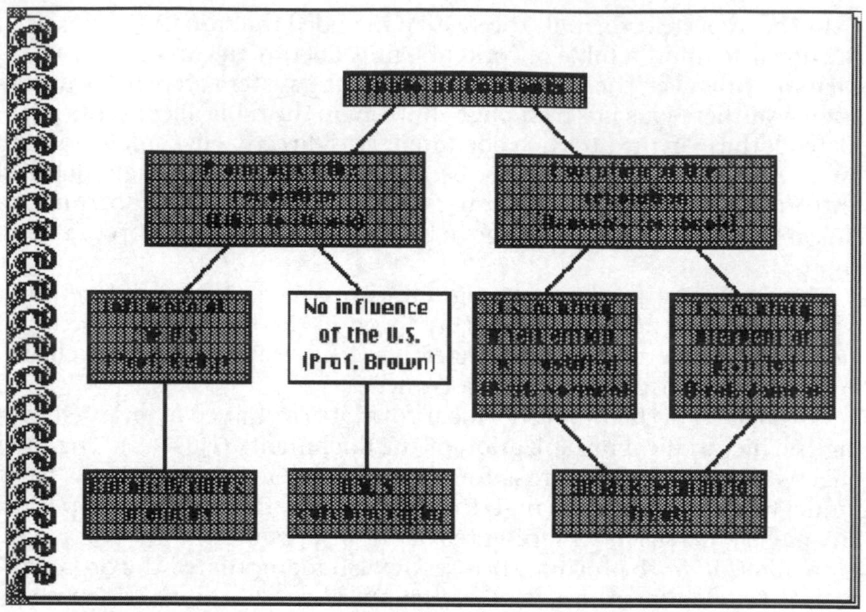

FIG. 6.3. The content map (hypertext version). The light square represents the document that the student was studying when he or she opened the map.

document, etc. In the scrambled condition, the order of presentation conveyed no sense of structure.

Forty-four college students with limited experience in history participated in the study. In session 1, the students were first tested on their history and geography knowledge, and they read a background text. Then the students were trained on the hypertext system using a sample set of documents about a different topic. The experimenter trained the students by introducing and demonstrating a study strategy that students were to use for all problems. In the hypertext condition, students were asked to use the embedded cross-reference links. In the linear condition, students were asked to read the documents by paging forward, reading one document at a time in a linear order. Prior to the second session, students were assigned to one of the four conditions to make the groups approximately balanced for gender, history knowledge, and reading ability. Twelve students were assigned to the structured-hypertext condition, 12 to the structured-linear condition, 10 to the scrambled-hypertext condition, and 10 to the scrambled-linear condition.

In the second session, the experimenter again modeled the study strategy and reminded the students to read the documents in the specified order. The students were given 20 minutes to study the document set. After the study period, they performed various posttests in order to assess their comprehension of the materials. In the third session, the students followed the same procedure as session 2 for the second problem.

Britt et al. analyzed students' online study strategies. They measured the number of document selections made through page-to-page links, and the number of selections made from the table of contents. The use of the table of contents significantly increased in both the hypertext and the scrambled conditions (Fig. 6.4).

In addition, there was a significant interaction between format, structure, and problem. This interaction reflected an increase in the use of the table of contents from problem 1 to problem 2, but only in the structured hypertext condition. Thus, during problem 2 students in the structured hypertext condition tended to give up the direct link strategy they had been taught, and to use the table of contents instead. Students in the scrambled hypertext condition used the table of contents much more often than other groups, in both problem 1 and problem 2.

Students' preference for overview structure over direct links is compatible with the results of previous studies (McKnight et al., 1990; see also chapter 5). It is generally interpreted as a symptom of cognitive overload (Wright, 1991). A possible source of cognitive load in Britt et al.'s study is that the two sets of links (table of contents, direct links) resulted in conflicting cognitive representations of the document set organization (e.g., a survey type versus a route type of representations; Perrig & Kintsch, 1985). In studies of hypertext navigation, mixed representations are often more difficult to understand (Edwards & Hardman, 1989).

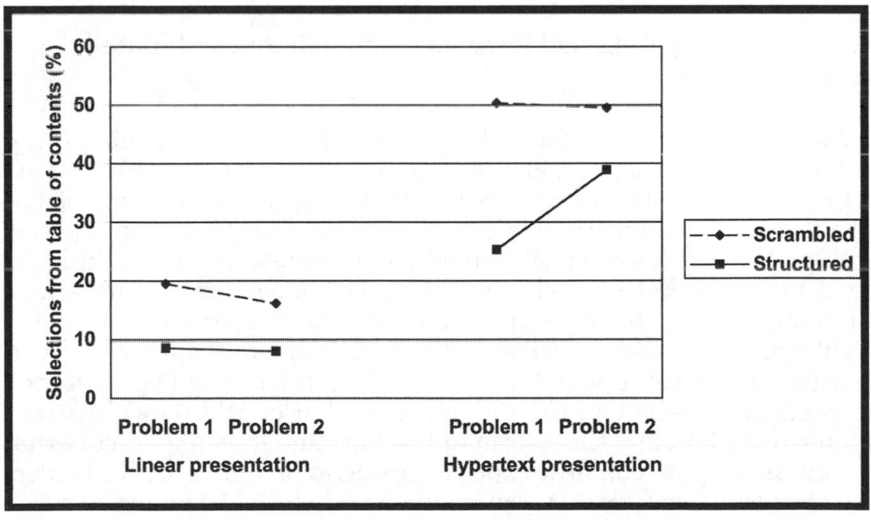

FIG. 6.4. Percentage of selections made through the table of contents (vs. page-to-page links). Based on the data presented in Britt, Rouet, and Perfetti (1996).

Britt et al.'s expectation that a *structured* hypertext presentation would improve subjects' representation of the argument model was not verified. Overall, students performed equally well in the structured hypertext and linear conditions. The only effect of presentation format was actually a deficit in the scrambled hypertext condition. Thus, the hypertext presentation of multiple documents was not beneficial per se. Britt et al. suggested that the specificity of the task (i.e., a complex, fuzzy problem-solving task) may have "overshadowed" any effect of presentation format. They suggested that different presentation formats be checked against different types of tasks or study contexts.

In conclusion, the benefits of using hypertext appear when learning requires the use of multiple documents, presenting different perspectives on a complex issue. In most higher education programs, students spend a lot of time studying documents (Lorch, Lorch, & Klusewitz, 1993; Nist & Simpson, 2000; Pressley et al., 1998). Their ability to understand and integrate facts, concepts, and theories from various sources is an important factor of academic success. When designed carefully, online information systems can provide useful assistance in those sophisticated, multitext comprehension activities. As illustrated in the studies reviewed here, however, the effectiveness of hypertext-based study activities is dependent on a number of conditions as regards task and system design.

6.3. CONDITIONS OF EFFECTIVE WEB-BASED LEARNING SITUATIONS

6.3.1. Designing Tasks and Presentation for Effective Web-Based Studying

Whether hypertext and the Web are effective media for learning is not an all-or-none issue. Just like any text-based activity, the effectiveness of Web-based reading experience varies as a function of task and document design parameters (see chapter 1, Fig. 1.2). Unlike simple text comprehension, however, Web-based comprehension is often characterized by the need to search and integrate information from various sources. Reading objectives are thus all the most essential because students cannot elaborate efficient task management strategies without an accurate representation of the purpose. Despite their rapid growth and popularity in recent years, the dissemination of Web-based instructional materials, and the reform of teaching and learning practice that proceeds, are based on little explicit consideration of learners as readers of complex documents. An emerging research field has nevertheless started to uncover the conditions that promote actual learning from the Web.

Based on research on text comprehension (see chapter 1), Wiley (2001) pointed out that reading yields several types of memory representation: a surface memory of the text, and deeper conceptual representations that are the building blocks of true learning. Wiley conjectured about the potential of Web-based instruction in history and other areas where documents play a central part in the dissemination of knowledge. Presenting students with online documents using multiple windows and hyperlinks may allow the students to corroborate text information and, hence, to construct high-level links across sources. She mentioned several important features in Web-based document learning situations. First is the issue of the number, length, and nature of the *documents* that students must read. In her study, Wiley (2001) preselected a small set of documents that were all relevant to the task. Second, the *comprehension task* was well-defined and specific, and it did require integration of information across sources. Third, the *interface* was designed so as to offer only those functions needed to perform the task: each document or image fitted in a single window, the browser had two side-by-side windows, an overview was available in its own window, and the documents did not include any embedded links. Fourth, the students received explicit *instructions* as to the task and to optimal procedures. They were told how to use the windows and the icons. Finally, *performance* was assessed through appropriate posttests focusing on conceptual learning.

In two experiments, Wiley tested the effectiveness of a two-window presentation combined with an argument writing task. In the first experiment, 10 pages about the 19th-century Irish potato famine were presented online in a single window or in two side-by-side windows (Fig. 6.5). The document set included five texts totaling 1,500 words, four tables, one graph, and one map. Thirty undergraduate students were asked to study the documents in order to write a narrative or an argument of what caused changes in Ireland's population. The argument writing tasks improved performance on measures of transformation of presented information, inference verification, and analogy rating. Furthermore, the two-window presentation improved students' performance on these measures but only in a condition where students were explicitly instructed about the use of the windows, and forced to do so by spreading the list of documents across windows. Wiley concluded that:

> (...) students need to have both a task and an environment that forces them to be more active in order for students to gain the benefits of Web resources. Only when both the task and the design support integration, and students are explicitly directed how to use the feature, do students take advantage of the flexibility of the multiple source environment. Only then do students integrate across sources, selectively re-read sources, and achieve the best level of understanding. (p. 1139)

Wiley (2001) conducted a second experiment in order to further confirm those conclusions. She used a set of documents about earthquakes

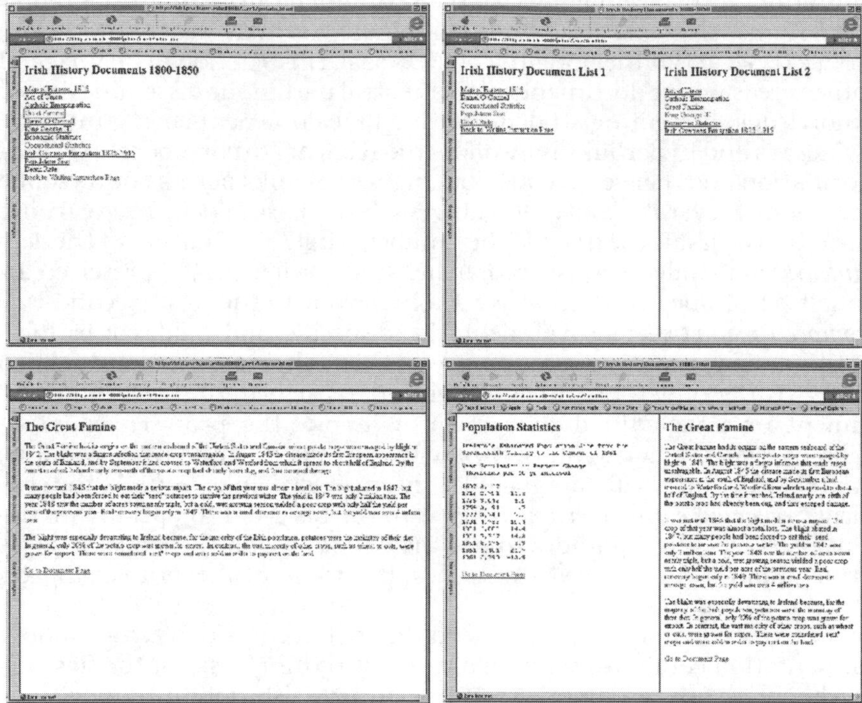

FIG. 6.5. Sample screen shots from the materials used in the Wiley (2001) experiments. Top left: single window condition, list of documents; bottom left: single window condition, sample document; top right: dual window condition, split list of documents; bottom right: dual window condition, two sample documents (Courtesy Jennifer Wiley).

and volcanoes that included ten texts, four diagrams, three maps, and two photographs. Forty students were assigned to one of the four conditions, and student learning was assessed using the same measures as in experiment 1. Again, the "two-window + argument" task outperformed the other conditions, but the display condition alone only had a marginal effect that, according to the author, may have resulted from the differences in the materials (topic and amount) used in the two experiments. These studies showed, nevertheless, that both task and interface parameters condition the effectiveness of Web-based document learning.

Positive effects of Web-based learning tasks have been observed in other areas. Hemmerich and Wiley (2002, experiment 2) asked 40 undergraduate students to study a set of Web documents about volcanoes in order to write an essay or an argument of "What caused the eruption of Mt. St. Helens in 1980." Half of the students read the documents through a single window, whereas the other half were given a browser with two windows and told that this was for the purpose of comparing information across documents. The participants had 30 minutes to read the documents and write their accounts. The authors found that argument writing had a beneficial effect on understanding, as assessed by the quality of students' accounts. Providing the students with a two-window browser showed a trend in the expected direction.

These studies confirm that at least three ingredients are needed in order to make a productive Web-based learning situation. First, the student must possess at least some basic document *comprehension skills*, that is, the ability to identify and evaluate source information, to integrate information across sources, and to assess the quality of content information from a given perspective (e.g., in order to solve a particular problem). I return to this issue in the next section. Next, the *task* must be explicit and require in-depth processing of the materials. In particular, the task must be synthetic, and it must require the student to transform document information. Text production tasks (e.g., argument writing) seem particularly appropriate in this perspective. As Spivey and King (1989) put it:

> Some hybrid reading-to-write tasks involve discourse synthesis, a process in which readers (writers) read multiple texts on a topic and synthesize them. They select content from the composite offered by the sources—content that varies in its importance. They organize the content, often having to supply a new organizational structure. And they connect it by providing links between related ideas that may have been drawn from multiple sources. (p. 11)

The perspective of argument writing may help students gauge the challenge of actually understanding the documents, and invest mental effort accordingly. Knowing that they will have to select, organize, and connect information across sources may encourage them to process each source deep enough so that they do extract gist idea and establish relevant connections among them. More generally, the task effects demonstrate that readers approach document reading with variable levels of attention.

Finally, the *environment* also plays a critical part, by providing students with informational resources necessary to gain the information needed in order to fuel the production process. Organizing, in the physical sense, a set of documents to study is never a trivial task. Again, the observation of academic working environments offers a good illustration. Students and research scientists use personal, often obscure methods to organize their stacks, piles, and folders. A photograph of the famous psychologist Jean Piaget working at his office amidst an apparent chaos of documents (Fig. 6.6) is probably the best example one could find of the intimate relationship between intellectuals and their information sources.

FIG. 6.6. A photograph of world-famous psychologist Jean Piaget working in his study (© Archives Jean Piaget. Reprinted with permission by the Université de Genève).

An example of a successful attempt to introduce Web-based activities within an introductory university course is the study by Maki, Maki, Patterson, and Whittaker (2000). But Maki and Maki observed that the mere provision of online resources does not transform students' learning strategies and tactics. For instance, the use of online adjuncts to an introductory psychology course mostly took place in the 2 days preceding a 3-week term examination. When students were granted course credit for answering additional quizzes attached to the adjunct materials, the self-reported use of the materials increased, as did students' performance to quiz-related items of the term exam. But this effect did not impact their success rate at the final semester exam. Furthermore, the use of online adjuncts seemed contingent on the navigational structure of the Web site, with the "deeper" materials (e.g., FAQ) accessed less often than the upper level pages (e.g., chapter outlines).

After over 20 years of research into the use of electronic information systems, one may still rightfully wonder if computerized systems offer as good and comfortable a working environment as the printed book does. There are no signs of the paperless student room yet, even though online studying is now part of students' schedule in most developed countries. Research studies by Wiley and her colleagues add to a growing body of evidence that design options have a great impact on the usability of these environments. Their conclusions join those of early hypertext researchers, that is, any reflection about educational engineering has to carefully adjust the parameters of task, environment, and student capabilities.

6.3.2. Teaching Advanced Web Learning Skills: Toward a Culture of Complexity?

Improving the quality of Web-based interfaces for learning is a necessary but not sufficient goal. Students also need to be taught appropriate

Web search strategies. Evidence comes from studies comparing people with more or less experience in using the Web. For example, Lazonder et al. (2000) examined the effect of Web experience on students' ability to locate Web sites and information within these sites. They considered that "seeking information on the WWW basically comes down to locating a Web site and, subsequently, to locating information on that site" (p. 580). Web experience was defined as a combination of the total number of hours of working with the Web and subjects' self-estimates of proficiency with a set of 12 Internet-related facilities. Twenty-five students, categorized as novices or experts, were asked to complete three Web search assignments. Each assignment involved locating a particular site, and then a particular piece of information within the site. Expert users were faster, more successful, more efficient (success/time ratio), and more effective (fewer actions) in the Web-site location task. No difference was found in the information location task. Similarly, Hölscher and Strube (2000) asked 12 Internet novices and 12 experts to solve five information problems related to the Euro currency (a prominent topic in the European media at that time), with a time limit of 10 minutes per task. Proxy traces and experimenter notes allowed the authors to categorize the participants' actions. "Double expert," that is, participants with experience both in Internet usage and in the content area of economy, were the most successful. They selected directly just a few target Web sites that they knew of, and were more likely to perform a deeper exploration of content. In contrast, "double novices" reformulated their queries more often and selected a larger number of documents, most of which were irrelevant. They also used the "back" button or other backward-oriented actions more often. Domain experts with little experience on the Web used formatted queries least often (37% of cases), whereas domain experts with Internet experience used formatted queries most often (81.5%).

Students' general opinions and attitudes toward the Web may also influence their judgment about Web-based learning situations. Mitchell, Chen, and Macredie (2005) evaluated a hypermedia tutorial on the topic of computation and algorithms. Seventy-four undergraduate computer science students worked for 1 hour with the tutorial. The students answered a questionnaire about their experience, confidence, and enjoyment in using computers and the Web, and they were asked to report their feelings about the hypermedia tutorial. Students with a positive Web attitude thought that the links were helpful, that they could choose topics according to their own needs, and so forth, whereas those with a negative Web attitude thought that "the structure was not clear," or that "it was difficult to know which links corresponded to the info they wanted."

These experiments show an impact of Web experience on the effectiveness of Web search independent of domain expertise. Whereas domain expertise has an impact on textbook search (Symons & Pressley, 1993), Web experience significantly affects students' manipulation of the search tools and the flexibility of their navigation behavior. Web experience also probably increases students' confidence in their information retrieval skills, which helps them develop more positive attitudes toward library and Internet resources (Collins & Veal, 2004).

Beyond the experience with Web tools and interfaces, students must also become experts in the art of selecting and evaluating Web information. The advent of the Web as a learning resource may not mean the end of paper resources, but it means that academic training will rely more extensively on students' ability to search and make use of a wide range of resources. Fescemeyer (2000) investigated geography students' citation behavior through the content analysis of students' term papers. She reported that 40% of students' cites were to electronic sources, a huge increase compared to a reported 7% in 1995. Nevertheless, most papers included cites to *both* print and electronic sources. Thus, the amount of library resources available to students is increasing in quantity and diversity, with electronic sources coming in addition to, rather than in replacement of, printed ones. As a result, "searching for information becomes more sophisticated as more types of print and electronic resources become widely available" (p. 315).

Students find themselves more and more frequently in situations where they have to set up their own study goals and get any information they can directly from the Web. As several authors have mentioned, the Web differs from traditional library resources in that it offers information of variable quality with no obvious way of distinguishing a priori useful from less useful sources (Eastin, 2001; Fescemeyer, 2000). Some researchers have proposed a classification of those skills. For example, Brem, Russell, and Weems (2001) designed a teaching module that implements four criteria for evaluating Web-based resources:

Source credibility depends on the author's expertise, purposes, potential conflicts of interest, and ethical behavior. It may be assessed through the author's identity (fame), credentials, institution.

Accuracy of content may be assessed in absolute terms by corroborating information across independent sources. It is, however, more commonly assessed through relative markers, such as the date of publication, the inclusion of author details, and bibliographic references.

Reasonableness consists in checking information against one's world knowledge or common sense. Information is reasonable when it is consistent with one's prior knowledge. Brem et al. insist that the independent assessment of reasonableness may be problematic because it depends on one's prior knowledge of the topic.

Finally, *support* represents the data and warrants brought to bear in order to make a claim more convincing. Support can be analyzed systematically (through, e.g., argument analysis), or through surface cues such as the presence of figures, references, scientific jargon, and so forth. Like reasonableness, the evaluation of support depends on one's prior knowledge of the topic.

Brem et al. (2001) examined 81 high school female students' ability to evaluate Web sites using the four criteria. The students worked alone or in pairs on three of six preselected web sites. Two sites were "highly sincere" sites presenting quality information, two were "weakly sincere" sites with more questionable information, and two were hoaxes, that is, sites deliberately aimed at conveying wrong information. Students were taught the criteria during one session, and worked on the sites in another session. Each student or pair of students could choose the three sites they wanted to work on. They wrote a report on each site they evaluated.

The researchers reported a series of interesting anecdotes on students' difficulties with the evaluation task. Students tended to cite mostly science and scientific work in their report. They seldom made references to reporting behavior, even though many texts were of journalistic genres. Thus, they overlooked many important rhetorical processes involved in reporting about scientific facts. Furthermore, students tended to be absolutists, that is, they tried to separate "real science" from hoaxes. However, they tended to show more relativist attitudes when evaluating more sincere sites. Thus, personal epistemology, or one's attitude toward knowledge (Schommer, 1990), appears to be partly dependent on the materials and task at hand.

Authors' credentials was the most prevalent criterion for judging *credibility*. Being a doctor, a scientist, or working for a university were often cited as credibility markers. Goodness of motives (i.e., the lack of quest for profit) or the existence of humanitarian motives were also used. *Accuracy* was mostly evaluated as a function of the amount of details given in a site. *Reasonableness* was assessed through the use of personal knowledge, but also by relying on some site characteristics. The use of common sense was higher when evaluating hoaxes (where the violations of common sense were more obvious). Finally, the *support* criterion was found easy to apply, but students tended to rely on surface markers (i.e., the presence of details or references). Evaluations were also based on the quality and sufficiency of information.

Overall, the study concluded that evaluating information on the Web is a difficult task and that students often are misled by surface markers found on the Web page. The authors concluded that students should be taught how to conduct evaluations, including how to differentiate science and reporting. They suggest, however, that evaluation is a multifaceted task and that there can be no general "cheap and easy" rule. Instead, a situated, context-sensitive approach must be promoted.

Eastin (2001) came to similar conclusions after he studied undergraduates' sensitivity to source information in online documents. He pointed out that, according to research on persuasion, people tend to rely both on source authority and content features such as accuracy, consistency, or bias when assessing the quality of a document. One hundred twenty-five students from introductory communication courses were asked to read a Web page containing information about a topic supposedly more familiar(AIDS) or less familiar (syphilis) to them. The page was presented as authored either by "Dr. William Blake—HIV (or syphilis) specialist," by "Esther Smith—widow of an AIDS (or syphilis) victim," or by "Tim Alster—a high school freshman." The dependent measure was perceived credibility of the content. Credibility was assessed with three items: accuracy, believability, and factualness, each on a 5-point Likert scale. Source and content manipulations both had a significant impact on credibility ratings. Ratings were higher for the more familiar topic, and for the more expert source compared to the less expert one. Contrary to the expectation, however, there was no significant source x familiarity interaction. It must be also pointed out that the information was originally from a highly reliable source (Center for Disease Control) and received rather high credibility ratings regardless of source attribution. Eastin concluded, "While the Internet is undoubtedly a valuable source of information, without some form of structure or educational intervention, its potential to help inform could be greatly diminished."

Recent work by my colleagues and me at Poitiers suggests that formal training into the evaluation and use of documents actually raises students' ability to assess Web documents' quality and credibility. We selected two sets of 12 documents from different Web sites. The first set dealt with the topic of "passive smoking and lung cancer"; the second set dealt with the topic of "workfare and social exclusion." Documents were classified for their quality and credibility based on criteria elicited in prior works: topical relevance, accuracy, currency, expertise, trustworthiness, and reliability. Each set included three documents of each of the following categories: good quality/good credibility; good quality/poor credibility; poor quality/good credibility; poor quality/poor credibility. We asked two groups of students to study the documents as if they were to select the best ones in order to write a short essay. One group of students had received training in Library and Information Sciences (LIS), whereas the other group was made of students from various, non-LIS programs. The two groups were matched for academic level and prior experience with the Web. None of the students had had any prior course or research experience with either topic. After studying the document set for 1 hour, the students were asked to rate the documents for content quality and source credibility, and to provide short written justifications for their ratings.

Students with LIS training gave quality and credibility ratings more consistent with the criteria-based (implicit) categorization of the documents. The control students tended to be less consistent in their ratings, resulting in less contrasted average marks across documents. In addition, the LIS students used a larger variety of criteria when justifying their ratings. Consistent with prior research, they used both content, source, and task-based considerations, whereas control students tended to focus on content only (Macedo-Rouet, Rouet, Bouin, Deshoullières, & Menu, 2004). The data support the view that training in LIS allows students to acquire generalized, content-free knowledge about document types and document features, as well as more efficient heuristics to identify those features as they study the documents.

But exactly what should be taught to inexperienced students in order for them to become mature Internet users? Based on earlier studies of multiple document comprehension (see chapter 3), Britt and Gabrys (2000) identified three skills needed for students to interact successfully with Web-based information. First is the skill of *integration*, that is, the ability to establish connections between prior knowledge and new information. Integrating information from the Web is difficult because the many links available tend to blur coherence relationships across text passages or pages (see also Foltz, 1996). Second, information on the Web tends to take the form of many short documents, forcing readers to establish more high level connections across documents, a difficult task for inexpert students. Third, students learning from the Web may encounter inconsistent or contradictory information that they have to reconcile. Finally, the Web does not offer the kind of guidance students normally find in printed sources, such as introductions, comments, explicit cross-references, and so forth.

Sourcing is a second skill needed when learning from the Web. Sourcing involves identifying a number of parameters that characterize the author and conditions of production of the information. Whereas knowing the source is normally easy with most printed documents, current editorial policies make it a challenge on many Web sites. Information about authors is often hidden or sometimes not available. Furthermore, Web documents do not include a number of cues that help readers of printed documents identify and evaluate the source. For instance, the size, texture, and thickness of the printed artifact is enough to tell a newspaper from a course handout, a handout from a magazine, and a magazine from a textbook. On the Web, none of these cues are available. And often, other useful visual or verbal cues that guide comprehension processes are also missing (see chapter 2).

The third skill mentioned by Britt and Gabrys is *corroboration*, or the activity of checking the accuracy of a piece of information against other sources. This is also difficult on the Web, due in part to the very large amount of information available, and on the difficulty of finding a second source that matches the information. Difficulties in sourcing also result in difficulties in corroboration.

Britt and Gabrys argued that integration, sourcing, and corroboration are "advanced literacy skills" that should be explicitly taught in order to prepare students for Web-based learning. The finding that learning from multiple, online information sources can make students' task harder does not mean, however, that students should learn only from single linear documents. But it does suggest that the Web should not be considered a "learning toy" that any student can use readily and effectively. Preparing students to learn from complex and ambiguous information sources poses new challenges for education.

Britt and Angliskas (2002) examined the skills needed for students to be able to learn from documents. They focused on *sourcing,* that is, the ability to identify and use information pertaining to the author or producer of a document. Based on a reanalysis of data collected as part of an earlier study by Rouet, Britt, Mason, and Perfetti (1996), they established a typology of source features cited by novice history students when evaluating documents. The first group of features describe the author of the document. These include position (or authority), motivation (or the author's purpose), participation (or the author's degree of personal involvement in the event described) and evaluation (i.e., the reader's personal beliefs and judgments about the author). The second main group of features characterize the *document as an artifact* (see also Wineburg, 1994). These include publication date, document type, and, again, readers' judgments about document contents.

Britt and Angliskas presented a series of three empirical studies aimed at assessing inexperienced history students' ability to use source information when reading multiple documents, and the benefits of a prototype training program. In the first study, they asked 60 high school students and 49 undergraduate psychology majors to study a set of documents about the United States's acquisition of the Panama Canal. They tested students' comprehension and memory for source information by asking them questions about sources and identifying correct references to sources in students' essays. They found that students' understanding and use of source information was generally low. Moreover, college students' performance was little affected by study directions that focused on identifying and using the sources.

In the next two studies, Britt and Angliskas used the Sourcer's Apprentice, a tutoring system that teaches the skills of sourcing, contextualization, and corroboration. The Sourcer's Apprentice is based on a set of instructional principles derived from cognitive and educational theories: (a) it simulates realistic problem-solving activities by letting students actually read and evaluate authentic documents; (b) it provides the students with structured, expert-like representations of the documents; (c) it decomposes the task of evaluating documentation into a set of simple subgoals; (d) it promotes transfer by using visual and functional analogies with the real-life document learning situations; (e) it includes modules providing direct instruction, in the form of a tutorial and help cards, and (f) it encourages students' engagement by setting up a game scenario in which students receive credit for the correct application of expert evaluation heuristics.

The Sourcer's Apprentice implements a rather simple scenario (see Fig. 6.7): The student is invited to study the evidence available about a particular problem. The student has to open and read each document in order to learn about the problem. While doing so, the student is prompted to identify relevant source details from each document, and to drag and drop the information onto icons that represent key source parameters (e.g., author's identity, position, motives, and so forth).

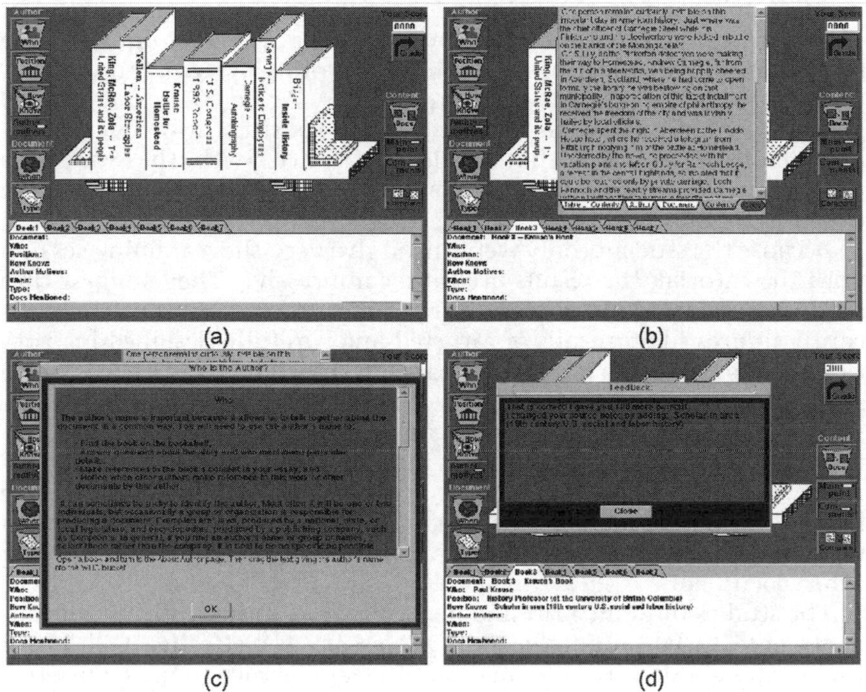

FIG. 6.7. Screen copies from the Sourcer's Apprentice. (a) bookshelf with a list of documents about the Homestead Steel Strike; (b) document opened on "content" page; (c) help card giving information about author's identity parameter ("who"); (d) feedback received on drag and dropping document information onto an evaluation category (downloaded from http://www.pitt.edu/~sourcers/ on April 15, 2003. Courtesy of Anne Britt).

Each correct selection is credited. If incorrect information is selected, then points are deducted and the student receives a hint. When the student feels that he or she has enough information to address the problem, he or she moves on to a questionnaire and an essay writing task.

Britt and Angliskas evaluated the benefits of using the Sourcer's Apprentice in two studies. In the first study, 15 high school students were trained during a 4-day period. Eight students worked with the Sourcer's Apprentice while the 7 control students took part in regular class. In the second experiment, 29 students from other high school classes participated, 10 in the experimental group and 19 in the control group. In both experiments, pre and posttest measures of students' sourcing skills were taken with a sourcing questionnaire and a content analysis of students' essays on two different problems. Students from the experimental groups made significant progress between the pre and posttests, and they outperformed control students on the sourcing posttest. In experiment 3, Britt and Angliskas performed a stricter test of the environment's effectiveness by letting the control group study the same materials as those presented in the tutoring system, but without the benefit of the scenario and interactivity. Again, the experimental group outperformed the control group on the posttest. Moreover, a content analysis revealed that students trained with the Sourcer's Apprentice wrote better causally connected essays than students in the control group.

Because the students only went through a very short training session with the tutorial, the results are rather impressive. They suggest that students' ability to identify and use source information can be significantly improved by means of targeted and carefully designed instructional sequences in an interactive learning environment. The study also supports learning situations based on genuine documents. Unlike studying from a textbook, students in a multiple documents environment have to engage in a real effort in order to read and interpret document information. Reading from textbooks may give students the impression that core information has already been processed and summarized in the feature text, which provides little incentive for studying other documents.

The studies by Anne Britt and her colleagues fully confirm that students need to be taught the skills necessary for effective Web-based learning. Such skills come in addition to those needed to use computers and computer software. They also come in addition to general knowledge of search engines, menus, URLs, and general Web-site organization. Instead, they amount to advanced literacy skills that may be of great use in printed as well as electronic information environments.

In conclusion, meaningful use of the Web as a learning resource requires new skills on the part of students. Navigating huge repositories of information is a skill by itself. Only students who can engage in reading with a "problem-solving framework" are able to set up, implement, and update efficient hypertext navigation strategies (Balcytiené, 1999; Winne & Hadwin, 1998). Beyond efficient study strategies, Web-learners need to know a great deal about documents and document production processes. Document knowledge is needed in order to appreciate the relevance, credibility, and usefulness of Web sources. It is also needed for the student to know what, when, and how to integrate information across documents. Study skills and document knowledge are not readily available to university students, let alone grade school students. They need to be taught and practiced in a principled and sustained way. This represents a whole new agenda for education.

CONCLUSIONS

In this chapter, I addressed the use of the Web as an instructional medium, focusing on the abilities that underlie people's efficient use of Web-based information resources. In recent years, the advent of the Internet and the accelerated production of Web-based services have boosted the use of computers as part of secondary and higher education. Most students in developed countries have access to online information resources through digital libraries, on-line classrooms, and personal computers. Many believe that the Web has a huge potential for improving education and training. In fact, some benefits are clearly apparent, like an easier access to course-related information and materials for students on and off-campus. The consequences in terms of instructional program quality, students' level of understanding, and, more generally, academic success or failure, are not yet obvious. This is, I believe, for three core reasons. First, the art of designing convenient and learning-effective Web-based instructional resources is still in its infancy. Computers remain relatively impractical for reading and manipulating documents; Web-site designers often use rules of thumb to organize the paging and linking of hypertext, sometimes resulting in rather complex and chaotic structures. Second, the Web merely provides a new resource that educators need to master in order to use it effectively. In the current state of the art, educators may not have a good grasp of how to design effective tasks and activities for students to interact successfully with the Web. Third, and most important, integrating online resources and activities as part of instructional programs requires students to master new skills, some of which have a lot to do with the advanced document processing skills discussed in chapters 3 and 4. Those skills may not have been fully recognized yet, let alone taught effectively in schools. I briefly return to each of these issues.

Usability is a critical factor in the development of any technology. It is an essential factor in the development of information systems. Throughout the centuries, instructional designers have learned to adjust the size, aspect, and contents of printed materials to the needs and capabilities of learners. This includes considerations of page size, page layout, print quality, content representation devices, and so forth. In contrast, today's computer is still a poor medium for sustained reading activities. Basic needs associated with document-based learning, like the need to scatter pages on a desk for the purpose of synopsis, the need to annotate, to carry on documents, and to archive them for easy retrieval are still not well fulfilled in the online medium. As regards the quality of Web-based resources in terms of readability, content representation, and navigation, there is yet some room for progress, to say the least. For sure, tomorrow's computers will improve on most of these fronts. They may be more portable, foldable, writable, truly multimodal, and so forth. This will, hopefully, alleviate most of the core usability problems that we know today.

In the meantime, those interested in the instructional applications of computer technology should keep in mind that computer technologies may not have reached a full level of maturity as media for publishing, reading and using text. Furthermore, designing quality online documents is not just an issue of technological sophistication. Quality design requires a careful consideration of readers' needs in terms of document structure, content representation, navigation tools, and so forth. Progress in this direction resides in the appropriate training of designers and Webmasters. There is a need to shift from a purely technocentered perspective to one that encompasses the reader as a cognitive agent, and also social and cultural dimensions. As Smith and Yetim (2004) pointed out:

> Effective strategies that address cultural issues in both the product and the process of information systems development now often are critical to systems success. In relation to the product of development, cultural differences in signs, meanings, actions, conventions, norms or values, etc., raise new research issues ranging from technical usability to methodological and ethical issues of culture in information systems. In relation to the process of development, cultural differences affect the manner in which users are able to participate in design and to act as subjects in evaluation studies. (p. 2)

Another critical issue for Web-based education is to design Web-based activities that are considerate of students' document search and evaluation skills. Teachers may be tempted to propose self-guided learning tasks that will require the student to take an active knowledge-building approach, freely searching and making use of documents available from the Web. As an anecdotal illustration, a young relative of mine, who was a 6th-grade student in a French suburban middle school at the time, was asked by her arts class teacher to "search the Web for information about traditional Irish dance and music." The result was to be a one-page essay "if possible, with pictures," and it was due within a week. A couple of hours on a Sunday afternoon were hardly enough for *me* to locate a few seemingly relevant, informative, and more or less appropriate sources given my relative's age, prior knowledge, and assigned purpose, amidst a deep forest of commercial, political, touristic, personal Web sites in various languages, all with "some kind of" relationship with the topic.

True, the Web offers a unique opportunity for students to access a huge diversity of sources on a given topic. But the risk here is for teachers to design "intelligent assignments for intelligent people," to paraphrase the title of an address by Resnick (1988). In other words, ill-structured assignments, requesting students to consider too many information sources of too poor quality in too little time, may lead to highly variable and, on average, less than acceptable outcomes. Such an excessive interpretation of the constructivist approach to learning might even increase the divide between students who already master advanced literacy skills and those who do not. Powerful computers and high-speed connections do not make every undergraduate student (let alone every 6th-grader) a reading Jean Piaget. The Web may prove to be the teacher's best friend, but teachers will have to learn how best to take advantage of it. Experiments reported in this chapter have shown that the best outcomes are obtained when study assignments have been carefully thought of and phrased. This includes specific guidelines as regards the type of information that must be used, and how this information actually is to be used. For instance, for students to become aware of qualitative differences between reliable and less reliable information sources, the assignments have to promote a critical reflection about the information (as for instance in argumentative essay writing). The topics chosen for such activities should be simple enough so that factual comprehension will not be a problem. Under such conditions, the Web may let students fruitfully confront multiple and diverse sources of information, a feature known to promote deeper understanding. Indeed, recent studies suggest that well-designed Web resources, along with appropriate tasks and directions, may allow the average student to deepen his or her understanding of complex subject matters.

Learning from open resources on the Web poses yet another daunting problem for teachers and educators. Even with simple and carefully framed Web learning assignments, the selection, evaluation, and integration of multiple sources is not a trivial task. As I tried to demonstrate in chapters 3 and 4, complex document comprehension relies on advanced skills that students do not readily master, as good a reader as they may be. Furthermore, when reading online, most of the cues that come traditionally with printed documents are lost, hidden, or transformed (Eastin, 2001). The student has to use advanced tactics to find out who the author is, why the author wanted to publish online, and whether the information is reliable and trustworthy. This type of expertise does not come with mere exposure to online resources. Instead, educators may want to include document comprehension and evaluation programs in their curricula if they want to prepare students for advanced Web-based instructional procedures. Fortunately, some researchers have started to design instructional strategies that may help students practice the skills of source identification and source evaluation. As I have tried to illustrate in this chapter, such strategies, used in the appropriate pedagogical contexts, might prove basic components of tomorrow's high school and college teachers' toolsets.

7

General Conclusions

OVERVIEW

My purpose in writing this book was to offer a synthetic view on the comprehension of complex documents, considered a psychological activity involving advanced knowledge structures and skills. More specifically, I wanted to present the state of the art in academic research, and to discuss more practical issues linked to the design of information systems and the training of advanced literacy skills. In this chapter, I summarize the main points, the lessons learned, and the agenda for further research and development.

7.1. FROM TEXT COMPREHENSION TO FUNCTIONAL LITERACY: WHAT HAVE WE LEARNED?

I started this book with the claim that there was something specific to the comprehension of complex documents, as opposed to the comprehension of single/simpler texts, which has been the focus of mainstream academic research. Modern cognitive psychology, like many other scientific disciplines, has used restricted, controlled situations and materials in order to understand the mental processes at work during language comprehension. There is, in my view, nothing wrong with this approach, which is the hallmark of scientific investigation. Among other important proposals, text processing theorists have established a distinction between reading processes, on the one hand, and text comprehension processes, on the other hand. Whereas skilled reading mainly rests on a restricted set of generalized processes (Perfetti, 1985; Gernsbacher, 1990), text comprehension is a more complex, memory-based process that allows the integration of information into a meaningful mental representation (Graesser et al., 2003; Kintsch, 1998;

van Oostendorp & Goldman, 1999). The purpose of a text is generally to fulfill a communicative process, in which the author tries to convey his or her knowledge about a real or fictitious situation to a reader. Thus, the text is both an external, symbolic representation of the situation, and a tool that allows the reader to construct an internal, cognitive representation of the situation. Because of the constraints of verbal sign systems and human visual–perceptual systems, reading usually proceeds in a linear and incremental fashion. In addition, it is a resource-demanding activity. For example, most people find it difficult to attend to unrelated speech (e.g., news on the radio), or to think deeply about something else (like a shopping list) while reading and comprehending text. Furthermore, reading comprehension speed is strongly constrained by the difficulty of mentally integrating incoming information. For these reasons, text continuity is very important, both in terms of reference (what the text is talking about) and coherence (how the different facts and events connect to each other).

The core research effort in the past 30 years has brought a detailed view of how readers manage to mentally reconstruct textual representations of situations. Numerous studies have found that when reading single texts for the purpose of comprehension, readers focus on coherence markers, trying to keep in line with the characters, objects, places, times, and events that make up the situation (Glenberg et al., 1987; Morrow et al., 1987; Zwaan et al., 1995). Consequently, shifts in any of those parameters may cause a difficulty or even a breakdown in the comprehension process (van den Broek et al., 1999; Zwaan, 1999). In chapter 2, I summarized research showing that the local and global devices that signal a text's organization generally help experienced readers construct a more coherent, stable memory representation of the situation described in the text. In sum, considerable advances have been made in our understanding of what goes on in a person's mind during the continuous reading of narrative, descriptive, or expository text.

I argued, however, that such an emphasis on text coherence and coherence-based strategies may have promoted a vision of text comprehension that is, maybe, a little restrictive compared to people's day-to-day interactions with naturalistic texts. Because the scientific study of text comprehension is difficult and costly, there has been little effort to shift from simplified laboratory tasks to more naturalistic text-based activities. However, as pointed out in reading practice surveys and inventories, people's purposes for reading text are highly variable, and sometimes very different from the prototypical read-to-comprehend situation considered in most text-processing experiments. In addition, the kinds of textual artifacts used in everyday life, whether at school, at work, or for private purposes like shopping, traveling, or paying taxes, are much more diverse than the short passages used in those experiments. Furthermore, in many cases, the reader uses more than just one source at a time. Very often people find themselves comparing information across catalogs, newspapers, essays, and other sources. In sum, I argued that there is a need for a broader psychological perspective on text -based activities, one that includes situations where people have to deal with vast amounts of textual information that is sometimes very heterogeneous.

In chapters 2 through 6, I tried to propose a detailed account of such a generalized view of text-based activities. I focused on dimensions of readers, texts, and reading contexts that are especially important in the comprehension of complex documents. I summarize those dimensions in Table 7.1.

Text Dimensions. Traditional text-processing research has focused on microlevel parameters, such as texts' lexical and propositional contents, and the organization of propositions into coherent causal and temporal structures. But there is more to texts than mere semantic content. Texts are artifacts that convey an author's communicative intent. They may be much longer and more complex than the short passages frequently used in text-processing research. Natur alistic texts include a broad range of content representation devices (e.g., titles, headings; see chapter 2) that guide the readers' information-seeking and comprehension strategies. Digital technologies contribute to increasing the types of

TABLE 7.1

Main Dimensions of Readers, Texts, and Situations Acknowledged in a Restricted Versus a Generalized View of Text-Based Activities

Source	*Restricted view*	*Generalized view*
Text	*Microlevel features*	*Macrolevel features*
	Lexical and propositional content	Content representation devices (chapters 2–6)
	Semantic organization (e.g., causal–temporal aspects)	Sources, genres, and communicative purposes (chapters 3 & 6)
Reader	*Reader as information processor*	*Reader as a literate agent*
	Verbal skills	Knowledge about texts as artifacts (chapters 2, 3, & 5)
	Working memory processes	
	Domain knowledge	Motivation and purposes (Chapters 4 & 6)
Context	*Content-oriented tasks*	*Purpose-oriented tasks*
	Short-term retention of information	Text-based reasoning (chapter 3)
	Inference generation	Information search (chapters 4 & 5)
		Document-based learning (Chapter 6)

text formats and representation devices that are available to the reader (chapters 5 and 6). Furthermore, source features are an important component of naturalistic texts, whether printed or online. Source features are important in that they allow the reader to qualify the semantic content of a text. To take a simple example, knowing *when* a text was published is sometimes essential. A scientist with experience in reading scholarly articles might read with very different perspective an article authored by "Rouet (1905)" as opposed to "Rouet (2005)," regardless of the article's actual content. The credentials, methods, and purposes of authors and publishers are also items of utmost importance when dealing with naturalistic materials.

Reader Dimensions. Whereas a restricted view of text comprehension focuses on readers' working memory, verbal skills, and domain knowledge, a generalized view would consider readers as literate agents, that is, individuals with knowledge about texts as artifacts. They know that texts convey their authors' communicative intents. Thus, literate readers normally care a lot about the origin or source of the text (chapter 3). They know whether the semantic content of a text can be trusted or not, whether it complements or contradicts other texts, and why. In addition, literate readers can elaborate sophisticated goal structures in order to manage the comprehension of complex, multiple texts. This includes generalized knowledge about text-based activities, as well as a range of processing heuristics (Wineburg, 1991). To apply such strategies, literate readers rely extensively on the content representation devices included in most naturalistic texts.

Task Dimensions. The restricted approach to text comprehension uses mostly content-oriented tasks. The reader is typically invited to read the text in order to get an understanding of what is being said, in order to get prepared for some kind of concurrent or delayed test. Comprehension is assessed through the measure of online performance indicators such as reading time and decision tasks, and through immediate or delayed memory tasks and questionnaires. Thus the reader's motivation for reading the text is often unspecific and even ill-defined. In contrast, naturalistic comprehension tasks often involve very specific information needs. For instance, the reader may be studying in order to write an essay about a historical event (chapter 3). Or, the reader may be looking for a specific piece of information, such as a name, a date, or a definition. More generally, printed and online texts are an integral part of a wide range of activities in which they play a variable, but often well-defined, part. I examined two such task domains, namely document integration (chapter 3) and information search (chapter 4). The evidence in both domains suggests that specific comprehension processes and strategies are brought to bear in each case.

A broader look at text, reader, and context features involved in naturalistic text-based activities help shape the contours of functional literacy. According to the restricted view of text comprehension, the competent reader must be a fluent decoder, and he or she must possess syntactic and background domain knowledge. The competent reader must also be able to exert text-based and knowledge-based processes that are constitutive of situation model construction. It is likely that a vast majority of everyday reading activities do involve the construction of mental models of the situations represented in texts. Functional literacy, however, involves more than just understanding situations from text. Quite often, single texts do not provide accurate, complete representations of the situation of interest. Readers need to interpret the complex and sometimes fuzzy relationship between a particular text and the situation it refers to. Furthermore, readers seldom construct knowledge from single, isolated texts. Instead, they need to integrate information across texts, even when the texts do not provide coherent or even consistent descriptions. More generally, many common text-based activities simply do not require readers to form an integrated model of the text's meaning. This does not mean that readers do not need to comprehend. Simply, the "situation" that needs to be comprehended does not strictly match the semantic contents of the text. Instead, it is defined by a preexisting problem or objective and will be fulfilled by matching some text information onto the problem representation.

What are the cognitive prerequisites of functional literacy? This is a difficult, not yet fully answered question. Research into the cognitive processes involved in complex documents comprehension is still in its infancy. Still, it is possible to list a few relevant dimensions. First, literate readers need to master a body of declarative and procedural knowledge *about* texts and documents. This includes knowing how to use visual and verbal cues that "shape" the information. Visual cues, such as paragraphing, help competent readers deal with topic transitions. Verbal adjuncts, such as headings, overviews, and connectors, also guide readers' formation of a mental representation of the text. This often includes identifying topics, categorizing, and structuring information according to various rhetorical schemata. Complex document comprehension requires extended knowledge about information resources characteristic of the discipline. These include typical document types, their internal structure, and the type of cues that will assist their comprehension. Expert readers do demonstrate ample explicit knowledge of text cues. Fine grain analysis of their reading patterns demonstrates that they also do make use of those cues while reading. Efficient use of text cues is critical when using complex documents.

What does it look like when people interact with complex documents? Whereas the restricted view of text comprehension would say, "They go through the text from top to bottom, trying to build a coherent representation of the text's content," a broader look at naturalistic text-based activities suggests a more conditional answer. I have, somewhat artificially, made a distinction between two types of activities: document integration (chapter 3) and information search (chapter 4). In document integration activities, people want to make use of information found in several sources in order to complete a single task. This situation is common in school and professional activities. Reading multiple documents requires readers to identify the origin of each document, to compare information across documents, and to integrate information into a coherent representation. These operations put a strong emphasis on the identification and use of source information. The phrase *source information* captures a complex set of parameters linked to a document. These include the author and context of production of the document. A powerful means to maintain coherence when taking information from multiple documents is to link source representations and content representations. Because high-level source integration is difficult and resource-demanding, however, only expert readers can successfully achieve the construction of complex document models. But regular students can be trained to do so, at least to some extent. In all cases, research studies indicate that letting students read from multiple texts can enrich their representation of the situation or topic.

Information search looks different from document integration, but the two activities share a number of characteristics. When searching from a text or set of texts, the reader must know what he or she is looking for. The clearer his or her mental representation of the objective, the easier the search. Even though this may seem trivial, research shows that people often stumble on search tasks because they cannot manage to remember what they are searching for (chapter 4). Remembering a search objective is a task in itself. It requires an active effort to hold in mind information while being permanently challenged by incoming new information. Information search also requires readers to evaluate information sources properly. This aspect of search is closely related to the "sourcing" heuristic in document integration. A source has to be both relevant and credible. These qualities may be established by looking at specific information pieces. But this is done only when the searcher engages in active, strategic reading.

Both document integration and information search require the mastery and use of memory control mechanisms, that is, thinking about the problem statement or question, looking at source parameters that come with a document, corroborating information sources, or quickly inhibiting irrelevant information. These skills are certainly not fluently used by students in secondary education. They are, nonetheless, compulsory elements of functional literacy, especially in a world that relies more and more strongly on sophisticated, digital information systems.

7.2. DOCUMENT USES IN A TECHNOLOGICAL WORLD

During the past decades, information technologies have deeply transformed our ways to interact with information systems. Microcomputers, graphic interfaces, and the Internet have brought powerful tools to search and make use of immense repertories of information. Early visionaries' dreams about a universal "information society" have, to some extent, come true. But to what extent do computer technologies actually make our lives easier when it comes to comprehending complex documents? To what extent do they improve learning environments, or facilitate written communication in professional environments?

In recent years, scientific investigation of hypertext use has brought somewhat disappointing answers to these questions (chapter 5). In no case did researchers find the tremendous benefits envisioned by early technology enthusiasts. To start with, people often seem to have trouble learning the functioning of a new information system. It is just as if the knowledge and skills that define competent readers should no longer apply when using hypertext. Even when people are more familiar with hypertext perusal, the nonlinear linking of information may still prove sometimes cumbersome or impractical. Among other things, it raises a persistent sense of disorientation and cognitive overload. Why is it so? I have suggested that the reason lies in part in a mismatch between the text, reader, and task features involved in effective text-based communication. People are competent at using printed documents because they rely on a standard organization, standard rhetorical schemata, and standard text organizers. The point of online information systems—at least, earlier ones—was exactly to depart from traditional ways to organize and to present information. No surprise, then, that users found themselves unable to make use of their usual strategies. Asking print-era readers to use hypertexts was a bit like asking 19th-century horse coach drivers to operate prototype automobiles.

Recent developments in digital information technology tend to focus on users' cognitive characteristics and needs. Designers have started to reuse some of the features typical of printed documents, for example, pages, margins, tables of contents, and numbered indexes. Compliance with standard text organizers is now part of Web-site design guidelines (e.g., National Cancer Institute, 2005). Contrary to what the hard-core hypertext idealists once believed, being a bit conservative with text formats does not prevent hypertext designers from also making use of the advanced navigation tools allowed by the electronic medium. In order for a new technology to be successful, however, it has to offer a palatable mixture of old and new.

Conversely, users have started to adjust to new presentation formats and search tools. Hypertext is becoming a fairly ordinary artifact—at least in the rather small portion of the world population that shares the privilege of online technologies. Virtually any connection to the Internet results in one making use of hypertext links. More and more people are learning to operate the navigation and search tools available online. Again, experiments demonstrate that powerful technologies do not automatically result in personal development and task effectiveness. To the lay person, searching for a piece of information through a Web portal is often a daunting task. Even after several months of use, laypersons are still surprisingly inefficient when it comes to performing precise tasks on the Web (Rouet, 2003). Studies of information evaluation and integration suggest that their source evaluation skills are much challenged—and often overwhelmed. Thus, user familiarity and improved design are necessary, but not sufficient to make the online world friendly and accessible to all. The advent of the Internet may not be creating "nations of strangers," but it is certainly widening the gap between those who are functionally literate and those who are not. Thus, powerful information technologies mean that more, not less, education and training are needed to ensure cohesion and solidarity among human communities.

7.3. NEW CHALLENGES TO LITERACY INSTRUCTION

For a long time, literacy was defined as being able to read and to write. The evolution of information technologies and their increasing importance in citizen's lives call for a new, extended definition of literacy, one that reflects the "broad range of skills that adults use in accomplishing the many different types of literacy tasks associated with work, home, and community contexts" (Kirsch et al., 2002). Such a definition will certainly encompass basic reading and text comprehension skills. For instance, word decoding, grapheme–phoneme conversion, or lexical access are involved in any reading activity, from single word reading to complex document-based reasoning, whether from printed materials or online. The literate reader must also be able to identify and use visual and verbal text organizers. To a large extent, those components of language literacy are known from research scientists, policymakers, and educators (Snow & the RAND Reading Study Group, 2002).

But literacy in the information age also means being able to cope with increased information quantity and complexity. In order to do this, the literate reader must be able to understand the text as a human artifact. That is, the reader must not only comprehend, but also interpret texts in light of the author's status and purpose. These processes are essential when one tries to establish the relevance of a piece of information with respect to one's needs. And relevance assessment is becoming increasingly important and difficult in today's world. In a world of scarce and expensive information, relevance was sometimes not an issue simply because there was no choice. When it was indeed an issue, relevance could be established through explicit though not always reliable markers. As information sources increase both in quantity and diversity, establishing information quality tends to become harder. For instance, it is sometimes difficult to find out who published a piece of information found on the Web through a search engine. It is an even bigger problem to understand the rationale behind a list of matches provided by the engine. Thus, the reader must be more than ever aware that this is part of comprehending the document, and be ready to engage in the effort to do so.

Comprehending complex documents also requires the ability to reason about them. In particular, the reader must be able to assess the respective contribution of multiple pieces of information in building an informed opinion about a complex issue. This demands a lot of knowledge about documents, and also the ability to perform resource-demanding mental operations. For instance, the reader has to hold in mind and compare information from several sources; he or she must be able to think about the problem or question at stake while actually reading and evaluating information; and at times, the reader must be able to discard, or "inhibit," any information that was considered but that turned out to be irrelevant, unimportant, or unreliable.

Clearly, most students do not master those types of literacy skills as they enter secondary education. Consequently, educational institutions must design programs to bridge the gap between "restricted literacy" (i.e., reading comprehension) and extended or functional literacy (i.e., being able to use documents in various contexts and for various purposes). Until recently, however, teaching reading skills was still seen by many as the primary school teacher's job. And most parents and educators expect students to be fully "literate" as they begin secondary education. This view is no longer sustainable under the comprehensive definition of functional literacy just outlined. There is, and there will be, more and more to be learned for secondary and higher education students as regards the skills of reading, evaluating, and making use of document information.

Many believe that computer technologies have a lot to offer with respect to those instructional objectives. Powerful and attractive as they may be, however, computer technologies do not bring any ready-made solution to the problem of functional literacy. In fact, computers are part of both the problem and of the solution, creating a new divide as much as they bring new resources. For instance, an international study found that in some countries, lower achieving students are found in schools with the highest ratio of students per computer (Sweet & Meates, 2004). Within those schools, low achievers frequently report that they have less access to computers than other students. And these problems get only worse in countries with a low Gross Development Product (GDP), even though blatant inequities are also found in countries with a high GDP, such as Australia and France. The study also points out that in many countries, low achievers have fewer computers, less educational software, and less Internet access at their homes than other students. And when computers are indeed available, their actual mastery (i.e., knowing how to operate software, how to manage information-related tasks, how to select and use Web sites) requires people to invest a lot of time and effort. Again, those with better learning skills may find themselves in a better position than the others.

In summary, the better, faster, and more powerful information technologies that are characteristic of postindustrial developed countries are setting up a new and challenging agenda for educators and policymakers. Because documents play an essential part in so many activities, the teaching of literacy skills must extend way beyond mere reading and comprehension skills. And because computers are complex artifacts, they represent an objective as much as a medium for modern instructional design.

7.4. IN CONCLUSION

The amount of printed materials available to citizens in the wealthiest parts of the world for learning, work, or leisure has kept increasing at an accelerated rate since the beginning of the industrial era. More recently, the advent of the information age has boosted the production and dissemination of information in printed and audiovisual formats. And in past decades, the rapid development of the Internet has made any computation of the quantity of information available virtually impossible. Millions of documents are created, edited, erased, or moved every day. Reading, comprehending, and using texts are fundamental skills in today's society. And chances are that their importance will increase, as societies rely more and more heavily on fast and powerful information systems. Therefore, a comprehensive theory of the psychological processes that underlie these skills is of utmost importance. Such a theory is necessary in order to understand the complex behaviors involved in using documents, and also how learners can be taught better skills.

I have tried to provide an overview of the tasks and activities that fall into the scope of a modern definition of functional literacy. Functional literacy is the art of interacting with printed and digital documents, in order to fulfill various types of tasks or activities. Finding out what this means in terms of psychological structures and processes, what factors influence their mastery in adult document users, and how they can be taught and practiced are problems of utmost importance for tomorrow's world. The ambition of this book was to introduce this new and fascinating agenda for researchers, designers, and educators. I have tried to present some of the core issues and recent research advances made by the small but fast growing research community interested in this topic. I hope that I have convincingly demonstrated that functional literacy can indeed be construed as a scientific concept, and turned into effective training programs and user-considerate technologies. Tempting as it may be, the vision of a universal information age with accessible and user-friendly information technologies remains a distant prospect. Tackling the intellectual, social, and technical challenges ahead will take many more comprehensive and sustained research programs that will include both a strong scientific culture and a broad perspective on the nature of human competence and skill acquisition.

References

Afflerbach, P. (1990). The influence of prior knowledge on expert readers' main idea comprehension. *Reading Research Quarterly, 25*(1), 31–46.

Albrecht, J. E., & O'Brien, E. J. (1993). Updating a mental model: Maintaining both local and global coherence. *Journal of Experimental Psychology: Learning, Memory and Cognition, 19*, 1061–1070.

Anderson, J. R. (2000). *Cognitive psychology and its applications* (5th ed.). New York: Worth.

Anderson, R. C., & Pichert, J. W. (1978). Recall of previously unrecallable information following a shift in perspective. *Journal of Verbal Learning and Verbal Behavior, 17*, 1–12.

Andre, T. (1979). Does answering higher level questions while reading facilitate productive reading? *Review of Educational Research, 49*, 280–318.

Andre, T., & Thieman, A. (1988). Level of adjunct question, type of feedback, and learning concepts by reading. *Contemporary Educational Psychology, 13*, 296–307.

Armbruster, B. B., & Armstrong, J. O. (1993). Locating information in text: A focus on children in the elementary grades. *Contemporary Educational Psychology, 18*, 139–161.

Baddeley, A. (1986). *Working memory*. New York: Oxford University Press.

Baillet, S. D., & Keenan, J. M. (1986). The role of encoding and retrieval processes in the recall of text. *Discourse Processes, 9*, 247–268.

Balcytiené, A. (1999). Exploring individual processes of knowledge construction with hypertext. *Instructional Science, 27*, 303–328.

Barr, R., Kamil, M. L., Mosenthal, P., & Pearson, P. D. (Eds.). (1991), *Handbook of reading research* (Vol. 2). Mahwah, NJ: Lawrence Erlbaum Associates.

Beck, I. L., McKeown, M. G., Sandora, C. A., Kucan, L., & Worthy, J. (1996). Questioning the author: A year-long classroom implementation to engage students with texts. *Elementary School Journal, 96*, 385–414.

Bernard, M., Hull, S., & Drake, D. (2001). Where should you put the links? A comparison of four locations. *Usability News, 3.2*. Retrieved May 10, 2004 from http://psychology.wichita.edu/surl/usabilitynews/3S/links.htm

Black, A., Wright, P., Black, D., & Norman, K. (1992). Consulting on-line dictionary information while reading. *Hypermedia, 4*, 145–169.

Blanc, N., & Brouillet, D. (2003). *Mémoire et Compréhension* [Memory and comprehension]. Paris: Armand Colin.

Bloom, C.P. (1988). The roles of schemata in memory for text. *Discourse Processes, 11*, 205–318.

Bransford, J. D., Barclay, J. R., & Franks, J. J. (1972). Sentence memory: A constructive vs. interpretative approach. *Cognitive Psychology, 3*, 193–209.

Bransford, J. D., & Johnson, M. K. (1972). Contextual prerequisites for understanding: Some investigations in comprehension and recall. *Journal of Verbal Learning and Verbal Behavior, 11*, 717–726.

Brem, S. K., Russell, J., & Weems, L. (2001). Science on the Web: Students' evaluation of scientific arguments. *Discourse Processes, 32*, 191–213.

Brewer, W. F. (1985). The story schema: Universal and culture-specific properties. In D. R. Olson, N. Torrance, & A. Hildyard (Eds.), *Literacy, language and learning: The nature and consequences of reading and writing* (pp. 167–194) . London: Cambridge University Press.

Britt, M. A., & Angliskas, C. (2002). Improving students' ability to identify and use source information. *Cognition and Instruction, 20*, 485–522.

Britt, M. A., & Gabrys, G. (2000). Teaching advanced literacy skills for the World Wide Web. In C. Wolfe (Ed.), *Webs we weave: Learning and teaching on the World Wide Web* (pp. 73–90). New York: Academic Press.

Britt, M. A., Rouet, J.-F., Georgi, M. C., & Perfetti, C. A. (1994). Learning from history texts: From causal analysis to argument models. In G. Leinhardt, I. Beck, & C. Stainton (Eds.), *Teaching and learning in history* (pp. 47–84). Hillsdale, NJ: Lawrence Erlbaum Associates.

Britt, M. A., Rouet, J.-F., & Perfetti, C. A. (1996). Using hypertext to study and reason about historical evidence. In J.-F. Rouet, J. J., Levonen, A. P. Dillon, & R. J. Spiro (Eds.), *Hypertext and cognition* (pp. 43–72). Mahwah, NJ: Lawrence Erlbaum Associates.

Britton, B. K, Glynn, S. M., Muth, K. D., & Penland, M. J. (1985). Instructional objectives in text: Managing the reader's attention. *Journal of Reading Behavior, 27*, 101–113.

Bush, V. (1945). As we may think. *Atlantic Monthly, 176*, 101–108. Retrieved September 24, 2005, from http://theatlantic.com/doc/194507/bush

Cacioppo, J. T., Petty, R. E., & Kao, C. F. (1984). The efficient assessment of need for cognition. *Journal of Personality and Assessment, 48*, 306–307.

Calisir, F., & Gurel, Z. (2003). Influence of text structure and prior knowledge of the learner on reading comprehension, browsing and perceived control. *Computers in Human Behavior, 19*, 135–145.

Carmel, E., Crawford, S., & Chen, H. (1992). Browsing in hypertext: A cognitive study. *IEEE Transactions on Systems, Man, and Cybernetics, 22* 5), 865–884.

Cataldo, M. G., & Cornoldi, C. (1998). Self-monitoring in poor and good reading comprehenders and their use of strategy. *British Journal of Developmental Psychology, 16*, 155–165.

Charney, D. (1994). The impact of hypertext on processes of reading and writing. In S. J. Hilligoss & C. L. Selfe (Eds.), *Literacy and computers: The complications of teaching and learning with technology* (pp. 238–263). New York: Modern Language Association.

Chen, C., & Czerwinski, M. (1997). Spatial ability and visual navigation: An empirical study. *The New Review of Hypermedia and Multimedia, 3*, 67–90.

Chen, S. Y., & Macredie, R. D. (2004). Cognitive modelling of student learning in Web-based instructional programs. *International Journal of Human–Computer Interaction, 17*, 375–402.

Chen, C., & Rada, R. (1996). Interacting with hypertext: A meta-analysis of experimental studies. *Human–Computer Interaction, 11,* 125–156.

Collins, K. M. T., & Veal, R. E. (2004). Off-campus learners' levels of library anxiety as a predictor of attitudes toward the Internet. *Library and Information Science Research, 26,* 5–14.

Conklin, J. (1987). Hypertext: an introduction and survey. *Computer, 20,* 17–41.

Cross, D. R., & Paris, S. G. (1988). Developmental and instructional analyses of children's metacognition and reading comprehension. *Journal of Educational Psychology, 80,* 131–142.

Dallal, N. P., Quibble, Z., & Wyatt, C. (2000). Cognitive design of home pages: An experimental study of comprehension on the World Wide Web. *Information Processing and Management, 36,* 607–621.

Davey, B., & McBride, S. (1986). Effects of question generation training on reading comprehension. *Journal of Experimental Psychology, 78,* 4, 256–262.

Dee-Lucas, D., & Larkin, J. H. (1986). Novices' strategies for processing scientific texts. *Discourse Processes, 9,* 329–354.

Dee-Lucas, D., & Larkin, J. H. (1988). Novice rules for assessing importance in scientific texts. *Journal of Memory and Language, 27,* 288–308.

Dee-Lucas, D., & Larkin, J. H. (1995). Learning from electronic texts: Effects of interactive overviews for information access. *Cognition & Instruction, 13,* 431–468.

Dell, G. S., McKoon, G., & Ratcliff, R. (1983). The activation of antecedent information during the processing of anaphoric reference in reading. *Journal of Verbal Learning and Verbal Behavior, 22,* 121–132.

Deschênes, A. J. (1988). Le rôle des connaissances initiales dans l'acquisition d'informations nouvelles à l'aide de textes [The role of prior knowledge in the acquisition of new information from text]. *European Journal of Psychology of Education, 3,* 137–143.

Dillon, A. (1991). Readers' models of text structures: The case of academic articles. *International Journal of Man–Machine Studies, 35,* 913–925.

Dillon, A. (1994). *Designing usable electronic text: Ergonomics aspects of human information usage.* London: Taylor and Francis.

Dillon, A., & Gabbard, R. (1998). Hypermedia as an educational technology: A review of the quantitative research literature on learner comprehension, control and style. *Review of Educational Research, 68,* 322–349.

Dillon, A., McKnight, C., & Richardson, J. (1993). Space—the final chapter or why physical representations are not semantic intentions. In C. McKnight, A. Dillon, & J. Richardson (Eds.), *Hypertext: A Psychological Perspective* (pp. 169–191). Chichester: Ellis Horwood.

Downing, R. E., Moore, J. L., & Brown, S. W. (2005). The effects and interaction of spatial visualization and domain expertise on information seeking. *Computers in Human Behavior, 21,* 195–209.

Dreher, M. J., & Guthrie, J. T. (1990). Cognitive processes in textbook chapter search tasks. *Reading Research Quarterly, 25,* 323–339.

Eastin, M. S. (2001). Credibility assessments of online health information: The effects of source expertise and knowledge of content. *Journal of Computer-Mediated Communication, 6.* Retrieved April 12, 2005, from http://jcmc.indiana.edu/vol6/issue4/eastin.html

Edwards, D., & Hardman, L. (1989). Lost in hyperspace: Cognitive mapping and navigation in a hypertext environment. In R. McAleese (Ed.), *Hypertext: Theory into practice* (pp. 105–125). Oxford, UK: Intellect.

Egan, D. E., Remde, J. R., Landauer, T. K., Lochbaum, C. C., & Gomez, L. M. (1989). Behavioral evaluation and analysis of a hypertext browser. In K. Bice & C. Lewis (Eds.), *Proceedings of CHI '89* (pp. 205–210). New York, NY: ACM Press.

Ehrlich, M. F., Kurtz-Costes, B., Rémond, M., & Loridant, C. (1995). Les différences individuelles dans la compréhension de l'écrit: Facteurs cognitivo-linguistiques et motivationnels [Individual differences in written comprehension: Cognitive-linguistic and motivational factors]. *Cahiers d'acquisition et de la pathologie du langage, 13*, 37–58.

Einstein, G. O., McDaniel, M. A., Owen, P. D., & Coté, N. C. (1990). Encoding and recall of texts: The importance of material-appropriate processing. *Journal of Memory and Language, 29*, 566–581.

Elshout-Mohr, M., & van Daalen-Kapteijns, M. (2001). Situated regulation in scientific text processing. In J. Otero, J. A. León, & A. C. Graesser (Eds.), *The psychology of science text comprehension* (pp. 417–436). Mahwah, NJ: Lawrence Erlbaum Associates.

Eme, E., & Rouet, J.-F. (2001). Les connaissances métacognitives en lecture-compréhension chez l'enfant et l'adulte [Metacognitive knowledge in reading comprehension in children and adults]. *Enfance, 53*, 309–328

Englert, C. S., & Hiebert, E. H. (1984). Children's developing awareness of text structures in expository materials. *Journal of Educational Psychology, 76*, 65–74.

Ericsson, K. A., & Kintsch, W. (1995). Long term working memory. *Psychological Review, 102*, 211–245.

Eveland, W. P., & Dunwoody, S. (2001). User control and structural isomorphism or disorientation and cognitive load? Learning from the Web vs. print. *Communication Research, 28*, 48–78.

Farris, J. S., Jones, K. S., & Elgin, P. D. (2002). Users' schemata about hypermedia: What is so 'spatial' about a website ? *Interacting with Computers, 14*, 487–502.

Fescemeyer, K. (2000). Information-seeking behavior or undergraduate geography students. *Research Strategies, 17*, 307–317.

Fincher-Kiefer, R., & D'Agostino, P. (2004). The role of visuospatial resources in generating predictive and bridging inferences. *Discourse Processes, 37*, 205–224.

Fischer, P.M., & Mandl, H. (1984). Learner, text variables and the control of text comprehension and recall. In, H. Mandl, N. Stein, &, T. Trabasso (Eds.), *Learning and comprehension of text* (pp. 213–254). Hillsdale, NJ: Lawrence Erlbaum Associates.

Foltz, P. W. (1996). Comprehension, coherence and strategies in hypertext and linear text. In J.-F. Rouet, J. J. Levonen, A. P. Dillon, & R. J. Spiro (Eds.), *Hypertext and Cognition* (pp. 109–136). Mahwah, NJ: Lawrence Erlbaum Associates.

Foss, C. L. (1989). *Detecting lost users: Empirical studies on browsing hypertext*. Sophia-Antipolis, France: Institut National de Recherche en Informatique et Automatique. Technical report #972.

Freudenthal, D. (2001). Age differences in the performance of information retrieval tasks. *Behaviour and Information Technology, 20*, 9–22.

Gaddy, M. L., van den Broek, P., & Sung, Y.-C. (2001). The influence of text cues on the allocation of attention during reading. In T. Sanders, J. Schilperoord, & W. Spooren (Eds.), *Cognitive approaches to text coherence* (pp. 89–110). Amsterdam/Philadelphia: Benjamins.

García-Arista, E., Campanario, J. M., & Otero, J. (1996). Influence of subject-matter setting on comprehension monitoring. *European Journal of Psychology of Education, 11*, 427–441.

Garner, R. (1987). Strategies for reading and studying expository text. *Educational Psychologist, 22*, 299–312.

Garner, R., Alexander, P., Slater, W., Chou Hare, V., Smith, T., & Reis, R. (1986). Children's knowledge of structural properties of expository text. *Journal of Experimental Psychology, 78*, 411–416.

Garnham, A. (1992) *Minimalism versus constructionism: A false dichotomy in theories of inference during reading*. PSYCOLOQUY 3(63) reading-inference-1.1. Downloaded September 21, 2004, from http://www.cogsci.ecs.soton.ac.uk/psycoloquy/

Gernsbacher, M. A. (1990). *Language comprehension as structure building*. Hillsdale, NJ: Lawrence Erlbaum Associates.

Gernsbacher, M. A. (Ed.). (1994). *Handbook of psycholinguistics*. New York: Academic Press.

Gernsbacher, M. A. (1995). The Structure Building Framework: What it is, what is might also be, and why. In B. K. Britton & A. C. Graesser (Eds.), *Models of text understanding* (pp. 289–311). Hillsdale, NJ: Lawrence Erlbaum Associates.

Gernsbacher, M. A., Robertson, R. R., Palladino, P., & Werner, N. K. (2004). Managing mental representations during narrative comprehension. *Discourse Processes, 37*, 145–164.

Gerrig, R. J., & McKoon, G. (1998). The readiness is all: The functionality of memory-based text processing. *Discourse Processes, 26*, 67–86.

Gilabert, R., Martinez, G., & Vidal-Abarca, E. (2005). Some good texts are always better: Text revision to foster inferences of readers with high and low prior background knowledge. *Learning and Instruction, 15*, 45–68.

Gillingham, M. G. (1993). Effects of question complexity and reader strategies on adults' hypertext comprehension. *Journal of Research on Computing in Education, 26*, 1–15.

Giroux, L., Bergeron, G., & Lamarche, J.-P. (1987). Organisation sémantique des menus dans les banques de données [Semantic organization of menus in databases]. *Le Travail Humain, 50*, 97–107.

Glenberg, A. M., & Epstein, W. (1985). Calibration of comprehension. *Journal of Experimental Psychology, 11*, 702–718.

Glenberg, A. M., & Langston, W. E. (1992). Comprehension of illustrated text: Pictures help build mental models. *Journal of Memory and Language, 31*, 129–151.

Glenberg, A. M., Meyer, M., & Lindem, K. (1987). Mental models contribute to foregrounding during text comprehension. *Journal of Memory and Language, 26*, 69–83.

Golder, C., & Coirier, P. (1994). Argumentative text writing: Developmental trends. *Discourse Processes*, 187–210.

Golder, C., & Rouet, J.-F. (2000). Comprendre un texte hétérogène: Modèle de situation ou modèle d'argument? [Comprehension of heterogeneous text: Situation model or argument model?] *Psychologie Française, 45*, 253–260.

Goldman, S. R., & Durán, R. P. (1988). Answering questions from oceanography texts: Learner, task and text characteristics. *Discourse Processes, 11*, 373–412.

Goldman, S. R., & Saul, E. U. (1990). Flexibility in text processing: A strategy competition model. *Learning and Individual Differences, 2*, 181–219.

Goldman, S. R., Saul, E. U., & Coté, N. C. (1995). Paragraphing, reader, and task effects on discourse comprehension. *Discourse Processes, 20*, 273–305.

Goldman, S. R., Varma, S., & Coté, N. C. (1996). Extending capacity-constrained construction integration: Toward "smarter" and more flexible models of text comprehension. In B. K. Britton & A. C. Graesser (Eds.), *Models of understanding text* (pp. 73–113). Mahwah, NJ: Lawrence Erlbaum Associates.

Gordon, S., Gustavel, J., Moore, J., & Hankey, J. (1988). The effect of hypertext on reader knowledge representation. *Proceedings of the 32nd Annual Meeting of the Human Factors Society* (pp. 296–300). Santa Monica, CA: Human Factors Society.

Graesser, A. C., & Black, J. B. (1985). *The psychology of questions*. Hillsdale, NJ: Lawrence Erlbaum Associates.

Graesser, A. C., Bowers, C., Olde, B. A., & Pomeroy, V. (1999). Who said what? Source memory for narrator and character agents in literary short stories. *Journal of Educational Psychology, 91*, 284–300.

Graesser, A. C., & Franklin, S. P. (1990). QUEST: A model of question answering. *Discourse Processes, 13*, 279–303.

Graesser, A. C., Gernsbacher, M. A., & Goldman, S. R. (2003). *Handbook of discourse processes*. Mahwah, NJ: Lawrence Erlbaum Associates.

Graesser, A. C., Golding, J. M., & Long, D. L. (1991). Narrative representations and comprehension. In R. Barr, M. L. Kamil, P. Mosenthal, & P. D. Pearson (Eds.), *Handbook of reading research* (Vol. 2, pp. 171–205). New York: Longman.

Graesser, A. C., Millis, K. K., & Zwaan, R. A. (1997). Discourse comprehension. *Annual Review of Psychology, 48*, 163–189.

Graesser, A. C., & Olde, B. A. (2003). How does one know whether a person understands a device? The quality of the questions the person asks when the device breaks down. *Journal of Educational Psychology, 95*, 524–536.

Graesser, A. C., Singer, M., & Trabasso, T. (1994). Constructing inferences during narrative text comprehension. *Psychological Review, 101*, 371–395.

Graesser, A. C., & Wiemer-Hastings, K. (1999). Situation models and concepts in story comprehension. In S. R. Goldman, A. C. Graesser, & P. van den Broek (Eds.), *Narrative comprehension, causality, and coherence: Essays in honor of Tom Trabasso* (pp. 77–92). Mahwah, NJ: Lawrence Erlbaum Associates.

Graff, M. (2005). Individual differences in browsing hypertext. *Behaviour and Information Technology, 24*, 93–99.

Grahame, M., Laberge, J., & Scialfa, C. T. (2004). Age differences in search of Web pages: The effects of link size, link number, and clutter. *Human Factors, 46*, 383–398.

Gray, S. H. (1990). Using protocol analysis and drawings to study mental model construction during hypertext navigation. *International Journal of Human–Computer Interaction, 2*, 359–377.

Gray, S. H., & Shasha, D. (1989). To link or not to link? Empirical guidance for the design of nonlinear text systems. *Behavior Research, Methods, Instruments and Computers, 21*, 326–333.

Guéraud, S., Harmon, M. E., & Peracchi, K. A. (2005). Updating situation models: The memory-based contribution. *Discourse Processes, 39*, 243–263.

Guéraud, S., & O'Brien, E. J. (2005). Components of comprehension: A convergence between memory-based processes and explanation-based processes. *Discourse Processes, 39*, 123–124.

Guthrie, J. T. (1988). Locating information in documents: Examination of a cognitive model. *Reading Research Quarterly, 23*, 178–199.

Guthrie, J. T., & Greaney, V. (1991). Literacy acts. In R. Barr, M. L. Kamil, P. Mosenthal, & P. D. Pearson (Eds.), *Handbook of reading research* (Vol. 2, pp. 68–96). New York: Longman.

Guthrie, J. T., & Kirsch, I. S. (1987). Distinctions between reading comprehension and locating information in text. *Journal of Educational Psychology, 79*, 210–228.

Hacker, D. J. (1998). Self-regulated comprehension during normal reading. In D. Hacker, J. Dunlowsky, & A. Graesser (Eds.), *Metacognition in educational theory and practice* (pp. 165–191). Mahwah, NJ: Lawrence Erlbaum Associates.

Haenggi, D., & Perfetti, C. A. (1994). Processing components of college-level reading comprehension. *Discourse Processes, 17*, 83–104.

Halpain, D. R., Glover, J. A., & Harvey, A. L. (1985). Differential effects of higher and lower order questions: Attention hypotheses. *Journal of Educational Psychology, 77*, 703–715

Hamilton, R. J. (1985). A framework for the evaluation of the effectiveness of adjunct questions and objectives. *Review of Educational Research, 55*, 47–85.

Hannon, B., & Danneman, M. (2004). Shallow semantic processing of text: An individual differences account. *Discourse Processes, 37*, 187–204.

Happ, A. J., & Stanners, S. L. (1991). Effects of hypertext cue on knowledge representation. *Proceedings of the Human Factors Society 35th Annual Meeting*, 305–309.

Hartley, J., & Davies, I. K. (1976). Preinstructional strategies: The role of pretests, behavioral objectives, overviews and advance organizers. *Review of Educational Research, 46*, 239–265.

Heath, S. B. (1991). The sense of being literate: Historical and cross-cultural features. In R. Barr, M. L. Kamil, P. Mosenthal, & P. D. Pearson (Eds.), *Handbook of reading research* (Vol. 2, pp. 641–668). New York: Longman.

Hemmerich, J., & Wiley, J. (2002) Do argumentation tasks promote conceptual change about volcanoes? *Proceedings of the Twenty-Fourth Annual Conference of the Cognitive Science Society*. Hillsdale, NJ: Lawrence Erlbaum Associates.

Hofman, R., & van Oostendorp, H. (1999). Cognitive effects of a structural overview in a hypertext. *British Journal of Educational Technology, 30*, 129–140.

Hölscher, C., & Strube, G. (2000). Web search behavior of Internet experts and newbies. *Computer Networks, 33*, 337–346.

Holt, P. O'B., & Howell, G. (1992). Making connections: the logical structuring of hypertext documents. *Instructional Science, 21*, 169–181.

Hsu, Y., & Schwen, T. M. (2003). The effects of structural cues from multiple metaphors on computer users' information search performance. *International Journal of Human–Computer Studies, 58*, 39–55.

Hyönä, J., & Lorch, R.F. (2004). Effects of topic heading on text processing: Evidence from adult readers' eye fixation patterns. *Learning and Instruction, 14*, 131–152.

Jacobs, J. E., & Paris, S. G. (1987). Children's metacognition about reading: Issues in definition, measurement and instruction. *Educational Psychologist, 22*, 255–278.

Jacobson, M. J., & Spiro, R. J. (1995). Hypertext learning environments, cognitive flexibility, and the transfer of complex knowledge: An empirical investigation. *Journal of Educational Computing Research, 12*, 301–333.

Jégou, G., Andréo, P., & Rouet, J.-F. (2001). Le rôle de la structuration de la tâche lors de la recherche d'informations dans un site Web [The role of task structure in information search in a Web site]. In E. de Vries, J.-P. Pernin, & P.-P. Peyrin (Dir.), *Actes du Cinquième Colloque Hypermédias et Apprentissages* (pp. 291–298. Paris: Institut National de la Recherche Pédagogique.

Johnson, H. M., & Seifert, C. M. (1994). Sources of the continued influence effect: When misinformation in memory affects later inferences. *Journal of Experimental Psychology: Learning, Memory & Cognition, 20*, 1420–1436.

Johnson, H. M., & Seifert, C. M. (1999). Modifying mental representations: Comprehending corrections. In H. van Oostendorp & S. Goldman (Eds.), *The construction of mental representations during reading* (pp. 303–318). Mahwah, NJ: Lawrence Erlbaum Associates.

Johnson-Laird, P. N. (1983). *Mental models*. Cambridge, MA: Cambridge University Press.

Kaestle, C. F., Campbell, A., Finn, J. D., Johnson, S. T., & Mickulecky, L. J. (2001). *Adult literacy and education in America*. National Center for Education Statistics. Retrieved July 25, 2004, from http://nces.ed.gov/naal/resources

Kardash, C. M., & Noel, L. K. (2000). How organizational signals, need for cognition, and verbal ability affect text recall and recognition. *Contemporary Educational Psychology, 25*, 317–331.

Kardash, C.-A. M., & Scholes, R. J. (1996). Effects of preexisting beliefs, epistemological beliefs, and need for cognition on interpretation of controversial issues. *Journal of Educational Psychology, 88*, 260–271.

Khan, K., & Locatis, C. (1998). Searching through cyberspace: The effects of link display and link density on information retrieval from hypertext on the World Wide Web. *Journal of the American Society for Information Science, 49*, 176–182.

Kieras, D. E. (1980). Initial mention as a signal to thematic content in technical passages. *Memory and Cognition, 8*, 345–353.

Kiewra, K. A. (1989). A review of note-taking: The encoding–storage paradigm and beyond. *Educational Psychology Review, 1*, 147–172.

Kiger, J. I. (1984). The depth/breadth trade-off in the design of menu-driven user interfaces. *International Journal of Man–Machine Studies, 20*, 201–213.

Kim, K. S. (2001). Implications of user characteristics in information seeking on the World Wide Web. *International Journal of Human–Computer Interaction, 13*, 323–340.

Kim, H., & Hirtle, S. C. (1995). Spatial metaphors and disorientation in hypertext browsing. *Behaviour and Information Technology, 14*, 239–250.

Kintsch, W. (1974). *The representation of meaning in memory*. Hillsdale, NJ: Lawrence Erlbaum Associates.

Kintsch, W. (1988). The role of knowledge in discourse comprehension: A construction–integration model. *Psychological Review, 95*, 163–182.

Kintsch, W. (1998). *Comprehension: A paradigm for cognition*. Cambridge, MA: Cambridge University Press.

Kintsch, W., Kozminsky, E., Streby, W. J., McKoon, G., & Keenan, J. M. (1975). Comprehension and recall of text as a function of content variables. *Journal of Verbal Learning and Verbal Behavior, 14*, 196–214.

Kintsch, W., & Yarbrough, J. C. (1982). Role of rhetorical structure in text comprehension. *Journal of Educational Psychology, 74*, 828–834.

Kintsch, W., & van Dijk, T. A. (1978). Toward a model of text comprehension and production. *Psychological Review, 85*, 363–394.

Kirsch, I. S., Jungeblut, A., Jenkins, L., & Kolstad, A. (2002). *Adult literacy in America: A first look at the findings or the national adult literacy survey* (3rd ed.). U.S. Department of Education. Downloaded April 6, 2005, from http://nces.ed.gov/pubsearch/

Koriat, A., & Levy-Sadot, R. (1999). Processes underlying metacognitive judgments: Information-based and experience-based monitoring of one's own knowledge. In S. Chaiken & Y. Trope (Eds), *Dual process theories in social psychology* (pp. 483–502). New York: Guilford.

Koved, L., & Shneiderman, B. (1986). Embedded menus: Selecting items in context. *Communications of the ACM, 29*, 312–318.

Kozminsky, E. (1977). Altering comprehension: The effect of biasing title on text comprehension. *Memory and Cognition, 5*, 482–490.

Kuhn, D. (1991). *The skills of argument*. New York: Cambridge University Press.

Lachman, R. (1989). Comprehension aids for online reading of expository text. *Human Factors, 31*, 1–15.

Lazonder, A. W., Biermans, H. J. A., & Wopereis, I. G. J. H. (2000). Differences between novice and experienced users in searching information on the World Wide Web. *Journal of the American Society for Information Science, 51*, 576–581.

Lee, M. J., & Tedder, M. L. (2003). The effects of three different computer texts on readers' recall: Based on working memory capacity. *Computers in Human Behavior, 19*, 767–783.

Lehman, S., & Schraw, G. (2002). Effects of coherence and relevance on shallow and deep processing. *Journal of Educational Psychology, 94*, 738–750.

Lin, D.-Y. M. (2003). Hypertext for the aged: Effects of text typologies. *Computers in Human Behavior, 19*, 201–209.

Lindblom-Ylänne, S., & Lonka, K. (1999). Individual ways of interacting with the environment: Are they related to study success? *Learning and Instruction, 9*, 1–19.

Loman, N. L., & Mayer, R. E. (1983). Singalling techniques to increase the understandability of expository prose. *Journal of Educational Psychology, 75*, 402–412.

Lonka, K., Lindblom-Ylänne, S., & Maury, S. (1994). The effect of study strategies on learning from text. *Learning and Instruction, 4*, 253–271.

Lorch, R. F. (1989). Text-signalling devices and their effects on reading and memory processes. *Educational Psychology Review, 1*, 209–234

Lorch, R. F., & Lorch, E. P. (1995). Topic structure representation and text recall. *Journal of Educational Psychology, 87*, 137–148.

Lorch, R. F., & Lorch, E. P. (1996). Effects of organizational signals on free recall of expository text. *Journal of Educational Psychology, 88*, 38–48.

Lorch, E. P., Lorch, R. F., Gretter, M. L., & Horn, D. G. (1987). On-line processing of topic structure by children and adults. *Journal of Experimental Child Psychology, 43*, 81–95.

Lorch, R. F., Lorch, E. P., & Inman, W. E. (1993). Effects of signalling topic structure on text recall. *Journal of Educational Psychology, 85*, 281–290.

Lorch, R. F., Lorch, E. P., & Klusewitz, M. A. (1993). College students' conditional knowledge about reading. *Journal of Educational Psychology, 85*, 239–252.

Lorch, R. F., Lorch, E. P., Ritchey, K., McGovern, L., & Coleman, D. (2001). Effects of headings on text summarization. *Contemporary Educational Psychology, 26*, 171–191.

Lovett, S. B., & Flavell, J. H. (1990). Understanding and remembering: Children's knowledge about the differential effects of strategy and task variables on comprehension and memorization. *Child Development, 61*, 1842–1858.

Lovett, S. B., & Pillow, B. H. (1995). Development of the ability to distinguish between comprehension and memory: Evidence from strategy-selection tasks. *Journal of Educational Psychology, 87*, 523–536.

Macedo, M. (2002). *Du texte à l'hypertexte: Argumentation et lisibilité des revues de vulgarisation scientifique* [From text to hypertext: Argumentation and readability of popular science magazines]. Unpublished doctoral dissertation, Methodist University of são Paulo and University of Poitiers, France.

Macedo-Rouet, M., Rouet, J.-F., Bouin, E., Deshoullières, B., & Menu, P. (2004, August 1–4). *Effects of documentary expertise in the assessment of information quality and source credibility on the Web*. Paper presented at the Fourteenth Annual Meeting of the Society for Text and Discourse, Chicago.

Macedo-Rouet, M., Rouet, J.-F., Epstein, I., & Fayard, P. (2003). Reading and understanding a science report through paper and hypertext—an experimental study. *Science Communication, 25*, 99–128.

Magliano, J. P., Zwaan, R. A., & Graesser, A. C. (1999). The role of situational continuity in narrative understanding. In H. van Oostendorp & S. Goldman (Eds.), *The construction of mental representations during reading* (pp. 219–245). Mahwah, NJ: Lawrence Erlbaum Associates.

Maki, R. H., Maki, W. S., Patterson, M., & Whittaker, P. D. (2000). Evaluation of a Web-based introductory psychology course: I. Learning and satisfaction in on-line versus lecture courses. *Behavior Research Methods, Instruments and Computers, 32*, 230–239.

Mani, K., & Johnson-Laird, P. N. (1982). The mental representation of spatial descriptions. *Memory and Cognition, 10*, 181–187.

Mannes, S. (1994). Strategic processing of text. *Journal of Educational Psychology, 88*, 577–588.

Mannes, S., & Kintsch, W. (1987). Knowledge organization and text organization. *Cognition and Instruction, 4*, 91–115.

Marchionini, G. (1995). *Information seeking in electronic environments*. New York: Cambridge University Press.

Marchionini, G., & Crane, G. R. (1994). Evaluating hypermedia and learning: Methods and results from the Perseus project. *ACM Transactions on Information Systems, 12*, 5–34.

Marchionini, G., Dwiggins, S, Katz, A., & Lin, X. (1993). Information seeking in full-text end-user-oriented search systems: The roles of domain and search expertise. *Library and Information Science Research, 15*, 35–69.

Marchionini, G., & Shneiderman, B. (1988). Finding facts versus browsing knowledge in hypertext systems. *IEEE Computer, 20*, 70–80.

Martin, L. A., & Platt, M. W. (2001). Printing and screen reading in the medical school curriculum: Guttenberg vs. the cathodic ray tube. *Behaviour and Information Technology, 20*, 143–148.

Mayer, R. E. (1984). Aids to text comprehension. *Educational Psychologist, 19*, 30–42.

Mayer, R. E. (2001). *Multimedia comprehension*. New York: Cambridge University Press.

McDonald, S., & Stevenson, R. J. (1996). Disorientation in hypertext: The effects of three text structures on navigation performance. *Applied Ergonomics, 27*, 61–68.

McDonald, S., & Stevenson, R. J. (1998). An evaluation of the effects of navigational tools and subject matter expertise on browsing and information retrieval in hypertext. *Interacting with Computers, 10*, 129–142.

McKnight, C., Dillon, A., & Richardson, J. (1990). A comparison of linear and hypertext formats in information retrieval. In R. McAleese & C. Green (Eds.), *Hypertext: State of the art* (pp. 10–19). Oxford, UK: Intellect.

McKnight, C., Dillon, A., & Richardson, J. (1993). *Hypertext: A psychological perspective*. Chichester: Ellis Horwood.

McKoon, G., & Ratcliff, R. (1992). Inference during reading. *Psychological Review, 99*, 440–466.

McNamara, D. S., Kintsch, E., Songer, N. S., & Kintsch, W. (1996). Are good texts always better? Interactions of text coherence, background knowledge, and levels of understanding in learning from text. *Cognition and Instruction, 14*, 1–43.

McNamara, T. P., Miller, D. L., & Bransford, J. D. (1991). Mental models and reading comprehension. In R. Barr, M. L. Kamil, P. Mosenthal, & P. D. Pearson (Eds.), *Handbook of reading research* (Vol. 2, pp. 490–511). New York: Longman.

Means, M. L., & Voss, J. F. (1985). Star wars: A developmental study of expert and novice knowledge structures. *Journal of Memory and Language, 24*, 746–757.

Meyer, B. J. F. (1975). *The organization of prose and its effects on memory*. Amsterdam: North Holland.

Meyer, B. J. F. (1985). Prose analysis: Purposes, procedures, and problems. In B. K. Britton & J. B. Black (Eds.), *Understanding expository text* (pp. 11–64). Hillsdale, NJ: Lawrence Erlbaum Associates.

Meyer, B. J. F., Brandt, D. M., & Bluth, G. J. (1980). Use of top-level structure in text: Key for reading comprehension of sixth-grade students. *Reading Research Quarterly, 16*, 73–103.

Meyer, B. J. F., & Poon, L. W. (2001). Effects of structure strategy training and signalling on recall of text. *Journal of Educational Psychology, 93*, 141–159.

Meyer, B. J. F., & Rice, G. E. (1982). The interaction of reader strategies and the organization of text. *Text, 2*, 155–192.

Meyer, B. J. F., & Rice, G. E. (1984). The structure of text. In P. D. Pearson (Ed.), *Handbook of reading research* (pp. 319–351). New York: Longman.

Miller, D. P. (1981). *The depth/breadth tradeoff in hierarchical computer menus*. Proceedings of the Human Factors Society, 296–300.

Mitchell, T. J. F., Chen, S. Y., & Macredie, R. D. (2005). Hypermedia learning and prior knowledge: Domain expertise vs. system expertise. *Journal of Computer-Assisted Learning, 21*, 53–64.

Miyake, N., & Norman, D. A. (1979). To ask a question, one must know enough to know what is not known. *Journal of Verbal Learning and Verbal Behavior, 18*, 357–364.

Mohageg, M. F. (1992). The influence of hypertext linking structures on the efficiency of information retrieval. *Human Factors, 34*, 351–367.

Möller, J., & Müller-Kalthoff, T. (2000). Learning with hypertext: The impact of navigational aids and prior-knowledge. *German Journal of Educational Psychology, 14*, 116–123.

Morrow, D. G., Greenspan, S. L., & Bower, G. H. (1987). Accessibility and situation models in narrative comprehension. *Journal of Memory and Language, 16*, 165–187.

Mosenthal, P. (1996). Understanding the strategies of document literacy and their conditions of use. *Journal of Educational Psychology, 88*, 314–332.

Mosenthal, P. B., & Kirsch, I. S. (1991). Toward an explanatory model of document literacy. *Discourse Processes, 14*, 147–180.

Murray, J. D., & McGlone, C. (1997). Topic overviews and the processing of topic structure. *Journal of Educational Psychology, 89*, 251–261.

Myers, J. L., & O'Brien, E. J. (1998). Accessing the discourse representation during reading. *Discourse Processes, 26*, 131–157.

Myers, M., & Paris, S. G. (1978). Children's metacognitive knowledge about reading. *Journal of Educational Psychology, 70*, 680–690.

Mynatt, B. T., Leventhal, L. M., Instone, K., Farhat, J., & Rohlman, D. S. (1992). Hypertext or book: Which is better for answering questions? *Proceedings of CHI'92* (pp. 19–25). New York: ACM Press.

Narvaez, D., van den Broek, P., & Ruiz, A. B. (1999). Reading purpose, type of text and their influence on think-alouds and comprehension measures. *Journal of Educational Psychology, 3*, 488–496.

Nash, J. G., Schumacher, G. M., & Carlson, B. W. (1993). Writing from sources: A structure-mapping model. *Journal of Educational Psychology, 85*, 159–170.

National Cancer Institute (2005). Research-based Web design and usability guidelines. Retrieved April 29, 2005, from http://usability.gov/guidelines/index.html

National Center for Education Statistics (2004). *Defining literacy and sample items*. Retrieved July 25, 2004, from http://nces.ed.gov/naal/defining/measprose.asp

Newell, G. E., & Winograd, P. (1989). The effects of writing on learning from expository text. *Written Communication, 6*, 196–217.

Nielsen, J. (1995). *Multimedia and hypertext: The Internet and beyond*. London: Academic Press.

Nielsen, J. (1999). *Designing Web usability: The practice of simplicity*. Indianapolis, IN: New Riders.

Nielsen, J., & Tahir, M. (2002). *Homepage usability: 50 Websites deconstructed*. Indianapolis, IN: New Riders.

Nilsson, R. M., & Mayer, R. E. (2002). The effects of graphical organizers giving cues to the structure of a hypertext document on users' navigation strategies and performance. *International Journal of Human–Computer Studies, 57*, 1–26.

Nist, S. L., & Simpson, M. L. (2000). College studying. In M. L. Kamil, P. Mosenthal, P. D. Pearson, & R. Barr (Eds.), *Handbook of reading research* (Vol. 3, pp. 645–666). Mahwah, NJ: Lawrence Erlbaum Associates.

Noordman, L. G. M., & Vonk, W. (1992) Readers' knowledge and the control of inferences in reading. *Language and Cognitive Processes, 7*, 373–391.

Norman, K. L. (1991). *The psychology of menu selection*. Norwood, NJ: Ablex.

O'Brien, E. J., & Albrecht, J. E . (1992). Comprehension strategies and the development of a mental model. *Journal of Experimental Psychology: Learning, Memory and Cognition, 18*, 777–784.

OECD-PISA (n.d.). Retrieved April 1, 2004, from http://www.pisa.oecd.org/pisa/read.htm

O'Hara, K., & Sellen, A. (1997). A comparison of reading paper and on-line documents. In S. Pemberton (Ed.), *Proceedings of the CHI'97 Conference*. Retrieved May 10, 2004, from http://www.acm.org/sigchi/chi97/proceedings/paper/koh.htm

Otero, J., & Campanario, J. M. (1990). Comprehension evaluation and regulation in learning from science texts. *Journal of Research in Science Teaching, 27*, 447–460.

Otero, J., & Graesser, A. C. (2001). PREG: Elements of a model of question asking. *Cognition and Instruction, 19*, 143–175.

Otero, J., León, J. A., & Graesser, A. C. (Eds.). (2002). *The psychology of science text comprehension*. Mahwah, NJ: Lawrence Erlbaum Associates.

Paris, S. G., & Jacobs, J. E. (1984). The benefits of informed instruction for children's reading awareness and comprehension skills. *Child Development, 55*, 2083–2093.

Paris, S. G., Wasik, B. A., & Turner, J. C. (1991). The development of strategic readers. In R. Barr, M. L. Kamil, P. Mosenthal, & P. D. Pearson (Eds.), *Handbook of reading research* (Vol. 2, pp. 609–640). New York: Longman.

Parkinson, S. R., Sisson, N., & Snowberry, K. (1985). Organization of broad computer menu displays. *International Journal of Man–Machine Studies, 23*, 289–297.

Passerault, J.-M., & Chesnet, D. (1991). Le marquage des paragraphes: Son rôle dans la gestion des traitements pendant la lecture [Paragraph marking: Its role in process management during reading]. *Psychologie Française, 36*, 159–165.

Paxton, R. J. (1997). "Someone with like a life wrote it": The effects of a visible author on high school history students. *Journal of Educational Psychology, 89*, 235–250.

Perfetti, C. A. (1985). *Reading ability*. New York: Oxford University Press.

Perfetti, C. A., & Britt, M. A. (1995). Where do propositions come from? In C. A. Weaver III, S. Mannes, & C. R. Fletcher (Eds.), *Discourse comprehension: Essays in honor of Walter Kintsch* (pp. 11–34). Hillsdale, NJ: Lawrence Erlbaum Associates.

Perfetti, C. A., Britt, M. A., & Georgi, M. C. (1995). *Text-based learning and reasoning: Studies in history*. Hillsdale, NJ: Lawrence Erlbaum Associates.

Perfetti, C. A., Rouet, J.-F., & Britt, M. A. (1999). Towards a theory of documents representation. In H. van Oostendorp & S. Goldman (Eds.), *The construction of mental representations during reading* (pp. 99–122). Mahwah, NJ: Lawrence Erlbaum Associates.

Perrig, W., & Kintsch, W. (1985). Propositional and situational representations of text. *Journal of Memory and Language, 24*, 503–518.

Peterson, I. (2001). Touring the scientific Web. *Science Communication, 22*, 246–255.

Potelle, H., & Rouet, J.-F. (2001, July 12–14). *Structural representations in the comprehension of expository text*. Paper presented at the 11th Annual Meeting of the Society for Text and Discourse, Santa Barbara, CA.

Potelle, H., & Rouet, J.-F. (2003). Effects of content representation and readers' prior knowledge on the comprehension of hypertext. *International Journal of Human–Computer Studies, 58*, 327–345.

Pressley, M., & Afflerbach, P. (1995). *Verbal protocols in reading: the nature of constructively responsive reading*. Hillsdale, NJ: Lawrence Erlbaum Associates.

Pressley, M., Van Etten, S., Yokoi, L., Freebern, G., & Van Meter, P. (1998). The metacognition of college studentship: A grounded theory approach. In D. J. Hacker, J. Dunlosky, & A. C. Graesser (Eds.), *Metacognition in educational theory and practice* (pp. 347–366). Mahwah, NJ: Lawrence Erlbaum Associates.

Raphael, T. E. (1984). Teaching learners about sources of information for answering comprehension questions. *Journal of Reading*, January, 303–311.

Raphael, T. E., & Pearson, P. D. (1985). Increasing students' awareness of sources of information for answering questions. *American Educational Research Journal, 22*, 217–235.

Rapp, D. N., Taylor, H. A., & Crane, G. R. (2003). The impact of digital libraries on cognitive processes: Psychological issues of hypermedia. *Computers in Human Behavior, 19*, 609–628.

Rayward, W. B. (1991). The case of Paul Otlet, pioneer of information science, internationalist, visionary: Reflections on biography. *Journal of Librarianship and Information Science, 23*,135–145.

Reason, J. (1990). *Human Error*. New York: Cambridge University Press.

Reder, L. (1987). Strategy selection in question answering. *Cognitive Psychology, 19*, 90–138.

Reinking, D., & Rickman, S. S. (1990). The effects of computer-mediated text on the vocabulary learning and comprehension of intermediate grade readers. *Journal of Reading Behavior, 12*, 395–411.

Resnick, L. B. (1988, October 3–5). *Machines intelligentes pour personnes intelligentes* [Intelligent machines for intelligent people]. First European Congress on "Artificial Intelligence and Training." Lille, France.

Rickards, J. P. (1979). Adjunct postquestions in text: A critical review of methods and processes. *Review of Educational Research, 49*, 181–196.

Rizk, A., Streitz, N. A., & André, J. (Eds.). (1990). *Hypertexts: Concepts, systems, and applications*. Cambridge, UK: Cambridge University Press.

Robinson, D. H., Robinson, S. L., & Katayama, A. D. (1999). When words are represented in memory like pictures: Evidence for spatial encoding of study materials. *Contemporary Educational Psychology, 24*, 38–54.

Rosenshine, B., Meister, C., & Chapman, S. (1996). Teaching students to generate questions: A review of the intervention studies. *Review of Educational Research, 66*, 181–221.

Rothkopf, E. Z. (1982). Adjunct aids and the control of mathemagenic activities during purposeful reading. In W. Otto & S. White (Eds.), *Reading Expository material* (pp. 109–138). New York: Academic Press.

Rothkopf, E. Z., & Bisbicos, E. (1967). Selective facilitative effects of interspersed questions on learning from written materials. *Journal of Educational Psychology, 58*, 56–61.

Rouet, J.-F. (1990). Interactive text processing by inexperienced (hyper-) readers. In A. Rizk, N. A. Streitz, & J. André (Eds.), *Hypertexts: Concepts, systems, and applications* (pp. 250–260). Cambridge, UK: Cambridge University Press.

Rouet, J.-F. (1991). *Compréhension de textes didactiques par des lecteurs inexpérimentés dans des situations d'interaction sujet-ordinateur* [Comprehension of expository text by inexperienced readers in subject–computer interaction situations]. Unpublished doctoral dissertation, University of Poitiers, France.

Rouet, J.-F. (1992). Cognitive processing of hyperdocuments: When does nonlinearity help? In D. Lucarella, J. Nanard, M. Nanard, & P. Paolini (Eds.), *Proceedings of the Fourth ACM Conference on Hypertext* (pp. 131–140). New York: ACM Press.

Rouet, J.-F. (2003). "What was I looking for?" The influence of task specificity and prior knowledge on students' search strategies in hypertext. *Interacting with Computers, 15*, 409–428.

Rouet, J.-F. (2005). Cent fenêtres sur Internet [A hundred windows on the Internet]. Poitiers: Atlantique.

Rouet, J.-F., Britt, M. A., Mason, R. A., & Perfetti, C. A. (1996). Using multiple sources of evidence to reason about history. *Journal of Educational Psychology, 88*, 478–493.

Rouet, J.-F., & Chollet, K. (2000, July 19–21). *The acquisition of information search skills in 9 to 13 year-old students*. Paper presented at the Tenth Annual Meeting of the Society for Text and Discourse, Lyon, France.

Rouet, J.-F., Deleuze-Dordron, C., & Bisseret, A. (1995). Documentation as part of design: Exploratory field studies. In K. Nordby, P. H. Helmersen, D. J. Gilmore, & S. A. Arnesen (Eds.), *Human–computer interaction—Interact'95* (pp. 213–218). London: Chapman & Hall.

Rouet, J.-F., & Eme, E. (2002). The role of metatextual knowledge in text comprehension: Issues in development and individual differences. In P. Chambres, M. Izaute, & P. J. Marescaux (Eds.), *Metacognition: Process, function and use* (pp. 121–134). Amsterdam: Kluwer.

Rouet, J.-F., Favart, M., Britt, M. A., & Perfetti, C. A. (1997). Studying and using multiple documents in history: Effects of discipline expertise. *Cognition and Instruction, 15*, 85–106.

Rouet, J.-F., Favart, M., Gaonac'h, D., & Lacroix, N. (1996). Writing from multiple documents: Argumentation strategies in novice and expert history students. In G. Rijlarsdaam & H. van den Bergh (Eds.), *Theories, models and methodologies in writing* (pp. 44–60). Amsterdam: Amsterdam University Press.

Rouet, J.-F., & Levonen, J. J. (1996). Studying and learning with nonlinear documents: Empirical studies and their implications. In J.-F. Rouet, J. J. Levonen, A. P. Dillon, & R. J. Spiro (Eds.), *Hypertext and cognition* (pp. 9–24). Mahwah, NJ: Lawrence Erlbaum Associates.

Rouet, J.-F., Levonen, J. J., & Biardeau, A. (Eds.). (2001). *Multimedia learning: cognitive and instructional issues*. Oxford, UK: Elsevier Science.

Rouet, J.-F., Levonen, J. J., Dillon, A. P., & Spiro, R. J. (Eds.). (1996). *Hypertext and cognition*. Mahwah, NJ: Lawrence Erlbaum Associates.

Rouet, J.-F., Ros, C., Jégou, G., & Metta, S. (2003). Locating relevant categories in Web menus: Effects of menu structure, aging and task complexity. In D. Harris, V. Duffy, M. Smith, & C. Stephanidis (Eds.) *Human-centered computing: Cognitive social and ergonomic aspects* (pp. 547–551). Mahwah, NJ: Lawrence Erlbaum Associates.

Rouet, J.-F., & Tricot, A. (1996). Task and activity models in hypertext usage. In H. van Oostendorp & S. de Mul (Eds.), *Cognitive aspects of electronic text processing* (pp. 239–264). Norwood, NJ: Ablex.

Rouet, J.-F., & Vidal-Abarca, E. (2002). Mining for meaning: A cognitive examination of inserted questions in learning from scientific text. In J. Otero, J. A. Leon, & A. C. Graesser (Eds.), *The psychology of science text comprehension* (pp. 417–436). Mahwah, NJ: Lawrence Erlbaum Associates.

Rouet, J.-F., Vidal-Abarca, E., Bert-Erboul, A., & Millogo, V. (2001). Effects of information search tasks on the comprehension of instructional text. *Discourse Processes, 31*, 163–186.

Scardamalia, M., & Bereiter, C. (1987). Knowledge telling and knowledge transforming in written composition. In S. Rosenberg (Ed.), *Advances in applied psycholinguistics* (Vol. 2, pp. 142–175). Cambridge, UK: Cambridge University Press.

Schmalhofer, F., & Glavanov, D. (1986). Three components of understanding a programmer's manual: Verbatim, propositional and situational representations. *Journal of Memory and Language, 25*, 279–294.

Schommer, M. (1990). Effects of beliefs about the nature of knowledge on comprehension. *Journal of Educational Psychology, 82*, 498–504.

Sears, A., & Shneiderman, B. (1994). Split menus: effectively using selection frequency to organize menus. *ACM Transactions on Computer–Human Interaction, 1*, 27–51.

Shapiro, A. M. (1999). The relationship between prior knowledge and interactive overviews during hypermedia-aided learning. *Journal of Educational Computing Research, 20*, 143–163.

Shears, C., & Chiarello, C. (2004). Knowledge-based inferences are not general. *Discourse Processes, 38*, 31–55.

Shneiderman, B. (1987). User interface design and evaluation for an electronic encyclopedia. In G. Salvendy (Ed.), *Cognitive engineering and the design of human computer interaction and expert systems* (pp. 207–223). New York: Elsevier.

Shneiderman, B. (1989). Reflections on authoring, editing and managing hypertext. In E. Barrett (Ed.), *The society of text: Hypertext, hypermedia and the social construction of information* (pp. 115–131). Cambridge, MA: MIT Press.

Simpson, A., & McKnight, C. (1990). Navigation in hypertext: Structural cues and mental maps. In R. McAleese & C. Green (Eds.), *Hypertext: The state of the art* (pp. 74–83). Oxford, UK: Intellect Books Ltd.

Singer, M. (1990). Answering questions about discourse. *Discourse Processes, 13*, 261–278.

Singer, M. (2003). Processes of question answering. In G. Rickheit, T. Herrmann, & W. Deutsch (Eds.), *Psycholinguistik-Psycholinguistics* (pp. 422–431). Berlin: Walter de Gruyter.

Smith, J., Halasz, F., Yankelovich, N., Schwartz, M., & Weiss, S. (Eds.). (1987). *Proceedings of the Hypertext '87 Conference*. New York: ACM Press.

Smith, E. E., & Swinney, D. A. (1992). The role of schemas in reading text: A real-time examination. *Discourse Processes, 15*, 303–316.

Smith, A., & Yetim, F. (2004). Global human–computer systems: Cultural determinants of usability. *Interacting with Computers, 16*, 1–5.

Snow, C., & the RAND Reading Study Group (2002). *Reading for understanding. Toward a R&D program for reading comprehension*. Santa Monica, CA: RAND.

Snowberry, K., Parkinson, S., & Sisson, N. (1983). Computer display menus. *Ergonomics, 26*, 699–712.

Spilich, G. H., Vesonder, G. T., Chiesi, H. L., & Voss, J. F. (1979). Text processing of domain-related information for individuals with high and low domain knowledge. *Journal of Verbal Learning and Verbal Behavior, 18*, 275–290.

Spiro, R. J., Feltovitch, P. J., Jacobson, M. J., & Coulson, R. J. (1991). Cognitive flexibility, constructivism and hypertext: Random access instruction for advanced knowledge acquisition in ill-structured domains. *Educational Technology, 31*, 24–33.

Spivey, N. S., & King, J. R. (1989). Readers as writers composing from sources. *Reading Research Quarterly, 24*, 7–27.

Spyridakis, J. H., & Standal, T. C. (1987). Signals in expository prose: Effects on reading. *Reading Research Quarterly, 22*, 285–298.

Stahl, S. A., Hynd, C. R., Britton, B. K., McNish, M. M., & Bosquet, D. (1996). What happens when students read multiple source documents in history? *Reading Research Quarterly, 31*, 4, 430–456.

Stanton, N. A., Taylor, R. G., & Tweedie, L. A. (1992). Maps as navigational aids in hypertext environments: An empirical evaluation. *Journal of Educational Multimedia and Hypermedia, 1*, 431–444.

Stark, H. A. (1988). What does paragraph marking do? *Discourse Processes, 11*, 275–303.

Stein, N. L., & Miller, C. A. (1993). A theory of argumentative understanding: Relationships among position preference, judgments of goodness, memory and reasoning. *Argumentation, 7*, 183–204.

Sternberg, R. J. (1999). *Cognitive psychology*. Belmont, CA: Wadsworth.

Streitz, N. A. (1987). Cognitive compatibility as a central issue in human–computer interaction: Theoretical framework and empirical findings. In G. Salvendy (Ed.), *Cognitive engineering in the design of human–computer interaction and expert systems* (pp. 75–82). Amsterdam: Elsevier Science.

Strømsø, H. I., & Bråten, I. (2002). Norwegian students' use of multiple sources while reading expository texts. *Reading Research Quarterly, 37*, 208–227.

Sweet, R., & Meates, A. (2004). ICT and low achievers: What does PISA tell us? In A. Karpati, (Ed.), *Promoting equity through ICT in education: Projects, problems, prospects*. Budapest: Hungarian Ministry of Education and OECD. Downloaded July 20, 2004, from http://www.pisa.oecd.org/Docs/Download/sweet.pdf

Sweller, J. (1994). Cognitive load theory, learning difficulty, and instructional design. *Learning and Instruction, 4*, 295–312.

Symons, S., & Pressley, M. (1993). Prior knowledge affects text search success and extraction of information. *Reading Research Quarterly, 28*, 250–261.

Townsend, M. A. R., Hicks, L., Thompson, L., Wilton, K. M., Tuck, B. F., & Moore, D. W. (1993). Effects of introductions and conclusions in assessment of student essays. *Journal of Educational Psychology, 85*, 670–678.

Trench, B. (2000, November). *Science journalism on the Web*. Paper presented at the seminar on Nouveaux Territoires de la Communication Scientifique [New Territories for Scientific Communication]. Paris, France: Cité des Sciences et de l'Industrie.

Trumbo, C., Sprecker, K., Dumlao, R., Yun, G., & Duke, S. (2001). Use of e-mail and the Web by science writers. *Science Communication, 22*, 347–378.

Turner, K., & Greene, E. (1977). *The construction and use of a propositional text base*. Boulder, CO: University of Colorado.

UNESCO (2000). *Education pour tous. Bilan à l'an 2000, document statistique* [Education for all. 2000 assessment, statistical document]. United Nations Educational, Scientific and Cultural Organization. Retrieved June 11, 2003, from http://www.uis.unesco.org/en/pub/doc/efaexsum_en.pdf

van den Broek, P., Risden, K., Fletcher, C. R., & Thurlow, R. (1996). A "landscape" view of reading: Fluctuating patterns of activation and the construction of a stable memory representation. In B. K. Britton & A. C. Graesser (Eds.), *Models of understanding text* (pp. 165–187). Mahwah, NJ: Lawrence Erlbaum Associates.

van den Broek, P., Virtue, S., Everson, M. L., Tzeng, Y., & Sung, Y. (2002). Comprehension and memory for science texts: Inferential processes and the construction of a mental representation. In J. Otero, J. A. León, & A. C. Graesser (Eds.), *The psychology of science text comprehension* (pp. 131–154). Mahwah, NJ: Lawrence Erlbaum Associates.

van den Broek, P., Young, M., Tzeng, Y., & Linderholm, T. (1999). The landscape model of reading: Inferences and the online construction of a memory representation. In H. van Oostendorp & S. R.Goldman (Eds.), *The construction of mental representations during reading* (pp. 71–98). Mahwah, NJ: Lawrence Erlbaum Associates.

van Dijk, T. A., (1980). *Macrostructures*. Hillsdale, NJ: Lawrence Erlbaum Associates.

van Dijk, T. A., & Kintsch, W. (1983). *Strategies of discourse comprehension*. Hillsdale, NJ: Lawrence Erlbaum Associates.

van Oostendorp, H. (1996). Updating situation models derived from newspaper articles. *Medienpsychologie, 8*, 21–33.

van Oostendorp, H. (2002). Updating mental representations during reading scientific text. In J. Otero, J. A. León, & A. C. Graesser (Eds.), *The psychology of science text comprehension* (pp. 309–329). Mahwah, NJ: Lawrence Erlbaum Associates.

van Oostendorp, H. (Ed.), (2003). *Cognition in a digital world*. Mahwah, NJ: Lawrence Erlbaum Associates.

van Oostendorp, H., & Bonebakker, C. (1999). Difficulties in updating mental representations during reading news reports. In H. van Oostendorp & S. Goldman (Eds.), *The construction of mental representations during reading* (pp. 319–340). Mahwah, NJ: Lawrence Erlbaum Associates.

van Oostendorp, H., & Goldman, S. (Eds.). (1999). *The construction of mental representations during reading*. Mahwah, NJ: Lawrence Erlbaum Associates.

Vidal-Abarca, E., Gilabert, R., & Rouet, J.-F. (1998, July 8–10). *El papel del tipo de preguntas en el aprendizaje de textos cientificos* [The role of question type on learning from scientific text]. Seminario "Comprension y produccion de textos cientificos" (Comprehension and production of scientific texts). Aveiro, Portugal.

Vidal-Abarca, E., Mengual, V., Sanjose, V., & Rouet, J.-F. (1996, September 4–6). *Levels of comprehension of scientific prose: The role of text and task variables*. Paper presented at the International Seminar on Using Complex Information Systems, Poitiers, France.

Voss, J. F., Greene, T. R., Post, T. A., & Penner, B. C. (1983). Problem-solving skill in the social sciences. In G. H. Bower (Ed.), *The psychology of learning and motivation: Advances in research theory* (pp. 165–213). New York: Academic Press.

Voss, J. F., Vesonder, G. T., & Spilich, G. J. (1980). Text generation and recall by high knowledge and low knowledge individuals. *Journal of Verbal Learning and Verbal Behavior, 19*, 661–667.

Wagner, R. K., & Sternberg, R. J. (1987). Executive control in reading comprehension. In B. K. Britton & S. M. Glynn (Eds.), *Executive control processes in reading* (pp. 1–22). Hillsdale, NJ: Lawrence Erlbaum Associates.

Walczyk, J. J., Marsaglia, C. S., Bryan, K. S., & Naquin, P. J. (2001). Overcoming inefficient reading skills. *Journal of Educational Psychology, 93*, 750–757.

Waller, R. (1991). Typography and discourse. In R. Barr, M. L. Kamil, P. Mosenthal, & P. D. Pearson (Eds.), *Handbook of reading research* (Vol. 2, pp. 341–380). New York: Longman.

Wang, X. H., & Liebscher, P. (1988). Information seeking in hypertext. Effects of physical format and search strategy. *Proceedings of the American Society for Information Science Annual Meeting, 25*, 200–204.

Weaver, C. A., III, & Kintsch, W. (1991). Expository text. In R. Barr, M. L. Kamil, P. Mosenthal, & P. D. Pearson (Eds.), *Handbook of reading research* (Vol. 2, pp. 230–245), New York: Longman.

Wenger, M. J., & Payne, D. G. (1996). Comprehension and retention of nonlinear text: Considerations of working memory and material-appropriate processing. *American Journal of Psychology, 109*, 93–130.

Westerman, S. J. (1995). Computerized information retrieval: Individual differences in the use of spatial vs. nonspatial navigational information. *Perceptual and Motor Skills, 81*, 771–786.

Westerman, S. J., Davies, D. R., Glendon, A. I., Stammers, R. B., & Matthews, G. (1995). Age and cognitive ability as predictors of computerized information retrieval. *Behaviour and Information Technology, 14*, 313–326.

Weyer, S. A. (1982). The design of a dynamic book for information search. *International Journal of Man–Machine Studies, 17*, 87–107.

Whilite, S. C. (1985). Differential effects of high-level and low-level postpassage questions. *American Journal of Psychology, 98*, 41–58.

Wiley, J. (2001). Supporting understanding through task and browser design. *Proceedings of the Twenty-Third Annual Conference of the Cognitive Science Society* (pp. 1136–1143). Edinburgh, Scotland.

Wiley, J., & Rayner, K. (2000). Effects of titles on the processing of text and lexically ambiguous words: Evidence from eye movements. *Memory and Cognition, 28*, 1011–1021.

Wiley, J., & Voss, J. F. (1997). The effects of "playing historian" on learning in history. *Applied Cognitive Psychology, 10*, 63–72.

Wiley, J., & Voss, J. F. (1999). Constructing arguments from multiple sources: Tasks that promote understanding not just memory for text. *Journal of Educational Psychology, 91*, 301–311.

Wilkes, A. L., & Leatherbarrow, M. (1988). Editing episodic memory following the identification of error. *Quarterly Journal of Experimental Psychology: Human Experimental Psychology, 40A*, 361–387.

Wineburg, S. S. (1991). Historical problem solving: A study of the cognitive processes used in the evaluation of documentary and pictorial evidence. *Journal of Educational Psychology, 83*, 73–87.

Wineburg, S. S. (1994). The cognitive representation of historical texts. In G. Leinhardt, I. Beck, & C. Stainton (Eds.), *Teaching and learning in history* (pp. 85–135). Hillsdale, NJ: Lawrence Erlbaum Associates.

Winne, P. H., & Hadwin, A. F. (1998). Studying as self-regulated learning. In D. Hacker, J. Dunlowsky, & A. Graesser (Eds.), *Metacognition in educational theory and practice* (pp. 277–304). Mahwah, NJ: Lawrence Erlbaum Associates.

Wixson, K. K. (1983). Postreading question–answer interactions and children's learning from text. *Journal of Educational Psychology, 75*, 413– 423.

Wright, P. (1991). Cognitive overheads and prostheses: Some issues in evaluating hypertexts. In R. Furuta & D. Stotts (Eds.), *Proceedings of the Third ACM Conference on Hypertext* (pp. 1–12). New York: ACM Press.

Yu, B.-M., & Roh, S.-Z. (2002). The effects of menu-design on information seeking performance and users' attitude on the World Wide Web. *Journal of the American Society for Information Science and Technology, 53*, 923–933.

Yuill, N., & Oakhill, J. (1991). *Children's problems in text comprehension. An experimental investigation*. Cambridge, UK: Cambridge University Press.

Zaphiris, P., Shneiderman, B., & Norman, K. L. (2002). Expandable indexes versus sequential menus for searching hierarchies on the World Wide Web. *Behaviour & Information Technology, 21*, 201–207.

Zwaan, R. A. (1999). Five dimensions of narrative comprehension: The event-indexing model. In S. Goldman, A. C. Graesser & P. van den Broek (Eds.), *Narrative comprehension, causality and coherence: Essays in honor of Tom Trabasso* (pp. 93–110). Mahwah, NJ: Lawrence Erlbaum Associates.

Zwaan, R. A., & Madden, C. (2004). Updating situation models. *Journal of Experimental Psychology: Learning, Memory and Cognition, 30*, 283–288.

Zwaan, R. A., Magliano, J. P., & Graesser, A. C. (1995). Dimensions of situation model construction in narrative comprehension. *Journal of Experimental Psychology: Learning, Memory and Cognition, 21*, 386–397.

Author Index

H

I

J

K

L

M

N

T

U

V

W

Y

Z

Subject Index